Cambridge English

SECOND EDITION

Complete Advanced

D1471482

Student's Book **without** answers

Guy Brook-Hart

Simon Haines

CAMBRIDGE
UNIVERSITY PRESS

University Printing House, Cambridge CB2 8BS, United Kingdom

One Liberty Plaza, 20th Floor, New York, NY 10006, USA

477 Williamstown Road, Port Melbourne, VIC 3207, Australia

4843/24, 2nd Floor, Ansari Road, Daryaganj, Delhi – 110002, India

79 Anson Road, #06–04/06, Singapore 079906

Cambridge University Press is part of the University of Cambridge.

It furthers the University's mission by disseminating knowledge in the pursuit of education, learning and research at the highest international levels of excellence.

www.cambridge.org
Information on this title: www.cambridge.org/9781107631069

© Cambridge University Press 2014

First published 2009
Second edition 2014
20 19 18 17 16 15 14 13 12

Printed in Dubai by Oriental Press

A catalogue record for this publication is available from the British Library

ISBN 978-1-107-63106-9 Student's Book without answers with CD-ROM
ISBN 978-1-107-67090-7 Student's Book with answers with CD-ROM
ISBN 978-1-107-69838-3 Teacher's Book with Teacher's Resources CD-ROM
ISBN 978-1-107-63148-9 Workbook without answers with Audio CD
ISBN 978-1-107-67517-9 Workbook with answers with Audio CD
ISBN 978-1-107-68823-0 Student's Book Pack (Student's Book with answers with CD-ROM and Class Audio CDs (2))
ISBN 978-1-107-64450-2 Class Audio CDs (2)
ISBN 978-1-107-66289-6 Presentation Plus DVD-ROM

Contents

Map of the units

Listening	Speaking	Vocabulary	Grammar
Part 4: Unusual occupations	Part 1	Collocations with *give* and *make*	Verb forms to talk about the past
Part 1: Language learning, Spelling reform, Job interviews	Part 2	Collocations with *make, get* and *do*	Expressing purpose, reason and result
Part 2: 'Face-blindness' – a psychological condition	Part 3	Nouns which can be countable or uncountable Formal or informal?	*no, none, not* The passive
Part 2: The co-operative movement	Part 4	Dependent prepositions Adjective–noun collocations (1)	Expressing possibility, probability and certainty
Part 1: Dramatic past experiences	Part 2	Idiomatic language	Verbs followed by *to* + infinitive or the *-ing* form
Part 3: An interview with a portrait artist and his sitter	Part 3	Adjective–noun collocations (2)	Avoiding repetition
Part 4: Talking about music	Part 4	Complex prepositions Money words	Linking ideas: relative and participle clauses; apposition
Part 3: An interview about news reporting	Part 3	'Talking' verbs	Reported speech Transitive verbs
Part 1: Rail travel, Olympic records, Space travel	Part 2	*action, activity, event* and *programme*	Time clauses Prepositions in time expressions
Part 2: Studying Arabic in Abu Dhabi	Part 4	*chance, occasion, opportunity* and *possibility*	Expressing ability, possibility and obligation
Part 1: Travelling on a river, A sponsored walk, A conversation between two travellers	Part 1	Phrasal verbs *at, in* and *on* to express location	Conditionals
Part 2: Climate change and the Inuit	Part 3	Prepositions following verbs Word formation	Nouns and articles
Part 3: Allergies	Part 2	Prepositions following adjectives	Ways of contrasting ideas The language of comparison
Part 4: Migration	Part 4	*learn, find out* and *know; provide, offer* and *give*	Comment adverbials and intensifying adverbs Cleft sentences for emphasis

Introduction

Who this book is for

Complete Advanced 2nd Edition is a stimulating and thorough preparation course for students who wish to take the **Cambridge English: Advanced** exam from 2015). It teaches the reading, writing, listening and speaking skills necessary for the exam as well as the grammar and vocabulary which, from research into the **Cambridge Learner Corpus**, are known to be essential for exam success. For those of you who are not planning to take the exam in the near future, the book provides you with skills and language highly relevant to an advanced level of English (Common European Framework of Reference level C1).

What the book contains

In the **Student's Book** there are:

- 14 units for classroom study. Each unit contains:
  - practice in two parts of the Reading and Use of English paper and one part of each of the other three papers in the Cambridge English: Advanced exam. The units provide language input and skills practice to help you deal successfully with the tasks in each part.
  - essential information on what each part of the exam involves, and the best way to approach each task.
  - a wide range of enjoyable and stimulating speaking activities designed to increase your fluency and your ability to express yourself.
  - a step-by-step approach to doing Cambridge English Advanced writing tasks.
  - grammar activities and exercises for the grammar you need to know for the exam. When you are doing grammar exercises you will sometimes see this symbol: ⊙. These exercises are based on research from the Cambridge Learner Corpus and they deal with the areas which are known to cause problems for students in the exam.
  - vocabulary necessary for the exam. When you see this symbol ⊙ by a vocabulary exercise, the exercise focuses on words which Advanced candidates often confuse or use wrongly in the exam.
  - a unit review. These contain exercises which revise the grammar and vocabulary that you have studied in each unit.

- A **Language reference section** which clearly explains all the main areas of grammar which you will need to know for the exam.

- **Writing and Speaking reference sections**. These explain the possible tasks you may have to do in the Writing and Speaking papers, and they give you examples together with additional exercises and advice on how best to approach these two papers.

- A **CD-ROM** which provides you with many interactive exercises, including further listening practice exclusive to the CD-ROM. All these extra exercises are linked to the topics in the Student's Book.

Also available:

- **Two audio CDs** containing listening material for the 14 units. The listening material is indicated by different-coloured icons in the Student's Book as follows: ▶02, ▶02

- A **Workbook** containing:
  - 14 units for homework and self-study. Each unit contains full exam practice in one or two parts of the Reading and Use of English paper.
  - full exam practice in one part of the Listening paper in each unit.
  - further practice in the grammar and vocabulary taught in the Student's Book.
  - exercises for the development of essential writing skills such as paragraph organisation, self-correction, spelling and punctuation based on the results from the Cambridge Learner Corpus.
  - an audio CD containing all the listening material for the Workbook.

Cambridge English: Advanced content and overview

Part / timing	Content	Test focus
Reading and Use of English 1 hour 30 minutes	**Part 1** A modified cloze test containing eight gaps, followed by eight multiple-choice questions **Part 2** A modified cloze test containing eight gaps **Part 3** A text containing eight gaps. Each gap corresponds to a word. The stems of the missing words are given beside the text and must be changed to form the missing word. **Part 4** Six separate questions, each with a lead-in sentence and a gapped second sentence to be completed in three to six words, one of which is a given 'key' word **Part 5** A text followed by six 4-option multiple-choice questions **Part 6** Four short texts, followed by four cross-text multiple-matching questions **Part 7** A text from which six paragraphs have been removed and placed in jumbled order, together with an additional paragraph, after the text **Part 8** A text or several short texts, preceded by ten multiple-matching questions	Candidates are expected to be able to: demonstrate the ability to apply their knowledge and control of the language system by completing a number of tasks at text and sentence level; demonstrate a variety of reading skills, including understanding of specific information, text organisation features, implication, tone and text structure.
Writing 1 hour 30 minutes	**Part 1** One compulsory question	Candidates are expected to write an essay in response to a proposition to discuss, and accompanying text.
	Part 2 Candidates choose one task from a choice of three questions.	Candidates are expected to be able to write non-specialised text types such as a letter, a report, a review or a proposal.
Listening Approximately 40 minutes	**Part 1** Three short extracts or exchanges between interacting speakers. There are two multiple-choice questions for each extract. **Part 2** A monologue with a sentence-completion task which has eight items **Part 3** A text involving interacting speakers, with six multiple-choice questions **Part 4** Five short, themed monologues, with ten multiple-matching questions	Candidates are expected to be able to show understanding of feeling, attitude, detail, opinion, purpose, agreement and gist.
Speaking 15 minutes (for pairs)	**Part 1** A short conversation between the interlocutor and each candidate (spoken questions) **Part 2** An individual 'long turn' for each candidate followed by a response from the second candidate (visual and written stimuli, with spoken instructions) **Part 3** A two-way conversation between the candidates (written stimuli, with spoken instructions) **Part 4** A discussion on topics related to Part 3 (spoken questions)	Candidates are expected to be able to respond to questions and interact in conversational English.

1 Our people

Starting off

1 Work in small groups. How do you think these things reflect our personality? (Give examples.)

- the job we choose
- the subject(s) we choose to study
- our free-time interests
- the clothes we wear
- the friends we choose

What sort of personalities do you imagine the people in the photographs have?

2 These adjectives can be used to describe personality. Complete the table by writing each adjective in the correct column.

competent conscientious genuine idealistic imaginative insecure insensitive modest naïve open-minded outgoing protective self-centred unconventional

Personality attributes		
Usually positive	Usually negative	Could be either

3 Choose adjectives from Exercise 2 and talk to your partner.

1 Explain how three of the adjectives form part of your personality.
2 Use three different adjectives to describe one of your close friends.

Listening | Part 4

1 Work in pairs. You will hear five short extracts in which people are talking about a family member they admire. Before you listen, look at the list of occupations (A–H) in Task One.

  1 What do you think attracts people to these occupations?

  2 Which do you think is easiest and which is the most difficult to learn?

Exam information

In Listening Part 4

- you hear five short monologues on related subjects and you do two listening tasks
- in each task you have to choose one answer for each speaker from a list of eight options
- you hear each speaker twice.

This part tests your ability to identify the gist of what the speakers say, their attitude and the main points, and to interpret the context they are speaking in.

TASK ONE

For questions 1–5, choose from the list (A–H) the person who each speaker is talking about.

A a deep-sea diver

B a fisherman/fisherwoman   Speaker 1   1

C a gardener

                           Speaker 2   2

D a magician

                           Speaker 3   3

E a musician

F an actor   Speaker 4   4

G an archaeologist   Speaker 5   5

H an explorer

TASK TWO

For questions 6–10, choose from the list (A–H) the quality the speaker admires about the person.

A a positive outlook on life

B ability to anticipate problems   Speaker 1   6

C an enquiring mind

                               Speaker 2   7

D attention to detail

                               Speaker 3   8

E calmness under pressure

F readiness to explain things   Speaker 4   9

G kindness to children   Speaker 5   10

H originality and inventiveness

2 Which of these phrases would you associate with each occupation? (You can associate some of the phrases with more than one occupation.)

- a few of his/her recordings
- complete dedication to his/her craft
- perform a new trick
- underwater adventures
- out in all weathers
- the first person to set foot in a place
- suffer from stage fright
- digging at some excavation or other

Now think of one more phrase you might associate with each occupation.

3 Look at the list of qualities (A–H) in Task Two and paraphrase each of them using your own words. Which quality would you associate with each occupation?

4 ▶02 Now listen to the five speakers and do Tasks One and Two.

5 Work in pairs. Tell each other about someone interesting or unusual in your family or circle of friends.

- What do they do?
- What are they like?
- What is your relationship with them like?

Grammar
Verb forms to talk about the past

1 Look at these extracts 1–8 from Listening Part 4. Match the underlined verb forms with the explanations a–g. There are two verb forms you can match with one explanation.

1 We loved his stories of the strange creatures he'd seen.
2 When she invited me to come out on one of her trips it was a real eye-opener to see what she was doing.
3 When she invited me to come out on one of her trips …
4 We've listened to them so many times.
5 He'd drop whatever he was doing.
6 She never used to panic.
7 Even if he'd been working all day, he'd be really conscientious about giving them a complete tour of the site.
8 He's been spending a lot of time recently getting this new show ready.

a something that happened at a specific time in the past
b a repeated action or habit in the past which doesn't happen now
c an activity which started before and (possibly) continued after an event in the past
d something which happened before another activity or situation in the past
e something which happened before another activity or situation, with an emphasis on the length of time
f an activity that started in the past and is still happening, with an emphasis on the length of time
g something that has happened more than once at times which are not stated between the past and the present

➡ page 177 Language reference: Verb forms to talk about the past

2 Put the verbs in brackets into the simple or continuous form of the past, past perfect or present perfect. (In some cases more than one answer is possible.)

1 Chen ......has been working...... (work) in Singapore since he .... (leave) university two years ago, but next year he expects to be transferred to Hong Kong.
2 Alexander takes university life very seriously. He .... (study) here for six months and he still .... (not go) to a single party!
3 Maria .... (come) round to dinner last night. She .... (start) telling me her life story while I .... (make) the salad and .... (continue) telling it during dinner.
4 Ivana .... (have) a splitting headache yesterday evening because she .... (work) in the sun all day and she .... (not wear) a hat.
5 I .... (grow) up in a house which .... (belong) to my great-great-grandfather. We .... (sell) it now because it was too big for our small family.

3 Circle the correct alternative in *italics* in each of the following sentences.

a My teachers (1) *were often getting / often used to get* annoyed with me when I was at school because I (2) *never used to bring / had never brought* a pen with me and I (3) *would always ask / have always asked* someone if I could borrow theirs.
b The village (4) *used to be / would be* very quiet and remote until they (5) *built / had built* the motorway two years ago. In those days everybody (6) *would know / used to know* everyone else, but since then, a lot of new people (7) *came / have come* to live in the area and the old social structures (8) *gradually changed / have gradually been changing*.
c When I was a child, both my parents (9) *used to go / were going* out to work, so when they (10) *would be / were* out, my grandmother (11) *was looking / would look* after me.

4 🎯 Exam candidates often make mistakes with present perfect, past and past perfect tenses. In the sentences below, circle the correct alternative in *italics*.

1 In recent times people *had / have had* more contact with their friends through email and mobile phones than they did in the past.
2 The feedback we received from our clients meant we *have been / were* able to provide excellent advice to the people developing the product, which they then acted on.
3 The party was great and the best bit for me *has been / was* the jazz band.
4 We should have had a really good holiday for what we paid, but unfortunately we discovered that they *didn't organise / hadn't organised* anything very much so it was rather a disappointment.
5 While I was studying in England, I *haven't taken / didn't take* an examination because it was not offered to me or to any of my fellow students either.
6 Are you going to the dinner on Saturday? A lot of my other friends *were invited / have been invited* and I know they'd love to meet you.
7 I *have only lived / have only been living* in Geneva for the past few months, though Madeleine, who you met yesterday, *lived / has lived* here all her life.
8 Petra looks after my children very well. I *haven't noticed / didn't notice* any weaknesses in her character, so I'm sure you'll be happy to offer her a job.

Reading and Use of English | Part 8

Exam information

In Reading and Use of English Part 8, you must match ten questions or statements with a text divided into four to six sections or four to six separate short texts.

This task tests your ability to read quickly and understand details, opinions and attitudes and to locate specific information.

Rafael Nadal

Julia Roberts

Nelson Mandela

Beyonće

1 Work in small groups. You are going to read extracts from four autobiographies. Before you read, discuss these questions.

1 What things make an autobiography entertaining?
2 What things do you expect to find out by reading an autobiography?
3 Of the people photographed above, whose autobiography would you be interested in reading? Why?

2 Work in pairs. Read questions 1–10 carefully and for each question

a underline the key idea

b paraphrase it as if you were the person speaking.

Example

1 *My mother worries too much about the danger I might be in.*

Who says

one of their parents can be unnecessarily protective?	1
they have changed during the course of their working life?	2
their parents never imagined the consequences of something they said?	3
they discovered the job they wanted in an unlikely place?	4
one parent saw the project as an opportunity for both the parents?	5
they gain satisfaction from the way their work affects others?	6
they thought the future promised them surprising experiences?	7
their upbringing was unusual?	8
they were enthusiastic but nervous about the job they were going for?	9
they achieved promotion by staying in the job longer than other people?	10

3 For questions 1–10 in Exercise 2, choose from the extracts A–D. The extracts can be used more than once.

4 Work in small groups. Discuss these questions.

1 Which of the people in the texts would you be most interested to meet?

2 How important do you think parents' opinions are when choosing a career?

3 What other factors should young people take into account when choosing a career?

My early career

A Linda Greenlaw

I am a woman. I am a fisherman. Neither abused nor neglected, I am the product of a blissful and unique childhood, a rare claim these days. Like all young children, I believed wholeheartedly in the words of my mother and father. It was only natural that I took seriously the assertions of my parents that I could do whatever I liked with my life, become anything I wanted. Although the advice they gave was well intentioned, my parents never dreamed that it might come back to haunt them when I decided that what I liked and wanted to become was a fisherman.

Fishing my way through college, I made my first deep-sea trip at the age of nineteen aboard the *Walter Leeman*. By the time I graduated from college I had outlasted the original crew members I had started with, most of whom moved on to boats of their own, and became captain of the boat by attrition. Promising my parents that I would postpone law school for just one year, I became a full-time fisherman.

Adapted from *The Hungry Ocean*

B Eric Idle

When you make an audience laugh, they really do love you, and that's one of the nicest things about being a comedian. Usually you've touched them at a time when they needed some kind of reassurance or they wanted something or they were feeling depressed and then you made them feel better. So there is a sort of healing thing to it.

But you don't sit and think, 'I'm going to have a career now.' Things just happen. I stumbled into performing at Cambridge University. I think there's something very seductive about the glamour of dressing up and playing someone else, and that comes from a sadness. I think I only became any good eventually through Monty Python* by being disguised and by being other people and it was only latterly in my life that I have been able to be funny as myself or be confident. I don't have to put on a disguise or wear a wig now but that's what I used to do.

*Monty Python's Flying Circus was a comedy series broadcast between 1969 and 1974.
Adapted from *The Pythons Autobiography*

D Kate Adie

Then, in a very odd act of serendipity, I read the local paper – the *Sunderland Echo* was no one under eighty's preferred reading, but I wasn't very busy; and there in the classifieds was an advertisement, headed *BBC Radio Durham*. I can still remember the jump it gave me, as the small private thought woke up at the back of my mind and leaped around shouting silently: this is it, this is it.

I didn't dare tell anyone, not my parents, nor my friends, and I realised with some trepidation that I wanted it very much indeed. Somehow the life with the BBC might satisfy a lot of unarticulated longing for … I wasn't sure what; just something to do with bigger events, the wider stage, the unexpected.

Adapted from *The Kindness of Strangers*

C Emma Richards

It had been only a few short months before that I'd made a flying visit to Scotland to tell my parents I was going to sail around the world. Dad had picked me up from Glasgow airport. He'd asked if I was up for a wedding or a party, the kind of occasions for which I'd normally make a flying visit.

'No,' I said. 'I've got something to tell you. I'm going to sail around the world alone.'

My mum often doesn't sleep when I'm at sea. She's the kind of mum who still instinctively goes to grab your hand when you cross the road, even though all four of us children left home at least ten years ago. She said it was a great idea, that she and Dad would travel round the world to visit me at the stopovers. She said it'd be great to see all those places, they'd be there to support me. She just kept talking.

Adapted from *Around Alone*

Vocabulary
Collocations with *give* and *make*

1 Look at this sentence from Reading and Use of English Part 8. Write the correct verb (A–D) in the gap.

> *Although the advice they .... was well intentioned, my parents never dreamed that it might come back to haunt them.*
>
> A made   B gave   C said   D expressed

2 ⊙ Exam candidates often use the wrong verb when they should use *give* or *make*. In most of the sentences below, the underlined verb is wrong. Replace the underlined verb with *give* or *make*, or write *correct* if you think there is no mistake.

1 When you print the article, we also expect you to <u>give</u> an apology.

2 Her report on the trip <u>did not show</u> accurate information so we were quite confused.

3 I have some suggestions to <u>give</u> before the forthcoming trip.

4 I hope your company will <u>give</u> me at least a partial refund.

5 I'm so grateful that you have <u>made</u> me the chance to attend the course.

6 In my boss's absence, I <u>give</u> telephone calls to customers, clean desks, and write emails.

7 Installing modern technology will <u>give</u> a good impression of the college.

8 Our evening lectures were <u>made</u> by 'experts' who knew nothing about the subject.

9 There is another recommendation I would like to <u>give</u> concerning the club.

3 Words which are often used together (e.g. *make an apology*) are called collocations. Which verb often forms a collocation with these nouns? Write *give* or *make* in each gap.

1 .... a speech, lecture, talk, performance

2 .... (someone) information, details, advice, instructions

3 .... a(n) recommendation, comment, apology, suggestion

4 .... someone a(n) chance, opportunity

5 .... someone a refund, their money back

6 .... a phone call

7 .... an impression on someone

8 .... someone an impression

Reading and Use of English | Part 4

1 Work in pairs. Study the exam instruction below. Then, for questions 1–4, read some answers that different students gave for each question. Decide which answer (A–C) is correct and say why the other answers are wrong.

> For questions 1–4, complete the second sentence so that it has a similar meaning to the first sentence, using the word given. Do not change the word given. You must use between three and six words, including the word given.

1 His actions were based on what his uncle advised him to do.
   ADVICE
   The basis for his actions .... him.
   A was some advice that his uncle gave
   B was the advice his uncle gave
   C was what his uncle advised

2 Alba made every effort to arrive at the meeting on time.
   BEST
   Alba .... to the meeting on time.
   A did her best to get
   B made the best to arrive
   C tried very hard to make it

3 Unless the product is in perfect condition, we cannot return your money.
   REFUND
   We will be unable .... the product is not in perfect condition.
   A to pay you a refund unless
   B to refund the money you paid if
   C to give you a refund if

4 Otto's teachers were favourably impressed by the presentation he gave to the class.
IMPRESSION
Otto's presentation to the class .... his teachers.
A gave a favourable impression to
B made a favourable impression on
C made an impression which was found very favourable by

2 For questions 1–6, complete the second sentence so that it has a similar meaning to the first sentence, using the word given. Do not change the word given. You must use between three and six words, including the word given.

1 I would often go cycling with my father when I was a child.
USED
My father .... cycling with him when I was a child .

2 Having apologised, Klaus shook my hand.
APOLOGY
When Klaus .... , he shook my hand.

3 Anna has been trying as hard as possible to take care of her children.
CAN
Anna has been doing the .... after her children.

4 For me, the second chapter was more convincing than the rest of the book.
PERSUASIVE
I found the second chapter .... other part of the book.

5 I never planned to annoy you.
AIM
It .... you angry.

6 I've never had problems with my car before.
TIME
This is the .... me problems.

Speaking | Part 1

Exam information

In Speaking Part 1 the examiner asks you questions about yourself. These may include questions about your life, your work or studies, your plans for the future, your family and your interests, etc.

This part is intended to break the ice and tests your ability to interact with the examiner and use general social language.

1 Work in pairs. Read the questions below from Speaking Part 1. Which questions are

a mainly about the present?   b mainly about the past?

How would you answer each question?

1 What do you most enjoy doing with your friends?
2 Have you ever had the opportunity to really help a friend? How?
3 Would you prefer to spend your holidays with your family or your friends?
4 What is the best way for people visiting your country to make friends?
5 Who do you think has influenced you most? Why?
6 What is your happiest childhood memory?
7 Who is the best teacher you've ever had?
8 Tell me about a friend of yours and how you got to know him or her.

2 ▶03 Listen to two students, Marta and Lukas. Which question does each of them answer?

Marta: ....   Lukas: ....

3 ▶04 Now listen to them again, with the examiner's questions, and say if the following statements are true (T) or false (F).

1 They both give very brief answers.
2 They give some details or reasons to support their answers.
3 They use a range of tenses appropriately.
4 They speak in a relaxed, natural way.

4 Think about how you could answer each of the questions in Exercise 1. Then work in pairs and take turns to ask and answer the questions.

➡ page 194 Speaking reference: Speaking Part 1

Writing | Part 1

An essay

Exam information

In Writing Part 1 you write an essay in which you discuss a question or topic. You are given

- three areas to consider and you must discuss two of them
- three opinions which you can use if you wish.

This part tests your ability to develop an argument or discussion, express your opinions clearly and support your ideas with reasons and examples.

1 Underline the key ideas in the writing task below.

> Your class has taken part in a seminar on whether the education system does enough to help young people to find jobs which fit their abilities and interests. You have made the notes below.
>
> > **Methods schools and universities use to help students find suitable jobs**
> >
> > - providing courses and qualifications
> > - work experience programmes
> > - careers advice
> >
> > > **Some opinions expressed in the seminar:**
> > >
> > > 'We study lots of things which we'll never use in any future job.'
> > >
> > > 'Without work experience you'd have no idea what to study at university.'
> > >
> > > 'Some of my teachers can't give me advice because they've never done any job other than teaching.'
>
> Write an essay discussing **two** of the methods in your notes. You should explain **which method is more effective**, giving **reasons** in support of your answer.
>
> You may, if you wish, make use of the opinions expressed in the seminar, but you should use your own words as far as possible.
>
> Write your answer in 220–260 words in an appropriate style.

2 Work in small groups.

- Discuss each of the methods and whether or not you agree with the opinions expressed in the seminar.
- During your discussion, express your own opinions on the methods and give reasons for your opinions.
- Take notes on the main ideas which arise during the discussion.

3 Read the writing task in Exercise 1 again. Do you think the following sentences are true (T) or false (F)? Why?

1 You must discuss all three methods.
2 You must decide which is the best method.
3 You must say whether you agree or disagree with the opinions expressed.
4 If you use any of the opinions, you should express them in a more formal style.
5 When you express your opinion, you should say why you hold that opinion.
6 You can expand the topic to talk about other issues related to work that interest you.
7 You can write your answer using a bulleted list of points instead of formal paragraphs.
8 The task contains a word limit, but if you write 300 words you will get higher marks.

4 Read Cristina's essay. Then complete the plan she wrote beforehand by matching the notes (a–e) with the paragraphs.

For many young people it is hard to find the sort of job they aspire to. **¹This** is in part due to a mismatch between what education provides and what employers believe **²they** require.

Schools and universities should offer students courses which provide **³them** with qualifications which will attract potential employers. However, employers often complain that courses are too theoretical and do not teach students the practical skills **⁴they** will need in the workplace.

While I understand **⁵this viewpoint**, I do not entirely share **⁶it**. I believe that the purpose of education is primarily to develop critical thinking skills, including the ability to analyse and solve problems. **⁷These abilities** will be useful throughout people's working lives. To achieve **⁸this**, I do not think it matters whether someone studies history or theoretical physics as long as the right teaching methods are used. Students will then pick up the specific job skills they require very quickly once they are in full-time employment.

It is often suggested that young people need to gain work experience in order to make an informed choice of university course and career. Although I believe **⁹this** helps to focus students' minds on what working life will be like, generally speaking it is not possible for students to get a wide enough range of experience to be able to choose **¹⁰their** career wisely.

I would therefore argue that the best way to help young people find suitable jobs is to give them an excellent general education while ensuring that employers realise how valuable **¹¹it** is.

Plan

Para 1: Introduction: ....

Para 2: ....

Para 3: ....

Para 4: ....

Para 5: Conclusion: ....

a education should teach students to think – useful for every job

b provide a good all-round education + persuade employers of its importance

c employers say courses not practical enough

d difficulty finding jobs – education vs. employers' needs

e work experience often too limited for students to make informed choices

5 Work in pairs. Discuss these questions.

1 Why is it important to underline the key ideas in the writing task?

2 Why should you write a plan before you write your essay?

3 Did Cristina follow her plan exactly?

4 Has she dealt completely with the instructions in the writing task?

5 What words and phrases does she use in her essay to introduce her opinions?

6 To what extent do you agree with Cristina's point of view?

7 Why is it important to make your opinions clear in an essay?

6 When you write, it is important that each paragraph should cover a different aspect of the subject and that sentences should be linked together using clear references. What do the underlined reference words in Cristina's essay refer to?

7 Write your own plan for the writing task in Exercise 1. When you have finished, compare your plan with a partner's.

8 Read Cristina's essay in Exercise 4 again and highlight any words or phrases you would like to use in your essay. Also, copy them to your plan and to your notebook.

Then write your essay following your plan.

➡ page 186 Writing reference: Essays

Starting off

1 Work in pairs. Read the following remarks and write a word or phrase from the box in each gap.

> a bit rusty   accurately   aims   an excellent command
> bilingual   fashionable loanwords   fluency
> highly articulate   mother tongue   pick up   switch

2 ▶05 Check your answers by listening to the speakers.

3 Work in pairs. Which of the speakers' opinions do you agree with? Which do you disagree with? Why?

People tend to be (1) ....
– they speak the regional and the national
language and they (2) ....
between languages with ease.

Lots of (3) .... are coming
into the language, particularly from English,
so my (4) .... is not at all the
same as it was, say, fifty years ago.

My English has got
(5) ....
because I don't use it very
often.

Living in the country, you just
(6) .... the
language naturally and that's just
about the best way to learn it.

I aim to achieve (7) ....
of English, which means becoming
(8) .... and being able to
use the language (9) ....

I wouldn't consider accuracy to be as
important as (10) ....
when learning a foreign language.

We should be teaching young people
how they can use language effectively to
achieve their (11) ....

Listening | Part 1

Exam information

In Listening Part 1

- you hear three short conversations on different themes
- you have to answer two multiple-choice questions with three options about each conversation.

This part tests your ability to identify both the gist and specific details in the conversation and to identify the speakers' attitudes and opinions and how they agree or disagree.

1 You will hear three different extracts. Before you listen, work in pairs. Read questions 1–6 and discuss the following.

a Why would you learn the local language of a place you are visiting?

b In question 2, which of the options A–C do you think is essential for adults who want to learn a new language?

c What do you think is meant by 'spelling reform'?

d In question 4, how are options A, B and C related to spelling reform?

e How would you answer question 5?

f In question 6, which of the options A–C would be most helpful for non-native speakers looking for jobs?

Extract One

You hear two travellers talking about language learning.

1 Why did the man learn the local language in Mongolia?
   A to deal with awkward situations
   B to learn other skills from local people
   C to have direct contact with the people around him

2 They both agree that people wanting to learn a new language must
   A have a talent for language learning.
   B be prepared to work hard.
   C be ready to take risks.

Extract Two

through   thorough   though
plough   rough   cough

You hear two teachers, Rajiv and Susan, discussing the need for English spelling reform.

3 Rajiv argues that spelling should be reformed because it would
   A make learning more pleasant for young children.
   B reduce the number of mistakes his students make.
   C make written publications shorter.

4 Rajiv and Susan agree that simplified spelling would
   A reduce learning difficulties.
   B improve foreign learners' pronunciation.
   C produce substantial economic savings.

Extract Three

You hear an conversation between two researchers who have studied job interviews conducted in English.

5 What does the woman consider the main problem for non-native speakers?
   A Their English is not good enough.
   B Their body language may be misleading.
   C Their answers are unsuitable.

6 They agree that the recruitment process might be improved by
   A training interviewers to ask clearer questions.
   B replacing interviews with practical tests.
   C changing interviewers' expectations.

2 ▶06 Now listen, and for questions 1–6, choose the answer (A, B or C) which fits best according to what you hear. There are two questions for each extract.

3 Discuss these questions.

- What are the main difficulties for people wanting to learn your language?
- What, for you, are the main difficulties of doing an interview in an exam or for a job in English?

Vocabulary
Collocations with *make, get* and *do*

1 Form collocations with the words in **bold** by writing *make, get* or *do* in the correct form in the gaps in these extracts from Listening Part 1.

   1 But you .... a conscious **decision** to learn it when you were in Mongolia, didn't you?
   2 What's essential, though, is .... **an effort**.
   3 I remembered .... those dictation **exercises**.
   4 As a language teacher it would .... my **life** a lot **easier**.
   5 .... **the questions right** would be useful training for many interviewers.

2 Exam candidates often use the wrong verb with the words and phrases in the box. Write each word or phrase in the correct column of the table below. Two words/phrases can be written in more than one column.

> a comment   a course   a decision   a mistake   a job
> an effort   a point   a proposal   a qualification
> a suggestion   activities   an apology   business
> complaints   changes   exercise   further information
> friends   harm   one's money back   one's best
> some shopping   sport   household chores   the cooking
> the right choice   use of something   an improvement

make	get	do
a comment	a job	a job

3 ◉ Each of the sentences below contains a mistake made by candidates with a collocation of *make, do* or *get*. Correct the mistakes.

   1 Before working in our shop you first make a one-week course in developing photos.
   2 A lot of my time was wasted, so I think I should receive some of my money back.
   3 She did everything possible to turn the trip more pleasant.
   4 We were made to work very hard at school and that certainly didn't make me any harm.
   5 We need to reduce the time taken to achieve all the tasks mentioned above.

6 Other members of the club have given suggestions about a quiz or karaoke night to form part of our social programme.
7 We'd be very grateful if you'd make your best to solve this problem.
8 You can spend lots of time at this holiday camp practising exercise and having a great time!

Reading and Use of English | Part 3

1 Work in small groups. How many words can you form from each of these base words?

> govern   care   critic   child   break   occasion   force
> deep   fragile   friend   repair

Example
govern: *government, governmental, governable, ungovernable, ungovernably, governing, governor*

2 Look at your answers to Exercise 1. Which of these suffixes did you use?

-ion, -ment, -less, -ise, -ally, -hood, -able, -ly, -ful, -en, -ity, -ship

Which of the suffixes above are used to form

   1 verbs?   2 nouns?   3 adjectives?   4 adverbs?

3 Can you think of other suffixes which are used in each of the categories 1–4 in Exercise 2? For each suffix, write one word as an example, e.g. nouns: *-ness*: *kindness*.

4 Which of the words in the box are spelled correctly? Correct the words which are spelled incorrectly.

occurrence happenning developement
statement referrence opening realy
factually beautifuly truthfull disappointed
disatisfied iregularrity reliable undenyable
useable refuseing basicaly arguement

➡ page 183 Language reference: Spelling rules for adding affixes

5 👁 Spelling mistakes are among the most frequent errors made by candidates in the exam. Find and correct the spelling mistakes made by candidates in the sentences below.

1 As you can see in the advertisment, the holiday is quite cheap.
2 People are begining to get tired of being promised things it's impossible to give them.
3 I'm sure you're going to be as succesful as your predecessor was.
4 He was sent to prison for expressing his disagreement with the goverment.
5 By implementing these proposals we will be doing more to protect the enviroment.
6 The family I stayed with was realy kind and helpful.

6 Work in small groups. You are going to read a text about names for new products. Before you read, suggest an attractive and an unattractive name for each of the products in the pictures.

7 Read the text below quite quickly to find out

1 how companies name products
2 what problems they have when naming products.

The naming of products

International companies are finding it (0) ....*increasingly*.... important to develop brand names that can be used in a wide range of countries. A product with a single, (1) .... recognised name can enable companies to make major (2) .... in production and promotion costs – especially now that world advertising is a (3) .... in such contexts as major sporting events.

INCREASE

UNIVERSE

SAVE

REAL

It is said that more time is actually spent deciding the name of a product than on the research and development leading to the (4) .... itself. Thousands of possible names may need to be investigated to find one that is internationally (5) ....

INNOVATE

ACCEPT

An indication of the scope of the problem can be seen from the experience of Dunlop, who spent over two years (6) .... researching a name for a new tyre. They then launched an international (7) .... amongst their employees, receiving over 10,000 entries. Around 30 names were selected from an enormous number of (8) .... but not one was found to be legally available in more than a small number of countries.

SUCCEED

COMPETE

SUBMIT

Adapted from *The Cambridge Encyclopedia of Language*

---

8 For questions 1–8, read the text again. Use the word given in capitals at the end of some of the lines to form a word that fits in the gap in the same line. There is an example at the beginning (0).

9 Work in pairs.

• How do people in your country choose names for their children?
• Are fashions in children's names changing?
• In Britain, people also name their pets and sometimes their houses. What things do people in your country name, and what sorts of name do they choose?

Reading and Use of English | Part 6

In Reading and Use of English Part 6, you

- read four short extracts from academic texts on the same subject
- answer four questions.

This part tests your ability to identify similarities, differences and connections between opinions and attitudes expressed in the extracts.

1 Work in small groups. You will read four extracts from texts about minority languages. Before you read, discuss these questions.

- What minority languages, or languages spoken by just a small number of people exist in your country, or do you know about?
- Are they in danger of dying out? Why (not)?
- Do you think it is important to protect endangered languages? Why (not)?

2 Before you do the exam task in Exercise 4, read the introductory sentence in *italics* and each extract carefully and answer these questions. Then discuss your answers in pairs.

Extract A

1 What effect has globalisation had on minority languages?
2 What suggestion does the writer have for keeping minority languages alive?

Extract B

3 What reasons does the extract give for not promoting regional languages?
4 What is the 'benign neglect' position?

Extract C

5 What problem do linguistics researchers face and how has this affected their research?
6 Why should languages be kept alive?

Extract D

7 When is it clear that a language is going to die?
8 Why is it important to prevent the loss of minority languages?

3 To follow the arguments of academic texts, it is important to understand the referencing within the texts. Work in pairs. What do the underlined words and phrases (1–16) in the texts refer to?

Endangered languages

The threat to minority languages in different parts of the world is an area of discussion amongst linguists.

A

In our connected globalised world, the languages which dominate communications and business, Mandarin, Hindi, English, Spanish and Russian amongst [1]others, are placing small languages spoken in remote places under increasing pressure. Fewer and fewer people speak languages such as Liki, Taushiro and Dumi as their children shift away from the language of their ancestors towards languages which promise education, success and the chance of a better life. While to many parents [2]this may appear a reasonable choice, giving their offspring the opportunity to achieve the sort of prosperity they see on television, the children themselves often lose touch with their roots. However, in many places the more reasonable option of bilingualism, where children learn to speak both a local and a national language, is being promoted. [3]This gives hope that many endangered languages will survive, allowing people to combine their links to local tradition with access to wider world culture.

B

While individuals are free to choose if they wish to speak a minority language, national governments should be under no obligation to provide education in an economically unproductive language, especially in times of budget constraints. It is generally accepted that national languages unite and help to create wealth while minority regional languages divide. Furthermore, governments have a duty to ensure that young people can fulfil their full potential, meaning that state education must provide [4]them with the ability to speak and work in their national language and so equip them to participate responsibly in national affairs. People whose language competence does not extend beyond the use of a regional tongue have limited prospects. [5]This means that while many people may feel a sentimental attachment to their local language, their government's position should be one of benign neglect, allowing people to speak the language, but not acting to prevent [6]its eventual disappearance.

The Breton language of Brittany, France, is classified as 'severely endangered'.

Of 250 known Australian Aboriginal languages, all but 35 have died out or are in critical danger.

There are just 50 speakers of Udege left in Siberia and most of them are over 50 years old.

C

Many PhD students studying minority languages lack the resources to develop their language skills, with the result that they have to rely on interpreters and translators to communicate with speakers of the language [7]they are studying. [8]This, I believe, has a detrimental effect on the quality of their research. At the same time, [9]they have to struggle against the frequently expressed opinion that minority languages serve no useful purpose and should be allowed to die a natural death. [10]Such a view fails to take into account the fact that a unique body of knowledge and culture, built up over thousands of years, is contained in a language and that language extinction and species extinction are different facets of the same process. [11]They are part of an impending global catastrophe which is beginning to look unavoidable.

D

A healthy language is [12]one which children learn to speak, so that however many adults use the language, if young people do not acquire [13]it, it will not survive. While the disappearance of a language may be a tragedy for the people who speak it, [14]it may appear to be an event of little importance to [15]others. However, I would argue that language diversity is as necessary as biological diversity and that we are simply not aware of all the things we lose when a language disappears. When an animal or plant becomes extinct, we seldom realise how its existence might have benefited us. [16]The same is true for many small languages. Moreover, the resources to prevent their loss are unlikely to ever be available simply because the economic benefits of keeping them alive cannot be demonstrated.

4 Now do the exam task. For questions 1–4, choose from the extracts A–D. The extracts may be chosen more than once.

Which extract	
shares Extract B's view of the economic significance of major languages?	1
expresses a different view from the others regarding the need to preserve minority languages?	2
takes a different view from the others regarding the future of small languages?	3
takes a similar view to Extract C on the effect of language disappearance?	4

5 Work in small groups.

- Which extract(s) do you think it would be interesting to read more of? Why?
- What can be done to keep endangered languages alive?

Speaking | Part 2

Exam information

In Speaking Part 2 you are each given three photos and are asked to choose two of the photos to speak about. You must speak on your own for one minute. You have to

- compare the two photos you have chosen
- answer two questions connected with the photos, which are printed on the task sheet.

When the other candidate is speaking, you need to listen and then answer a brief question about the photos.

This part tests your ability to speak at length, organise your ideas, compare, describe, express opinions and speculate about things connected with the photos.

1 Look at the photos and read the examiner's instructions. What are the three parts to the task?

> " In this part of the test I'm going to give each of you three pictures. I'd like you to talk about two of them on your own for about a minute, and also to answer a question briefly about your partner's pictures. Here are your pictures. They show people explaining things. I'd like you to compare two of the pictures and say what the speakers might be explaining and what problems the speakers might have. "

- What might the speakers be explaining?
- What problems might the speakers have?

2 In the Speaking test you will get higher marks if you use a range of appropriate vocabulary. Decide which of these phrases you could use with each photo. (Some can be used with more than one photo.)

argue a case   boost morale   defend a client
decide on / discuss / explain tactics   encourage the team
give a demonstration   influence the outcome
persuade the judge/jury   reach a verdict
take people through the steps

3 ▶07 Listen to Ivan doing the Speaking task.

1 Which phrases from Exercise 2 does he use?
2 When he compares the photos, does he just point out differences or does he also mention similarities?
3 Does he answer both of the examiner's questions?

4 Complete each of these sentences about the photos. You can use your own ideas or Ivan's ideas.

1 The coach looks as if …
2 They give the impression that … judging by …
3 The lawyer seems …
4 She appears …
5 The coach wants … while the barrister wants …
6 In both photos I imagine …

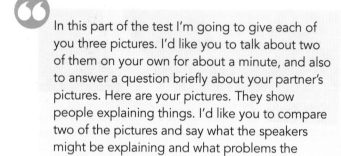

5 Work in pairs.

- Take turns to talk for a minute to do the Speaking task in Exercise 1. You can choose which two photos you wish to speak about.
- When your partner has finished speaking, briefly answer this question about the photos your partner chose: *Which of the two speakers do you think has the harder task?*

6 Work in pairs. Look at the photos and read the examiner's instructions. Then answer questions 1 and 2 below.

> Here are your pictures. They show adults and children talking to each other. I'd like you to compare two of the pictures and say why they might be talking to each other and how each of them might benefit from this.

1 Do you think you should choose the two easiest photos to talk about, or the two most difficult? Why?
2 When you answer the second question, should you just talk about how the children might benefit?

- Why might the people be talking to each other?
- How might each of them benefit from this?

7 Work in pairs. Which of these phrasal verbs and other phrases could you use with each of the photos?

bond with each other   cheer someone up
give encouragement   look through an album
put a brave face on things   remember good times
share family history   spend quality time together
teach someone basic skills

8 Work in pairs.

1 **Student A:** Follow the examiner's instructions in Exercise 6.
2 **Student B:** When Student A has finished, follow the examiner's instructions in Exercise 6 using the photo Student A didn't use and one of the others.
3 When your partner has finished speaking, briefly answer this question: *Which situation do you think the adult would find most rewarding?*

→ page 195 Speaking reference: Speaking Part 2

Grammar
Expressing purpose, reason and result

1 Match the beginnings of these sentences (1–8) with their endings (a–h).

1 I thought I should pick the language up while I was there, **so**

2 It might be better to set up a simulation of the job in question **so as to**

3 The candidate often lacks the sort of cultural background that would stand them in good stead in these situations, **with the result that**

4 They used to give us dictations in class **to**

5 I always write new vocabulary down in my notebook **in case**

6 Pavla is studying languages at university **with the intention of**

7 We found the lecturer difficult to hear **due to**

8 You'll need to use a microphone, **otherwise**

a eventually working as an interpreter.
b I forget it.
c I immersed myself in the life of the local community.
d the people at the back won't hear you.
e the poor acoustics in the hall.
f their responses take the interviewer by surprise.
g see whether the candidate has the skills and attitude they're looking for.
h make sure we knew things like putting a double 'p' in 'approve'.

2 Answer the following questions.

1 Which of the **bold** words/phrases in Exercise 1 express
  a a purpose?
  b a reason?
  c a result?

2 Which of the words/phrases are followed by
  a an infinitive?
  b a noun / verb + -ing?
  c a clause?

→ page 170 Language reference: Expressing purpose, reason and result

3 ⊙ Exam candidates often make mistakes with words and phrases to express reason, purpose and result. Circle the correct alternative in *italics* in each of the following sentences.

1 My Italian is excellent *because / due to* I lived in Italy for four years.

2 *By / For* technical reasons, the flight was delayed for several hours.

3 Over the last decade, our lives have changed a lot *because of / by* computers.

4 Could you please send us a brochure *so as / so that* we can see exactly what you are offering?

5 I hope the organisation's efficiency will improve *for not to / in order not to* waste people's time and money.

Writing | Part 2
A report

Exam information

- In Writing Part 2 you do one writing task from a choice of three.
- The possible tasks are an email/letter, a proposal, a report or a review.
- You must write between 220 and 260 words.

1 Read the following writing task and answer the questions below.

An international media company is investigating the influence that television programmes imported from English-speaking countries have on different countries around the world. You have been asked to write a report on English-language TV programmes in your country. In your report you should address the following:

- how popular these programmes are and why
- the effect they are having on local culture
- any changes you would recommend.

Write your **report**.

1 Who is expected to read this report?
2 Should you use a formal or informal style?
3 What are the four main points you should deal with?
4 In what order would you deal with them?

2 Read the sample report and write one word/phrase from the box in each gap.

accounted for   the aim   as a consequence   due to
means   meant   resulted   so as   the effect   the result

English-language TV programmes in my country

Introduction

¹.. of this report is to comment on the popularity of imported English-language television programmes in my country, to explain how they are affecting local culture and to recommend changes that could be made in the way these programmes are shown.

Popularity of imported programmes

Approximately fifty percent of the programmes shown on TV in this country have been made in an English-speaking country and were originally in English. The popularity of these programmes can be ².. by their larger budgets, which ³.. they are generally more spectacular than locally made programmes and may include internationally famous stars in their casts. On most channels, viewers can choose which language they wish to watch the programme in, with ⁴.. that people with a good command of English tend to watch programmes in their original versions.

Effects on local culture

The popularity of English-language programmes has ⁵.. that it is hard for local programme-makers to compete, given their limited budgets. ⁶.. , local culture has been heavily influenced by American values of consumerism. Moreover, exposure to mistranslations of English-language films has ⁷.. in words in our languages being used with new or wrong meanings. However, a positive effect has been that people have become more open and ready to change ⁸.. the fact that they see other ways of living and thinking.

Recommended changes

I would recommend that the government should subsidise national television companies ⁹.. to encourage them to make more quality programmes. This would have ¹⁰.. of reducing our reliance on imported programmes while at the same time promoting local values and culture.

3 Read the report again and answer these questions.

1 How is the layout of a report different from other types of writing?
2 Has the writer included all the points in the writing task? Where are they dealt with in the report?
3 Is the style appropriate for the target readers?

4 Read the following writing task and then

1 underline the points you must deal with
2 identify who will read the report
3 decide what style you will need to use
4 decide what title to give your report and what sections and section headings you will need.

A leading educational publisher is interested in language learning in different countries. You have been asked to write a report on foreign language learning in your country. In your report you should deal with

* the languages people learn, who learns them and where they learn them
* recommendations for improving language learning in your country.

Write your **report**.

5 Write the report, using the sample report in Exercise 2 as a model.

 page 191 Writing reference: Reports

Vocabulary and grammar review Unit 1

Vocabulary

1 Complete each of the sentences below by writing the correct form of *give*, *do* or *make* in each gap.

1 The minister .... a rousing speech at the end of the conference.

2 Carrie sat through the entire meeting without .... a single suggestion to solve the problem.

3 We .... our students plenty of opportunities to speak to ensure they become fluent.

4 Fergus .... a pretty bad impression in Saturday's match, so the manager is .... him just one last chance or he'll be dropped from the team.

5 If you'd just .... me the details, I'll take a note of them and pass them to the person responsible.

6 I never expected to see you at the concert because the last time we met, you .... me the impression that you didn't like classical music.

7 If you're not completely satisfied with the result, we'll .... you a full refund.

8 Patsy is just .... a phone call at the moment, so she'll be with us in a sec.

Grammar

2 For questions 1–6, complete the second sentence so that it has a similar meaning to the first sentence, using the word given. Do not change the word given. You must use between three and six words, including the word given.

1 I received some very useful advice from Gustavo.
FOUND
I .... me very useful.

2 The opportunity to study at university should be open to everyone.
BE
Everyone .... to study at university.

3 The first time Carla went skiing was last Monday.
NEVER
Carla .... last Monday.

4 We were all favourably impressed with Paola's lecture.
FAVOURABLE
The lecture .... on all of us.

5 Students don't spend their free time in the same way as fifty years ago.
CHANGED
The way students spend their free time .... fifty years.

6 Without a receipt, they will not return your money.
REFUND
They will not .... you have a receipt.

3 Circle the best alternative in *italics* in the sentences below.

1 We got to the park quite soon after lunch and fortunately the rain *stopped / had stopped* by then.

2 *We'd stood / We'd been standing* in the rain for at least twenty minutes before the bus arrived, by which time we *were feeling / had been feeling* pretty cold and wet, as you can imagine.

3 *I've driven / I've been driving* along this road a thousand times – I could almost do it with my eyes shut!

4 You'd expect Fran to be looking tired because *she's studied / she's been studying* for her final exams for the last three weeks.

5 Maisie *ate / had been eating* sweets all evening so it was not surprising she didn't want any supper!

6 I think people *used to work / would work* much harder in the past than they do nowadays.

7 So much noise *had come / had been coming* from our flat all afternoon that eventually the neighbours complained and we had to explain that we *repaired / were repairing* the heater and that we'd be finishing soon.

8 We always used to go to the Mediterranean for our holidays when I was a child. I think *we went / used to go* to Ibiza at least five times.

Vocabulary and grammar review Unit 2

Vocabulary

1 For questions 1–8, read the text below. Use the word given in capitals at the end of some of the lines to form a word that fits in the gap in the same line.

The evolution of linguistics

Linguistics has undegone two great revolutions in the past 70 years. In the late 1950s Noam Chomsky ....theorised.......... that all languages **THEORY** were built on an underlying **(1)** .... **UNIVERSE** grammar embedded in human genes. A second shift in linguistics – an **(2)** .... of **EXPLODE** interest in small and endangered languages – has focused on the **(3)** .... of **VARY** linguistic experience. Field linguists are more interested in the **(4)** .... that make **CHARACTER** each language unique and the ways that culture can be **(5)** .... in a language's form. **INFLUENCE** At present some 85 percent of languages have yet to be documented. Understanding them can only **(6)** .... our comprehension of **RICH** what is similar in all languages.

Different languages highlight the range of human experience, revealing that aspects of life that we have a **(7)** .... to think of **TEND** as true of all languages, such as our experience of time, number or colour, are in fact quite **(8)** .... In the Siberian language **CHANGE** Tuva, for example, the past is always spoken of as ahead of one and the future is behind one's back.

2 Complete each of these sentences with a word/phrase relating to language (the number of letters in each word is given at the end of the sentence).

1 You've got to be able to write .... for this job. We can't afford to have people making mistakes. (10 letters)
2 Amina expresses her ideas very clearly – but then she's a highly .... young woman. (10)
3 Having lived in Chile for seven years, Philippe has a perfect .... of Spanish. (7)
4 It takes a great deal of practice to achieve .... in a language. (7)

5 I prefer to .... the language while I'm visiting the country rather than going to classes. (4, 2)
6 Maria's English is virtually perfect although her .... is Greek. (6, 6)
7 With a Japanese father and a French mother, Motoko is completely .... (9)

3 Complete these sentences by writing the correct form of *make, get* or *do* in the gaps.

1 Lee has been working hard because he needs to .... better professional qualifications.
2 The new principal is planning on .... quite a few changes to the way this college is run.
3 How long have you been .... your current job?
4 It was a difficult decision, but I think you .... the right choice.
5 I don't understand you. What point are you trying to .... ?
6 It wouldn't .... you any harm to take a bit more exercise!

Grammar

4 Complete each of these sentences with a word or phrase from the box.

due to   in case   otherwise   so as   so that
with the intention of

1 I caught an earlier train .... finishing the report before my boss arrived in the office.
2 Natalie delivered the parcel herself .... to make sure it arrived safely.
3 If I were you, I'd take your bank card .... your money runs out.
4 You really should write new vocabulary in your notebook, ... you'll forget it.
5 Services on North-East Trains were cancelled today .... a train drivers' strike.
6 Amin covered his face as he left the building .... no one would recognise him.

3 All in the mind

Starting off

1 Discuss these questions.
   - Do you believe it is possible to measure a person's intelligence accurately? Why (not)?
   - Even if you believe it is possible, do you think we should measure intelligence? Why (not)?

2 Now consider what type of a thinker you are. Look at the nine types below and give yourself a score of 0–5 for each statement (0 = completely untrue for you, 5 = absolutely true for you).

   Compare yourself with other students. How similar or different are you?

Type of thinker	Characteristics	Score 0–5
Logical/ Mathematical	You like to understand patterns and relationships between objects or actions. You are good at thinking critically and solving problems creatively.	
Linguistic	You think in words and like to use language to express complex ideas. You are sensitive to the sounds and rhythms of words as well as their meanings.	
Interpersonal	You like to think about and try to understand people. You make an effort to cultivate good relationships with family, friends and colleagues.	
Intrapersonal	You spend a lot of time thinking about and trying to understand yourself. You understand how your behaviour affects your relationship with others.	
Naturalistic	You like to understand the natural world and the living beings that inhabit it. You have an aptitude for communicating with animals.	
Existential	You like to think about philosophical questions such as 'What is the meaning of life?'. You try to see beyond the 'here and now' and understand deeper meanings.	
Musical	You tend to think in sounds, and may also think in rhythms and melodies. You are sensitive to the sounds and rhythms of words as well as their meanings.	
Spatial	You tend to think in pictures and can develop good mental models of the physical world. You think well in three dimensions and have a flair for working with objects.	
Kinaesthetic	You think in movements and like to use your body in skilful and expressive ways. You have an aptitude for working with your hands.	

3 What type of thinkers do you think these famous people are/were? Focus on their occupations and use some of the expressions below.

I'd imagine someone like X would be / have been …
X is/was probably a … thinker, don't you reckon?
X could be / have been a … thinker or a … thinker.
X must have been a … thinker – he/she was so …
Would you agree?
That's just my opinion.
It's difficult/impossible to tell.

Louise Bourgeois, sculptor, France

Charles Darwin, scientist, UK

Chinua Achebe, novelist, Nigeria

Ayn Rand, philosopher, Russia

Judit Polgár, chess grandmaster, Hungary

Maria Callas, opera singer, Greece

Antoni Gaudí, architect, Catalonia, Spain

Lionel Messi, footballer, Argentina

4 What is your opinion of attempts like this to categorise people?

Listening | Part 2

1 Work in pairs. How good are you at recognising people you have only met once or twice before?

2 Look at this painting by the surrealist artist René Magritte. Do you find it amusing, disturbing, interesting, mystifying or just pointless? Compare your reaction with your partner's.

3 ▶08 You are going to listen to part of a radio programme about a psychological condition known as *prosopagnosia*. What is the more common name for this condition? Listen to the first part of the programme to find the answer.

4 ▶09 Listen to the whole programme and say if the following statements are true (T) or false (F).

1 The speaker compares face-blindness to the inability to hear.
2 Scientists do not understand how normal people remember faces.
3 The face-blind subjects could not distinguish between the faces or the objects.

5 Read the sentences below. How many of the gaps can you already fill? (The number of missing words is in brackets, but this information is not given in the exam.)

According to the speaker, the painting by René Magritte (1) .... the idea of face-blindness. (2 words)

People with face-blindness have no memory of a person's face once the person (2) .... their sight. (1 word)

Some people with this condition are so (3) .... that they cannot recognise members of their own family. (2 words)

It could help scientists to understand (4) .... if they knew more about face-blindness. (2 words)

Scientists do not yet know whether the ability to recognise faces has a (5) .... of its own or whether it is part of an individual's general ability. (3 words)

In an experiment, a number of (6) .... were shown images of people, places and objects. (3 words)

The experiment proved that the human brain processes (7) .... differently from faces. (2 words)

Other experiments have shown that people with this condition can improve their (8) .... (3 words)

6 ▶09 Listen again. For questions 1–8, complete the sentences with a word or short phrase.

Vocabulary
Nouns which can be countable or uncountable

1 Look at the nouns in *italics* in these extracts from Listening Part 2. Are they being used as countable or uncountable nouns?

1 As soon as someone leaves their *sight*, the *memory* of that person's face is blank.
2 This *ability* helps to hold *society* together and has enabled human beings to develop a complex *culture*.

2 Write sentences in which the uncountable nouns in Exercise 1 are used as countable nouns and vice versa.

3 In pairs, discuss the countable and uncountable meanings of these nouns.

art   business   chicken   disease   exercise   speech

➡ page 166 Language reference: Countable and uncountable nouns

Grammar
no, none, not

1 Complete these extracts with *no, none* or *not*.

1 The subjects were shown pictures of faces with .... hair on their heads.
2 .... of the subjects could recognise the faces well.
3 This is .... to say that prosopagnosia has .... advantages.

➡ page 173 Language reference: *no, none, not*

2 ◉ Five of these sentences contain mistakes that exam candidates have made in expressing negation. Correct the mistakes. (One sentence is correct.)

1 It was difficult to get around last weekend as there was not public transport.
2 Most students were no satisfied with the standard of food in the school canteen.
3 We've had hardly no communication from management for over a week.
4 As far as I can see, there's not much difference between Spanish grammar and Italian grammar.
5 I'm afraid I don't know nothing about psychology.
6 We couldn't get treated for two hours because none doctors were available.

Grammar
The passive

1 How are passive verbs formed? Compare these two sentences.

Active: They showed the subjects images of cars, tools, guns, houses and landscapes.

Passive: The subjects <u>were shown</u> images of cars, tools, guns, houses and landscapes.

2 Underline the passive verbs in these extracts from Listening Part 2.

a The subjects were asked to indicate whether each image they saw was new or repeated.

b Faces are handled differently by the brain from other objects.

c It has been shown in experiments that people with face-blindness can be taught to improve their face recognition skills.

3 Discuss these questions.

1 In which extract above is the doer of the action (the 'agent') mentioned?

2 Who or what could be the agents in the other extracts?

3 Why is the agent not mentioned in these extracts? (There are several possible reasons.)

4 Would you be more likely to find passive verbs
- in an email to a friend or an essay?
- in a scientific report or a magazine story?
- in a personal anecdote or a job application?

4 Change these active sentences into the passive form. Only include an agent if you think it is important.

1 Over a million people have watched this YouTube clip.

2 They made the film over twenty years ago.

3 At the time no one had seen anything like it.

4 Apparently, they are making a new version of the film at the moment.

5 They are going to release it next year.

5 In formal writing we often begin sentences with *It + passive*, especially if we want to focus attention on ideas and arguments, e.g. *It has been shown* in Exercise 2, extract c. Work in pairs to complete these beginnings with your own ideas. Choose any subject you find interesting.

1 It is commonly believed that …

2 It has been reported in the last few days that …

3 It has been proved beyond doubt that …

page 173 Language reference: The passive

6 Rewrite this text using passive verbs to replace the underlined active verbs. Only include an agent if you think it is important. Use one verb with *it*, as in Exercise 5.

Example: 1 *A new study on Albert Einstein has been completed …*

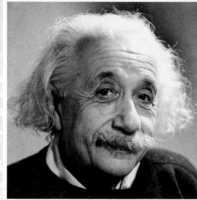

An expert **(1)** <u>has completed</u> a new study on Albert Einstein and she **(2)** <u>will publish</u> it next month in a journal on neurology. The study suggests that a uniquely shaped brain **(3)** <u>may have influenced</u> Einstein's extraordinary genius. When anthropologist Dean Falk and her team made a comparison with 85 'normal' human brains, **(4)** <u>they found</u> that Einstein's brain possessed some remarkable features.

The researchers were using 14 photos of the genius's brain which people **(5)** <u>had</u> only recently <u>rediscovered</u>. With permission from his family, scientists **(6)** <u>removed and photographed</u> Einstein's brain after his death in 1955. The National Museum of Health and Medicine **(7)** <u>hold</u> the photographs but people **(8)** <u>had</u> never fully <u>investigated</u> them before.

Reading and Use of English | Part 5

Exam information

In Reading and Use of English Part 5 you have to
- read a text of 650–750 words
- answer six questions about it by choosing A, B, C or D.

This part tests your ability to understand the main ideas and purpose of the text and the writer's opinions or attitude, and to understand text organisation features such as exemplification.

1 You are going to read an article about how digital technology is affecting people's lives. Before you read: how does it affect your life? Make a list of the ways you use digital technology. Then compare lists with a partner and discuss how important this technology is in your lives.

Examples: smart phone apps, downloading music, films or podcasts, creating a website …

2 Read this article quickly and decide whether you are more like Emily Feld or her mother, Christine.

The next step in brain evolution

Emily Feld is a native of a new planet. While the 20-year-old university student may appear to live in London, she actually spends much of her time in another galaxy – in the digital universe of websites, e-mails, smart phones and social networking sites. The behaviour of Emily and her generation, say experts, is being shaped by digital technology as never before. It may even be the next step in evolution, transforming our brains and the way we think.

'First thing every morning I check my mobile for messages, have a coffee and then go on Twitter,' says Emily. 'I look at Facebook, my favourite social networking site, update my status, add any photos and interesting articles or music clips I've found. And I've got about 300 friends so there are always messages to read and reply to. Then I'll browse the Internet, and if a news article on Google catches my eye, I'll read it.

'The other day, I went to meet a friend in town and realised I'd left my mobile at home. I felt so lost without it that I panicked and went back to collect it. I need to have it on me at all times. Technology is an essential part of my everyday life. I don't know where I'd be without it.'

That's what makes Emily a 'digital native', someone who has never known a world without instant communication. Her mother Christine, on the other hand, is a 'digital immigrant', still coming to terms with a culture ruled by the ring of a mobile and the zip of text messages. Though 55-year-old Christine happily shops online and e-mails friends, at heart she's still in the old world. 'Children today are permanently multitasking – downloading tracks, uploading photos, texting. It's non-stop,' she says. 'They find sitting down and reading, even watching TV, too slow and boring.'

Are digital natives like Emily charting a new course for human intelligence? Many parents fear that children who spend hours glued to computer screens will end up as zombies with the attention span of an insect. Cyberspace is full of junk, they worry, and computer games are packed with mindless violence. But it need not be like that, say some experts, and increasingly it isn't, as users exert more control and discrimination.

The sheer mass of information in the modern world is forcing digital natives to make choices that those who grew up with only books and television did not have to make. 'Younger people sift more and filter more,' says Helen Petrie, a professor of human–computer interaction. 'We have more information to deal with, and we pay less attention to particular bits of information, so it may appear that attention spans are shorter.'

The question, then, is how do digital natives learn to discriminate, and what determines the things that interest them? Parents who hope that skills, values and limits are instilled at school may be fighting a losing battle. According to some educationalists, the reason why many children today do not pay attention in school is that they find teaching methods dull compared with their digital experiences. Instead, parameters are increasingly set by 'wiki-thinking', peer groups exchanging ideas through digital networks. Just as the online encyclopedia Wikipedia has been built from the collective knowledge of thousands of contributors, so digital natives draw on the experience and advice of online communities to shape their interests.

Where is this all leading? Only one thing seems clear: changes propelled by the digital world are just beginning. Indeed, apart from age, one of the differences between the natives and the immigrants is the intuitive acceptance of rapid digital change. Parents may use the Internet as much as their children, but what they are not used to doing is upgrading. The younger generation are much more used to replacing old technology. Faster broadband speeds, smaller hardware – innovation is happening at such a pace that what was science fiction a few years ago will soon be fact.

Anecdotally, it seems, a lot of natives in this digital culture are adept at multitasking, doing several things simultaneously. But nobody knows exactly what the effect will be. In a sense, we are running a grand-scale experiment. We're bringing up a whole generation in this totally new environment – without any firm evidence of how they will be affected.

Adapted from *The Times online*

3 Read the article again and for questions 1–6, choose the answer (A, B, C or D) which you think fits best according to the article.

1 Why are the first three paragraphs of the article devoted to Emily Feld?
A She is particularly interested in technology.
B She is a typical university student.
C She is a representative of people of her age.
D She is studying the effects of digital technology on students.

2 How would you sum up Emily's relationship with digital technology?
A She is completely dependent on it.
B She uses it mainly to support her academic studies.
C It provides her with a meaningful social life.
D It is useful but she could live without it.

3 How is Emily's mother different from her daughter?
A She is very uncomfortable using digital technology.
B She rarely uses digital technology.
C She is still adjusting to digital technology.
D She prefers reading or watching TV.

4 Some parents worry that continued exposure to digital technology will result in children
A becoming uncontrollable and violent.
B becoming too reliant on technology.
C being unable to discriminate between right and wrong.
D losing the ability to pay attention for more than a few seconds.

5 Educationalists believe that digital natives may be developing their ideas and interests from
A older family members.
B online encyclopedias like Wikipedia.
C internet contacts of their own age.
D schools and teachers.

6 What, according to the writer, is the only certainty with regard to the future of digital technology?
A Children will always be happier with digital technology than their parents.
B The world is at the start of the digital age.
C Everybody will need to become accustomed to multitasking.
D People will accept that digital technology is changing their world.

4 Discuss these questions.

1 How do you feel about the idea expressed in the following extract?
The behaviour of Emily and her generation is being shaped by digital technology. It may even be the next step in evolution, transforming our brains and the way we think.

2 The writer says: *Many parents fear that children who spend hours glued to computer screens will end up as zombies.* Are parents right to be worried?

3 The article concludes: *We're bringing up a whole generation in this totally new environment – without any firm evidence of how they will be affected.* How do you think this generation will be affected?

Vocabulary
Formal or informal?

1 Which of the following examples would you be more likely to find in formal writing and which in informal writing? Pay particular attention to the words in **bold** type.

1 **They've** rung to say **they're** coming tomorrow.
2 What on earth are you doing?
3 **We will** be leaving as soon as the **fog has** lifted.
4 We have never **contemplated residing** in any other **neighbourhood**.
5 I can't **put up with** this situation for much longer.
6 'Community' can be defined as any individual or organisation **with whom** we interact.
7 A teenager **is believed** to have started the fire.
8 **Grub's up.** Come and get it.
9 That's the girl I go to school **with**.

2 Rewrite each of the sentences in Exercise 1, changing from formal to informal and vice versa.

3 Look again at paragraphs 3–7 in the article on page 34 and find examples of formal and informal language. Why is there a mixture of styles here?

Reading and Use of English | Part 2

1 You are going to read an article which considers the extent to which we inherit our personalities as well as our physical characteristics from our parents.

1 What is your opinion on this issue? Are we born with a ready-made personality, or does our personality develop from our experiences? Think about yourself and people you know.

2 Read *Nature vs nurture* quickly, without paying attention to the missing words. What conclusion does the article come to?

2 Work in pairs to complete the text. Use the list below to help you think of the type of word you need for each gap.

preposition   article   verb   adjective   pronoun
auxiliary verb   auxiliary verb   pronoun

Nature vs nurture

You know where your looks come from – for example, you may have your mother's nose or your father's eyes. But what about things that we cannot see, like your talent **(0)** ....for........... music? Is this something that you learned, or are your abilities and personality traits determined **(1)** .... your genes? What makes **(2)** .... individual behave in a certain way and display certain talents?

Scientists are not clear what the answer to this question **(3)** .... Those who support the 'nature' theory believe that humans are genetically programmed to behave in certain ways, regardless of culture and upbringing. On the **(4)** .... hand we have the 'nurture' theory, **(5)** .... argues that a person's behaviour and personality **(6)** .... developed by teaching and experience. There is evidence to support both of these theories and the debate **(7)** .... still to be resolved. **(8)** .... seems most probable that both theories have their validity and that nature and nurture each play a part in making us who we are.

Exam information

In Reading and Use of English Part 2 there is a text with eight gaps. You have to write one word in each gap. Most missing words are 'grammar words', e.g.

- articles (*the, a*)
- auxiliary or modal verbs (*are, is, can*)
- pronouns (*he, us*)
- conjunctions (*but, although*)
- possessive adjectives (*my, our*)
- prepositions (*at, to*)

A few may be 'meaning' words, e.g. nouns, verbs, adjectives. You must spell your answers correctly.

3 Now do the task below with no assistance. For questions 1–8, read the text and think of the word which best fits each gap. Use only one word for each gap. There is an example at the beginning.

Where do my talents come from?

Some people claim that the ability **(0)** ......to...... sing, dance or draw is acquired, rather than inherited. But you know what they also say: some people have it and some people don't. How do people actually acquire **(1)** .... individual talents? You could argue that you become good **(2)** .... something by determination and constant practice, but there are small children with **(3)** .... or no training who sing or dance beautifully or are clearly genius-level artists. Most children of musicians and actors seem to be talented **(4)** .... their parents. Then again, I personally can sing, dance and draw but my parents have none of those abilities. I was singing and drawing **(5)** .... I was little but had never been in a choir or to an art class in my life. It just came naturally to **(6)** .... I suppose you could say that being born **(7)** .... stronger lungs or longer legs and arms might give you **(8)** .... advantage.

4 Discuss these questions.

1 What physical characteristics have you inherited from your parents?

2 Where do your likes, dislikes, tastes and interests come from – your genes or your experience?

Speaking | Part 3

Exam information

In Speaking Part 3, you and the other candidate discuss a situation or issue together.

- The examiner gives you instructions and a set of written prompts.
- You have about 15 seconds to think about the task and then two minutes to discuss your ideas.
- The examiner then asks you another question, which requires you to come to a decision. You have one minute to do this.

This part tests your ability to interact with your partner by exchanging ideas, expressing and justifying opinions, agreeing and disagreeing, speculating, evaluating and reaching a decision through discussion. It is important that you keep talking.

1 Do the following tasks related to the causes of stress in today's society.

   1 Make a list of things that make people feel stressed, for example, overwork, difficult relationships, etc.
   2 Compare lists with a partner. How many causes of stress are in both your lists?
   3 Explain to your partner how you cope with stressful situations you find yourself in.

2 ▶ 10 Listen to two people discussing stress and how they cope with it. Do either of the speakers mention any of the causes of stress that you have discussed?

3 ▶ 10 To make sure you don't speak too much in the discussion, ask your partner questions. Listen to the conversation again and complete these questions which the speakers ask to involve their partner.

   1 Do you know what I ....?
   2 That's one of the worst effects of stress, ...?
   3 So what .... if you're feeling stressed?
   4 What .... you?
   5 Have you .... that?

4 Read the examiner's instructions. Then look at the written prompts below and prepare what you are going to say.

> Here are some of the actions that people take to prevent or cope with stress. Talk to each other about how effective these actions might be in helping people to prevent or cope with stress.

- avoiding stressful situations
- taking regular exercise
- How effective are these actions in preventing or coping with stress?
- expressing your feelings
- having an active social life
- practising relaxation techniques

5 Now discuss the prompts with your partner. Your discussion should last for about two minutes.

6 After your discussion, the examiner will give you a final instruction, like this:

> Now you have about a minute to decide which action would be the most effective in helping people prevent or deal with stress.

Try to reach agreement with your partner.

Writing | Part 1
An essay

1 Discuss these questions in pairs or groups and note down your ideas while you are talking.

   1 What are some causes of unhappiness or tension
   - for employees in the workplace?
   - for students at school or university?
   2 What can employers or educational organisations do to increase happiness and reduce tension?

2 Read the essay task below and discuss these questions.

   1 In the context of employment, what do you consider to be *good communications*?
   2 What do you understand by the term *work–life balance*?
   3 What does the phrase *feel valued* mean to you?
   4 Do you strongly agree or disagree with any of the three opinions?

Your class has listened to a debate about methods employers should use to ensure that their workforce is happy and motivated. You have made the notes below.

How can employers ensure that their employees are happy and motivated?

- establish good communications
- encourage a work–life balance
- make employees feel valued as people

Some opinions expressed in the debate:

'Most employees are satisfied if they are well paid'

'The happier employees are, the more efficient and productive they will be.'

'You need to be able to discuss problems with your colleagues and your manager.'

Write an essay discussing **two** of the methods in your notes. You should **explain which method you think is more important** for employers to adopt, **providing reasons** to support your answer.

You may, if you wish, make use of the opinions expressed in the debate, but you should use your own words as far as possible.

---

3 Read the following essay on the task in Exercise 2. Then discuss these questions with a partner.

   1 Has the writer
   a discussed two methods?
   b provided reasons for his/her opinion?
   c used his/her own words?
   2 Is the style of the essay appropriate?
   3 Is the essay roughly the correct length?

Methods employers should adopt to ensure that their employees are happy and motivated

There is no doubt, in my opinion, that the happier and more motivated employees are, the more productive they are likely to be. This almost certainly results in the organisation they are employed by being more successful than it would otherwise be. For this reason, it is in employers' interests to ensure that their workers are happy and motivated. I'll now consider methods which employers could adopt to achieve this.

Perhaps the most important thing employers can do is make employees feel valued, not just as paid workers but as individuals. In practice, this should involve establishing good relationships between staff at all levels. Employees should have access to those above them in their organisation, people with whom they can discuss their work or personal matters which affect their work. Employees will feel valued if they know that they are being listened to.

Employers should also, in my view, encourage employees to have a healthy work–life balance. This means accepting that employees need time to pursue leisure activities and to socialise with their friends and families. Employers should even discourage employees from starting work too early in the morning or from taking on a lot of overtime and finishing late in the evening.

I believe that both the approaches I've suggested are actually interdependent; one of the ways employers can make their employees feel valued is to recognise that they have lives outside work. This will help to ensure that employees remain happy and motivated.

4 Look at the structure of the sample essay and discuss the following.

   1 Summarise the purpose of each of the four paragraphs, like this:

     <u>Para 1:</u> *Introduction showing the writer's general approach to the topic*

     <u>Para 2:</u> *One of the methods ...*

   2 How do the paragraphs relate to the essay task?

   3 In which paragraph(s) does the writer express his/her opinions?

5 Read the essay task below.

   1 Discuss the topic of the essay with a partner, using your own experience of schools or universities.

   2 Do you agree with any of the opinions expressed?

You have taken part in a seminar discussing how schools and universities can help to make the exam period less stressful for students. You have made the notes below.

> #### <u>How can schools and universities help to ensure that students do not suffer from stress during the exam period?</u>
>
> - support from tutors
> - a structured revision timetable prior to exams
> - time for relaxation and leisure activities

> **Some opinions expressed in the seminar**
>
> 'Students need to remember that there is more to life than exam success.'
>
> 'Revising for 24 hours a day before exams doesn't necessarily lead to success.'
>
> 'You won't do well on the day if you feel stressed.'

Write an essay discussing **two** of the methods in your notes. You should **explain which method you think is more important** for schools and universities to adopt, **providing reasons** to support your answer.

You may, if you wish, make use of the opinions expressed in the seminar, but you should use your own words as far as possible.

---

6 Consider how you can adapt the paragraph structure in Exercise 4 for the new essay task. Discuss this question.

Which of the following paragraph openings would be appropriate for this essay and in which paragraph (1–4) would each of these fit best?

   1 One way in which schools can help is …

   2 Both of these methods …

   3 I feel incredibly stressed out when …

   4 Firstly, …

   5 For many students, exams are …

   6 Another method …

   7 Exams don't bother me much …

   8 In my opinion, the more important …

   9 Exam stress is a problem which …

  10 In addition, …

7 Plan and write your essay on the task in Exercise 5. Start by making a paragraph plan which is clearly related to the essay task, as in Exercise 4.

> ### Exam advice
>
> Make sure that you
>
> - read the question and notes carefully, underlining key words so that you know exactly what you have to do
> - answer the question, dealing with two of the three topic areas listed
> - use your own words if you decide to make use of any of the opinions expressed.
>
> Start by making a paragraph plan to ensure that you cover all the points in the question.

4 Just the job!

Starting off

1 Look at the photos of people in jobs. What aspects of working do you associate with each job?

Example

1 This person is probably a high-flying executive in a large multinational company. She is likely to be involved in high-level decision-making, so she has a lot of power, high status and a large salary. She probably works long hours and has to deal with a lot of stress.

2 Which of these aspects of work appeal to you?

- working under pressure
- being creative
- working with the public
- working in finance
- working as part of a team
- working independently
- being your own boss
- having managerial responsibilities
- problem solving and troubleshooting
- quick promotion

Reading and Use of English | Part 1

1 Work in pairs. How far do you agree with each of the following statements?

1 My best friends are the ones I've met through my work/studies.

2 I'd never consider going on holiday with someone I work/study with.

3 What I find most interesting about my work/studies are the people I come in contact with.

4 My friendships with colleagues help me to cope with my work/studies.

2 Quickly read the text. Which of the ideas in the statements above are reflected in the text?

Friends benefit firms

We have all heard tales about difficult people at work, usually managers, but the office is also where many people make friends, and friends (0) ......C...... us to feel that bit more enthusiastic about the job we do. Research has found that more than half of British workers (1) .... their best friends in the office and more than a third say that they go on holiday with (2) .... workers.

The changing nature of work with more flexibility and more multi-tasking means that people (3) .... stability from their workmates. Friendships bring (4) .... in a changing world. A collaborative working environment (5) .... the way for making job-sharing and expansion of roles more of an (6) .... for employers and employees.

So fun workplaces where friendships flourish (7) .... workers who can handle changing job roles. This is not (8) .... surprising since numerous experiments carried out by workplace psychologists over the years have clearly demonstrated that work is a social affair.

Adapted from *The Times*

3 For questions 1–8, read the text again and decide which answer (A, B, C or D) best fits each gap. There is an example at the beginning (0). Use the clues to help you (in the exam there are no clues).

0 A enliven   B influence   C inspire   D stimulate

1 A meet   B encounter   C find   D know
Clue: this word means 'to see and speak to someone for the first time'.

2 A peer   B colleague   C companion   D fellow
Clue: this word can be used as an adjective which collocates with 'worker' to describe someone who has the same job as you.

3 A desire   B search   C seek   D wish
Clue: a word which means 'look for' and is not followed by a preposition

4 A basis   B support   C assistance   D backing
Clue: a word which means 'help and encouragement'

5 A leads   B finds   C shows   D paves
Clue: If something … the way for/to something else, it makes the other thing possible.

6 A option   B opportunity   C opening   D occasion
Clue: a word which means 'one thing which can be chosen from a set of possibilities'

7 A appeal   B attract   C lure   D engage
Clue: these workplaces are pleasant and enjoyable, so people want to work there.

8 A extremely   B thoroughly   C entirely   D utterly
Clue: this word forms part of a phrase which means 'not completely' and collocates with 'surprising'.

4 Work in pairs.

• What do you think are the advantages and disadvantages of going on holiday with your colleagues?

• Do you think people find it easier or more difficult to make friends than they did in the past? Why?

Reading and Use of English | Part 8

1 Work in small groups.

In your country

- how easy is it for graduates to find jobs?
- what are the most usual methods of job hunting?
- what is the most effective way to find a job?
- how well do universities prepare students for the world of work?

2 You are going to read an article for graduates joining the job market. Before you read the article, read the title and introductory sentence in *italics*. What contradiction is the writer pointing out?

3 Underline the key idea in questions 1–10 below.

In which section does the writer	
advise graduates to continue job-hunting while already working?	**1**
explain why some graduates accept a certain type of employment opportunity?	**2**
make a suggestion for graduates whose job hunting has so far been unsuccessful?	**3**
mention a variety of ways of obtaining employment?	**4**
suggest how graduates can create a good impression?	**5**
mention the need to maintain relationships?	**6**
recommend a way of thinking positively?	**7**
explain why some jobs may have fewer applicants?	**8**
warn graduates that some information may be difficult to hide?	**9**
describe an employment opportunity he disapproves of?	**10**

4 For questions 1–10, choose from the sections (A–D). The sections may be chosen more than once.

Exam advice

Before reading the sections,
- read the questions carefully, underlining the main ideas
- read the first section and find which questions it answers
- deal with each section in turn in this way.

Graduate jobs: advice from an expert

You've got a beautiful new degree, a dazzling career ahead of you and the world is your oyster. Terrifying, isn't it?

A

You should be very conscious of your digital footprint and remember that nothing can ever really be deleted and this includes social media profiles as well as forums and websites. Although it helps if you activate the privacy settings on your social media accounts and control who you allow to see your account, the most foolproof solution is to behave well and treat these networks with a healthy respect. You might not be able to fully prevent some things from showing on search engines, but you can make the most of what shows up first by using public professional networking sites to build a much more professional footprint which you can then add to by getting mentioned for extra-curricular activity. In the job market this can be gold dust, so find opportunities to comment on blogs and articles, provide quotes for journalists and guest blog on things you're interested in or know a lot about.

B

By all means apply for vacancies on big job boards, but the major drawback is that if you've seen a vacancy, so has everybody else. If you've had no joy applying for positions this way, it may well be more productive to start hunting for less visible vacancies instead, because when you do find one, the competition will be a fraction of what you're up against for widely advertised positions. It's important to realise that different job-hunting methods work for different industries. If you're answering ads for junior jobs in media, applying blind is unlikely to reap rewards, but building a network of contacts will. On the other hand, for public-sector jobs all the talking in the world won't get you through the door: you'll have to apply through official channels like everybody else. If you've only targeted big companies, broaden your search to smaller outfits. They'll have tighter recruitment budgets and won't be advertising vacancies or hiring stands at recruitment fairs, so find out how they do recruit and see which small companies are thriving.

C

Strictly speaking, in some countries unpaid internships are illegal which means it's illegal for your employer not to pay you and for you to work for free, as you're both undermining the national minimum wage law. The problem is that in some countries this law isn't being enforced, so employers are free to exploit graduates who can afford to work for less than the minimum wage and exclude those who can't. Because many graduates are desperate for experience, the result is that most internships now pay nothing, even when interns are effectively doing a proper job and working long hours with a wide range of activities for months at a time. Until things change, you'll have to decide for yourself whether an unpaid internship is a good investment. This will depend on the calibre of the company and what you'll be doing while you're there. As there is no guarantee of a paid job at the end of it, you must keep applying for roles elsewhere before your internship ends.

D

It's normal to feel low just after graduation. For some graduates, it's because the energy they needed is still flowing but now has no outlet, so they feel anxious. For others, it's because they've realised how much effort they've expended, and they feel exhausted. Whatever the reason, pay attention to the words you use. Graduation represents an ending, it's true, but it also represents new beginnings and it's more energising to think in those terms. Instead of saying, "I need to start my career," you should break the task ahead into smaller steps and frame each step in a way that allows you to measure progress. So, for example, instead of expecting to "sort myself out", ask yourself to "prepare my CV", "find two referees", and "register with an employment agency". Put these goals in chronological order and focus on each one in turn until you have achieved it. In the long run you might easily conclude that the most treasured aspect of your university experience wasn't your academic education or any careers advice, but rather the friends you made, so you should make it a priority to stay in touch with those who mattered most to you during your university career.

Adapted from *The Guardian*

5 Work in small groups. Discuss these questions.

- Why should people be careful about using social media? How careful do you think people need to be?
- Which do you think is a better way to start your working life: in a big organisation or a small company?
- What are the advantages and disadvantages of doing an internship?
- How easy do you think it is to keep up with friends when you leave university?

Vocabulary
Dependent prepositions

Complete these extracts from Reading and Use of English Part 8 by writing a preposition in each gap.

1 You should be very conscious .... your digital footprint.
2 You might not be able to fully prevent some things .... showing on search engines, but you can make the most .... what shows up first by using public professional networking sites.
3 If you've had no joy applying .... positions this way, it may be more productive to start hunting .... less visible vacancies.
4 Because many graduates are desperate .... experience, the result is that most internships now pay nothing.
5 Pay attention .... the words you use.
6 Put these goals in chronological order and focus .... each one in turn until you have achieved it.
7 You should make it a priority to stay in touch .... those who mattered most to you.

 page 167 Language reference: Dependent prepositions

Adjective–noun collocations (1)

1 Look at these sentences from Reading and Use of English Part 8. Which of the words in *italics* form collocations with the words in **bold** that follow them?

1 The *large / major* **drawback** is that if you've seen a vacancy, so has everybody else.

2 Interns are effectively doing a proper job and working *many / long* **hours** with a *wide / long* **range** of activities.

2 👁 Exam candidates often make mistakes forming collocations with the words in **bold** in the following sentences. Which adjective from each set of three is not correct?

1 Karl has *wide / extensive / vast* **experience** of sorting out computer glitches.

2 Gustav's report made a(n) *huge / extreme / powerful* **impact** on his managers.

3 Our staff enjoy a *high / big / great* **degree** of flexibility in their working hours.

4 People working here have to work under *heavy / constant / high* **pressure**.

5 The company I work for has a(n) *excellent / big / unrivalled* **reputation** for quality.

6 There has been *big / fierce / intense* **competition** for the manager's job.

7 We have had a *high / large / great* **number** of applicants for this job.

8 There's been a *strong / huge / considerable* **increase** in the number of job applicants.

9 With her *expert / high / specialist* **skills**, Suzy is bound to get the job.

10 With Marianne's *vast / extensive / strong* **knowledge** of statistical theory, I'm sure she'll get the job.

Listening | Part 2

1 Work in small groups. You will hear a student giving a talk to his class about a project he has done on the co-operative movement. Before you listen, which of these statements do you agree with? Why (not)?

- Employees should have a say in decisions affecting the place where they work.
- To become a manager, you should start at the bottom and work your way up.
- Companies exist equally for the benefit of staff, clients and shareholders.

2 Work in pairs. Read the sentences below. What type of information do you think you need to fill each gap?

Example: **1** *a time or period of history*

The co-operative movement

Co-operatives were originally set up during the (1) .... to provide for workers.

The first successful co-operative was formed by (2) .... in northern England.

The co-operative opened a food store for its members and also sold (3) ....

Nowadays there are traditional co-operatives running chain stores or financial services and new ones active in areas ranging from (4) .... to web design.

Co-operatives are businesses owned and run by and for their members, who may be (5) .... , customers or employees.

All members share company profits and have an (6) .... in decisions.

Co-operatives are popular now because they are seen to have a strong (7) .... in comparison to conventional companies.

Some co-operatives avoid investing money in companies which harm the environment by producing (8) .... or participate in the arms trade.

3 ▶ 11 Listen and for questions 1–8, complete the sentences in Exercise 2.

4 Match phrases 1–9 from the recording with their definitions a–i. If necessary, listen to the recording again.

1 make a go of something
2 set up
3 go a step further
4 be around
5 share out
6 have a say (in something)
7 set something apart
8 go about things
9 put money into something

a be involved in making a decision about something
b begin to do something or deal with something
c divide food, money, goods, etc. and give part of it to someone else
d exist
e formally establish a new company, organisation, system, way of working, etc.
f invest in something
g show something to be different from, and usually better than, other things of the same type
h take an extra action which adds to a situation
i make something succeed, usually by working hard

5 Work in small groups.

• Would you be interested in working for a co-operative? Why (not)?
• Jessica mentioned two types of business she thinks are unethical. Do you agree with her?

Grammar
Expressing possibility, probability and certainty

1 Read the underlined phrases in these pairs of sentences. Which sentence in each pair expresses a stronger possibility?

1 a If you've had no joy applying for positions this way, it <u>may well be</u> more productive to start hunting for less visible vacancies instead.
  b If you've had no joy applying for positions this way, it <u>may be</u> more productive to start hunting for less visible vacancies instead.

2 a If you're answering ads for junior jobs in media, applying blind <u>is unlikely to</u> reap rewards.
  b If you're answering ads for junior jobs in media, applying blind <u>is highly unlikely</u> to reap rewards.

3 a In the long run you <u>might easily conclude</u> that the most treasured aspect of your university experience wasn't your academic education or any careers advice, but rather the friends you made.
  b In the long run you <u>might conclude</u> that the most treasured aspect of your university experience wasn't your academic education or any careers advice, but rather the friends you made.

➡ page 169 Language reference: Expressing possibility, probability and certainty

2 What do you think you will be doing in five years' time? Write five sentences about yourself, using the phrases underlined from Exercise 1.

Example

In five years' time I may well be working for an international company.

When you have finished, compare and discuss your sentences in pairs. Give reasons for your statements.

3 The sentences below all contain mistakes made by exam candidates. Find and correct the mistakes.

1 By reaching an advanced level of English, I am more probably to succeed in business.
2 If you come here for your holiday in July, you bound to enjoy it.
3 If you also watch television and films, then you're most likely to learn the language faster than if you just go to class.
4 I've studied the three posible options to try to solve the problem.
5 I'd like to recommend Grey's Academy as one of the possibly best schools in Barnsley.
6 This was the worst trip I probably have ever experienced.
7 That may be the possible reason why you're having such problems.

4 For questions 1–6, complete the second sentence so that it has a similar meaning to the first sentence, using the word given. Do not change the word given. You must use between three and six words, including the word given.

1 Madeleine felt sure that she would be offered the job.
BOUND
Madeleine felt she .... offered the job.

2 Boris is unlikely to win the prize.
LIKELIHOOD
There is little .... the prize.

3 There's a good chance that Takesi has seen your message.
WELL
Takesi .... your message.

4 I'm sure you didn't remember to post the letter.
MUST
You .... post the letter.

5 If you arrive late, the teacher may well get angry with you.
LIKELY
The teacher .... his temper with you if you arrive late.

6 Do you think you might be able to help me with the essay?
CHANCE
Is .... me with the essay?

Speaking | Part 4

Exam information

In Speaking Part 4, the examiner

- asks both candidates questions to find out their opinions on general topics related to Part 3. You may both be asked the same question, or each asked different questions.
- may also ask you to react to ideas and opinions which the other candidate expresses, so it is important to listen carefully to what he/she says.

This part tests your ability to express and justify opinions, agree and disagree.

1 Work in pairs. Before working on Speaking Part 4, follow the examiner's instructions for the first part of this Speaking Part 3 task.

Now, I'd like you to talk about something together for about two minutes. Here are some things that companies can do to make their employees' working lives more pleasant. Talk to each other about how effective these things might be in making employees' lives more pleasant.

A staff social club

How effective might these things be in making employees' working lives more pleasant?

Free transport to and from work

An inexpensive staff restaurant

A sports centre and gym

Flexible working hours

2 Now follow the examiner's instruction for the second part of the Part 3 task.

> Now you have about a minute to decide which two things would benefit staff most.

3 Work in pairs. Look at these Part 4 questions and decide which of them you should answer by

a   expressing just one point of view and a reason / reasons for it

b   giving a number of different ideas and perhaps reasons for them.

1   The world we live in is changing faster than ever before. How do you think our working lives will be different in the future?

2   Many people dream of being able to work from home. What do you think are the advantages and disadvantages of working from home?

3   Some people believe that people should continue working as long as they can, while other people believe that everyone should retire at 60 or 65. What is your view?

4   Which do you think is more important in a job: friendly colleagues or a good salary?

5   How can young people get the experience they need to be given a good job?

6   Many people complain about their managers. What qualities would you look for in a perfect manager, and why?

4 Work in pairs. Discuss and make brief notes on how you could answer questions 1–6.

5 In which answers to questions 1–6 could you use these words/phrases?

> achieve a good work–life balance   commute
> feel valued   give praise   a good communicator
> a feeling of isolation   a job vacancy   motivate/motivation
> a reasonable/heavy/light workload   recruit
> take somebody on   a trainee   a work environment
> a workplace

6 ▶ 12 Listen to Daniel and Laura answering three of the questions.

1   Which words/phrases from Exercise 5 did they use?

2   Which answers do you agree with?

7 Say if the following statements are true (T) or false (F).

1   Daniel and Laura suggest several different ideas to answer each question.

2   They give general answers to the questions.

3   They occasionally mention their personal situation but don't answer the question entirely with that.

4   They answer the question but also add other ideas which are not relevant.

5   When they agree with their partner, they add extra ideas.

6   When they disagree with their partner, they explain why.

8 Work in pairs. Take turns to ask and answer questions 1–6 in Exercise 3.

➡ page 198 Speaking reference: Speaking Part 4

Writing | Part 2
A report

1 Read the exam task below and underline the key points. Then answer these questions.

   1 Why does the organisation want to improve your work environment?
   2 Who will read the report?

The international organisation where you work has a sum of money available for making improvements to the work environment in your office to make it more productive. You have been asked to write a report for your manager in which you

- outline the problems with your work environment
- summarise the improvements you and your colleagues suggested
- recommend two changes.

Write your **report**. Write between 220 and 260 words.

---

2 Work in pairs.

   1 Brainstorm and note down a list of problems (e.g. noisy air-conditioning system) and their effects (e.g. headaches).
   2 Decide which problems you want to mention in your report (you need to limit the number of ideas so that you can deal with the whole task within the word limit). Then think of improvements to deal with them.
   3 You need to persuade your manager to implement your ideas. Discuss what you can say to explain how the improvements will make your office more productive.
   4 Decide which two changes you will recommend and the reasons for recommending them.

3 Work alone and write a brief plan for your report, including sections and section headings (see pages 26–27). When you have finished, compare plans with a partner.

4 Read the sample report below, without paying attention to the options in *italics* for the moment. Compare the contents of the report with your plan.

Report on workplace improvements

Introduction
The aim of this report is to [1]*sum up / outline* [2]*the deficiencies in / what's wrong with* our present office environment and the suggestions which have been made for improvements, and to [3]*make recommendations / give ideas* for two changes.

The office environment
At present, the office suffers from [4]*a number of / lots of* problems. Firstly, the air-conditioning system is [5]*antiquated / worn out* and therefore noisy. This causes headaches and occasionally makes it difficult to [6]*talk on the phone / hold telephone conversations*. Also, the open office plan makes it difficult for people to [7]*get on with / concentrate on* their work as they are frequently [8]*put off / distracted* by conversations in other parts of the office. Finally, many of the office chairs are uncomfortable and employees who spend [9]*lots of time / long hours* in front of their computers often complain of backache.

Staff suggestions
Staff were [10]*consulted / asked* and they made the following suggestions: first, the air-conditioning should be replaced by a more modern, quieter system which provides cool air in the summer and heating in the winter. It was felt that this would [11]*reduce / cut down on* tiredness and improve morale, which would enable staff to work more productively. To deal with distractions from conversations there were two suggestions: either dividing the office with screens round each work station, or having separate meeting rooms for [12]*necessary work discussions / the chats people need at work*. Staff also requested more ergonomic office chairs.

Recommendation
[13]*As a first measure, I would recommend / The first thing I'd recommend* is replacing the air conditioning and the office chairs. These two changes will [14]*have a direct effect on productivity / increase the amount of work people do* by reducing [15]*absence due to sick leave / time off because people are ill* and [16]*giving staff the chance / enabling staff* to work more efficiently and more comfortably.

5 Read the report again and choose the more formal alternatives from the options 1–16 in *italics*.

6 Work in pairs. Writing Part 2 often asks students to persuade the reader about something.

   1 Why is using a suitable style essential to persuading the reader?

   2 Which arguments in the sample report are used to persuade the manager?

7 Read this writing task and underline the key points you must deal with.

> You have been working in an international hotel chain for a month as part of a work experience programme. The training manager has asked you to write a report in which you
>
> - describe the tasks and activities you participated in
> - explain any problems with the programme
> - make recommendations for two improvements for future programmes.
>
> Write your **report**. Write between 220 and 260 words.

8 Work in pairs.

   1 Think of a number of tasks and activities you participated in.

   2 Decide what problems you want to mention and think of two improvements for future programmes.

   3 Discuss how you can persuade the training manager to implement them. (For example, will they make the programme more effective? Will they attract better trainees? Will they save money?)

9 Read the sample report again and underline words and phrases which you think might be useful when you write your own report. Compare ideas with a partner.

10 Write a plan for your report. Then in small groups, compare your plans.

11 Now write your report.

Exam information and advice

Writing a report tests your ability to organise and express information and to make recommendations or suggestions.

When writing a report

- you should give it a title
- you can divide it into sections and give each section a heading (the first and last sections could be *Introduction* and *Conclusion* or *Conclusion and recommendations*)
- if required by the task, make suggestions and recommendations
- make sure that you answer all parts of the task
- match your style to the situation and the target reader(s).

page 191 Writing reference: Reports

Vocabulary and grammar review Unit 3

Vocabulary

1 For questions 1–8, read the text below. Use the word given in capitals at the end of some of the lines to form a word that fits in the gap in the same line. There is an example at the beginning (0).

Problems between neighbours

Research shows that nearly a fifth of Britons have had a serious dispute with their neighbours in the past year, with the **(0)** ....._findings_..... suggesting that **FIND**
difficult **(1)** .... with our **RELATION**
fellow residents are generally the result of a breakdown in **(2)** .... **COMMUNICATE**
between people. Although there are many people who do get on well with their neighbours, the research shows that nearly a third of Britons **(3)** .... speak to them. **RARE**
One in seven of us don't even know the names of the people who live in our immediate **(4)** .... **NEIGHBOUR**
Consequently, many neighbours are finding it **(5)** .... difficult **INCREASE**
to settle disputes amicably. One in seven people have had verbal **(6)** .... with a neighbour **ARGUE**
in the past, and a small number of disputes have even ended in physical **(7)** .... Feuding neighbours **VIOLENT**
are also turning to the authorities to solve their **(8)** .... for them. **AGREE**
In fact, almost a fifth of people have reported their neighbours to the police or local council.

Grammar

2 The words *no*, *not* and *none* are used incorrectly in some of these sentences. Correct the mistakes.

1 I've searched everywhere for my passport but there is not sign of it.
2 Most of my family love all kinds of sport, but no my sister – she thinks all sport is a waste of time.
3 The exam was so difficult that I didn't get none of my answers right.
4 Humans are basically no different from any other animal.
5 I thought we had plenty of coffee but I've just looked in the cupboard and there's no left.
6 Not one of Patrick's friends remembered his birthday.
7 Our rate of pay is no the point – it's the actual working conditions that are so awful.
8 The group left for the North Pole three weeks ago and so far we've had none news of their progress.

3 Rewrite these short texts replacing active verbs with passive verbs where possible and appropriate.

1 We use the term 'amnesia' to refer to a partial or complete loss of memory. It is usually a temporary condition which only affects a certain part of a person's experience. Specific medical conditions can cause amnesia.

2 We all know very well that our real experiences form our memory. But could someone put a false memory into our heads? Could they persuade us that we had experienced something that never actually took place?

3 We use our semantic memory to store our knowledge of the world. Everyone has this knowledge base, and normally we can access it quickly and easily. Our semantic memory includes the meanings of words and the names of people and places.

4 Our working memory is a very important part of our memory system. You can think of it as the ability to remember and use a limited amount of information for a short amount of time. Our working memory can help us to perform a task, like following a set of instructions. However, this information is erratic. If someone distracts you, you can lose the information and you have to start the task again.

Vocabulary and grammar review Unit 4

Vocabulary

1 For questions 1–8, read the text below and decide which answer (A, B, C or D) best fits each gap.

The importance of internships

Recent research indicates that graduates **(1)** .... to some of the UK's leading employers **(2)** .... a much better chance of being **(3)** .... a job if they have already had some work experience with the same organisation – either through internships, industrial placements or vacation work. In fact three quarters of graduate vacancies are **(4)** .... to be snapped up by graduates who already had some work experience with the same employer. This latest research **(5)** .... that taking part in work placements or internships whilst at university is now just as important as getting a good degree.

A separate study warns that almost six in ten students finish university without a graduate job, highlighting the **(6)** .... competition for graduate jobs. It is not **(7)** .... that employers are going to be interested in your previous work experience and while this does not have to have been a glamorous internship with an investment bank, using your time at university to gain work experience is going to have a major **(8)** .... on your future job prospects.

1 A asking   B applying   C joining   D recruiting

2 A stand   B give   C hold   D take

3 A provided   B contracted   C found   D offered

4 A liable   B probable   C prone   D likely

5 A agrees   B declares   C confirms   D yields

6 A firm   B heavy   C intense   D impressive

7 A astonishing   B surprising   C amazing
   D shocking

8 A result   B consequence   C repercussion
   D impact

2 Complete each of the sentences with an adjective from the box. In some cases more than one answer is possible.

> constant   excellent   extensive   fierce   huge
> powerful   specialist   vast

1 Malik's positive attitude and .... experience make him the best person for the job.
2 Almodóvar's film has made a(n) .... impact on audiences throughout the country.
3 This is a highly stressful job and we're under .... pressure to meet our targets.
4 The Paradise Hotel has a(n) .... reputation in this town.
5 I want to join the football team but there's extremely .... competition for places.
6 The .... increase in house prices has made it very difficult for young people to buy a first home.
7 Ivan's .... knowledge of the market is invaluable to our operations.
8 We need someone with .... language skills to work as part of our expert team.

Grammar and vocabulary

3 Circle the correct alternative in *italics* in each of these sentences.

1 It's by far the best film of the festival so far. I think it *must / could* easily win first prize.
2 The weather forecast isn't too good so the outing *might not / could not* take place tomorrow.
3 Jay had a sprained ankle so he *mightn't have / couldn't have* run very far!
4 It's just about *probable / possible* that the train has been delayed.
5 We're *highly / strongly* likely to see Fran at the concert tonight.
6 You're looking exhausted! You *mustn't / can't* have had a very relaxing holiday.
7 Why don't you call Marcos? He's *bound / liable* to have the information you need.

Starting off

1 You receive an email telling you that you have won an adventure activity competition. Which of these three activities would you choose?

2 Compare and discuss your choice of activity with other students.

3 Work in pairs. Discuss these quotations. What do they mean? Do you agree with them?

- 'Do one thing every day that scares you.' (Eleanor Roosevelt)
- 'Distrust and caution are the parents of security.' (Benjamin Franklin)

HYDROSPEEDING

Hydrospeeding in Morzine, Switzerland, is not for everyone but the more extreme will love it. Equipped with a float, helmet, flippers and wetsuit, you will float, plunge and scream your way down the River Dranse!

Interested? **Click here>>**

York Skydiving Centre

Ready to skydive? We offer tandem skydiving, parachuting and freefalling at York Skydiving Centre. Come and experience the exhilaration of jumping from an aeroplane at 4,000 metres at the closest full-time parachute centre to York.

Interested? Click here

WILDERNESS HUSKY SAFARI

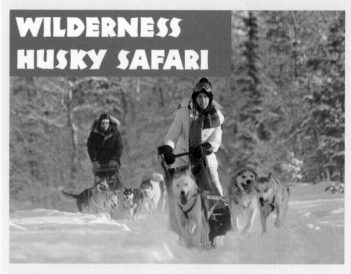

Quite simply, we love this and, judging by the feedback, so do our clients.

You will be provided with all the necessary equipment, including thermal clothing, and then taken to meet the dogs. You will be taught how to handle your team and the sled, and then you depart into Pallas-Ounas National Park in Western Lapland, one of Europe's few remaining wilderness areas.

Interested? **CLICK HERE**

Listening | Part 1

1 You will hear three people talking about dramatic past experiences. Before you listen, match 1–10 with a–j to make sentences which refer to frightening experiences.

1 It seemed to go on …	a nightmares about it.
2 Everything seemed to be happening …	b in a flash.
	c I'll never forget.
3 It was as though time …	d stood still.
4 It was all over …	e as if it was yesterday.
5 Everything was …	f much about it.
6 I remember it …	g in slow motion.
7 It's an experience …	h happening at once.
8 I still have …	i forever.
9 It's all …	j a bit of a blur now.
10 I don't remember …	

2 Now tell a partner about a dramatic experience that happened to you or someone you know. Use some of the sentences from Exercise 1 if possible.

3 Read the questions and options in Exercise 4. At this stage, think about what you can work out from the question and answers. Ask yourself questions like these.

1 In Extract One, what are we told about Harry? For example, where has he been? What has happened to him? Whose fault might it have been?

2 In Extract Two, what do we know about what happened to the motorist? Why do you think the police were involved?

3 In Extract Three, why might the person have to leave her home and why might moving back be a problem?

4 ▶ 13 Now listen and for questions 1–6, choose the answer (A, B or C) which fits the best according to what you hear.

Extract One

You hear two people, Harry and Jasmine, talking about an incident at a gym.

1 When did Harry's accident happen?
   A when he started to run fast
   B as soon as he got on the machine
   C when he tried to reduce his running speed

2 Why did Jasmine stop going to the gym?
   A She found the equipment to be unreliable.
   B She thought the machine might not work properly.
   C She found running on machines exhausting.

Extract Two

You hear a police officer interviewing a motorist who has been involved in a driving incident.

3 How does the motorist correct something the policeman says?
   A He tells him who was with him at the time.
   B He tells him why he was travelling late at night.
   C He tells him the time of the incident.

4 What was the driver's state of mind after he was hit by the stone?
   A He was convinced he was going to die.
   B He was confused but still able to steer the car.
   C He was optimistic that the trees would slow the car down.

Extract Three

You hear a news reporter interviewing someone who has had to leave her home.

5 Why isn't the reporter particularly surprised by the problem the woman is facing?
   A He is in a similar situation himself.
   B The same thing happened to him in the past.
   C He has heard similar stories from other people.

6 How does the woman feel about the whole incident?
   A She realises that it could have been much worse.
   B She can't stop thinking about the problems she faces.
   C She is afraid she'll never be able to move back.

Exam advice

- Before you listen to the recording, read the questions and options and infer as much information as possible from them about the topic. This should help you to understand the recording when you hear it for the first time.
- The words you hear will usually be different from the words in the question, so listen for the meaning rather than for specific words.

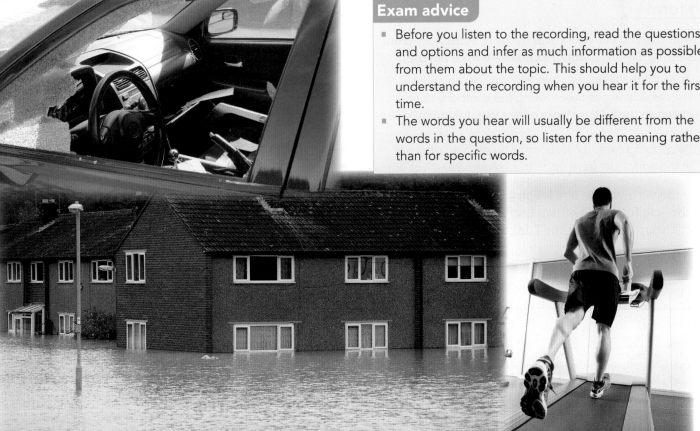

Vocabulary
Idiomatic language

1 Discuss these questions about words and phrases from Listening Part 1.

  1 Are *flashbacks* pleasant or unpleasant? What kinds of event cause flashbacks?
  2 What is the meaning of *treadmill* in this sentence? *There were days when child-rearing seemed like an endless treadmill of feeding and washing.*
  3 What might cause a memory to be *a blur*?
  4 What did the speaker mean by *I was sure we'd had it*?

2 Discuss the meaning of the idiomatic expressions in these sentences, which all include parts of the body.

  1 In the end all I could do was jump off and *keep my fingers crossed*.
  2 I'm really scared of heights but if you *twist my arm*, I suppose I'll go climbing with you.
  3 James may seem friendly but he's likely to *stab you in the back* when he has something to gain.
  4 Lots of people use their work computers for personal reasons, but managers usually *turn a blind eye to it*.
  5 He told me I'd won the lottery but I knew he was just *pulling my leg*.

Grammar
Verbs followed by *to* + infinitive or the *-ing* form

1 Circle the correct verb form in these sentences from Listening Part 1. Compare choices with a partner.

  1 Then I decided *to run / running* fast for ten minutes.
  2 I'm considering *to take / taking* the company to court.
  3 I keep *to think / thinking* how disastrous it could have been.
  4 I was trying *to stop / stopping* it by digging ditches.
  5 In the end, I just gave up *to dig / digging* and got out.

2 Are the verbs in the box followed by the *to* infinitive or the *-ing* form? Make two lists of verbs, and then check your answers in the Language reference.

admit afford agree avoid can't help choose
deny enjoy expect finish hope involve keep on
mind offer pretend promise put off refuse
resent risk suggest

➡ page 179 Language reference: Verbs + *to* infinitive or *-ing*

3 Some verbs have different meanings depending on whether they are followed by the *-ing* form or the infinitive. Discuss the differences in meaning between the verbs in *italics* in these pairs of sentences.

  1 a I *remember* waking up on the grass verge.
    b *Remember* to wake me up early tomorrow morning.
  2 a I *tried* putting my foot on the brake, but the car simply went faster.
    b I *tried* to hold on to the steering wheel, but it slipped out of my hand.
  3 a While we were driving along the motorway, we *saw* planes taking off.
    b When we went to the airport to meet my brother, we got there in time to *see* his plane land.
  4 a I *regret* saying anything now.
    b I *regret* to say that I won't be able to come to your wedding.
  5 a Being a careful driver *means* paying attention to other road users.
    b I'm sorry. I didn't *mean* to offend you.

4 👁 The following sentences contain mistakes made by exam candidates. Correct the mistakes.

  1 I suggest to take the overnight train to Vienna.
  2 Part of my job is to help maintaining the machinery in good working order.
  3 I would strongly recommend to sail rather than going by plane.
  4 I never considered to do anything except being a teacher.
  5 I told my department manager that I objected to work at weekends.
  6 Despite not being able to afford going abroad, I am interested in diving in other countries.

5 Work in small groups. Discuss some of these topics.

  • something I'm looking forward to
  • things I'd like to give up
  • things I put off doing
  • jobs I'd refuse to do
  • something I regret having done
  • something I've tried to do, but failed

Reading and Use of English | Part 4

1 Work in pairs. Look at this sample task for Reading and Use of English Part 4 and discuss the questions.

We only felt safe when we were on dry land again.
UNTIL
It <u>was only after we had finally got</u> on dry land again that we felt safe.

1 Does the completed second sentence have a similar meaning to the first sentence?
2 Is it grammatically correct?
3 Would this answer be correct in the exam?
4 If not, what should the answer be?

2 Read these sentences and discuss the clues under each one. (You do not have clues in the exam.) Then complete the second sentence with between three and six words, including the word given.

1 I have absolutely no interest whatever in adventure holidays.
APPEAL
Adventure holidays .... in the least.
Clue: What preposition do you need after the verb 'appeal'?

2 They had offered him a .38 gun for his own protection.
PROTECT
They had offered him a .38 gun so that ....
.... himself.
Clue: What kind of structure follows 'so that'?

3 Driving a car without insurance is illegal.
LAW
It .... a car without insurance.
Clue: Which phrase using 'law' means 'illegal'?

4 People generally think of tennis as a safe sport.
CONSIDERED
Tennis .... a safe sport.
Clue: How does starting with 'Tennis' affect the grammar of the second sentence?

5 Our surroundings became more primitive as we travelled further inland.
THE
The further we travelled .... our surroundings became.
Clue: What comparative structure includes the word 'the' twice?

6 It is advisable not to climb mountains after a heavy snowfall.
AVOID
You .... mountains after a heavy snowfall.
Clue: Which modal verb is normally used for advice?

Exam advice

- Use the word in CAPITALS without changing it.
- Count the words you have used to complete the gapped sentence. Contractions (*isn't*, *don't*, etc.) count as two words.
- Check that the words you have added are grammatically correct in the gapped sentence.
- Finally, read both sentences again to check that they have the same meaning.

3 Some questions in Part 4 test your knowledge of idiomatic expressions and phrasal verbs, such as those in *italics* below. Match the expressions in 1–6 with the meanings a–f.

1 After the meal we *settled up* and left.
2 *It's a wonder* that you got here at all.
3 *Keep an eye on* the weather.
4 I'm *tied up* until this afternoon.
5 Thank goodness, she's *on the mend*.
6 He's always trying to *pick a fight*.

a very busy   d surprising
b start an argument e watch carefully
c get better   f pay what you owe

4 Write sentences of your own using the six expressions in Exercise 3.

Reading and use of English | Part 7

1 Discuss these questions with a partner.

  1 Tell each other about an interesting unspoiled area you have visited. It could be a forest, a desert, a mountainous region or a wild coastal area. How did being in this area make you feel?

  2 Do you enjoy visiting wild, natural areas like this? Why (not)?

  3 Are there areas like these you would like to visit in the future?

2 Read the exam task. Then follow the sequence of activities below to complete the task.

> You are going to read an extract from a book by Bill Bryson. Six paragraphs have been removed from the text. Choose from paragraphs **A–G** the one which fits each gap (1–6). There is one extra paragraph which you do not need to use.

- Read the main part of the text quickly to build up a picture in your mind of what is happening.
- Underline any reference words or phrases in the text which you think may refer to either the previous or the following missing paragraph. These may include pronouns, time expressions, conjunctions and other linking phrases.
- Read the missing paragraphs and look for subject matter and language links.
- Match any gaps and missing paragraphs that you are sure of first.

3 Discuss these questions in pairs or small groups. Give reasons for your answers.

  1 If a friend suggested a walk in the woods, how would you respond?

  2 If you went for a walk in a wood or forest, would you prefer to go alone or with a friend?

  3 How would you feel if you had to spend the night in a wood or forest?

A WALK IN THE WOODS

Woods are not like other spaces. Their trees surround you, press in from all sides. Woods choke off views, and leave you without bearings. They make you feel small, confused and vulnerable, like a child lost in a crowd. Standing in a desert, you know you are in a big space. Standing in a wood, you only sense it. They are a vast, featureless nowhere. And they are alive.

1 _____

Though you tell yourself it's preposterous, you can't quite shake off the feeling that you are being watched. You order yourself to be calm – it's just a wood, but you are feeling jumpy. Every sudden noise makes you spin in alarm. Whatever mechanism within you is responsible for adrenalin, it has never been so prepared to pump out the warm adrenal fluid. Even asleep, you are a coiled spring.

2 _____

But tougher men were sobered by this strange menace. Daniel Boone, who wrestled bears, described corners of the southern Appalachians as 'so wild that it is impossible to behold them without terror'. When Daniel Boone is uneasy, you know it's time to watch your step.

3 _____

Most of this vast forest area is now gone, but what survives is more impressive than you might expect. The Chatahoochee is part of four million acres of forest stretching up to the Great Smoky Mountains. On a map of the USA it is just a smudge of green, but on foot, the scale of it is colossal. It would be four days before Katz and I crossed a highway and eight till we came to a town.

> **4**

In a normal year we would be walking into the dynamic abundance of a southern mountain spring, through a radiant, productive world alive with insects and birds. Above all, there would be wild flowers blossoming from every twig and pushing through the forest floor. Instead, we trudged through a silent world of bare trees. In this way, we fell into a simple routine.

> **5**

Sometimes other hikers would come along, and tell me where he was. Because everyone walks at different rates and rests at different times, several times a day you bump into fellow hikers, especially on mountain tops or beside streams, and at the wooden shelters that stand at distant intervals.

> **6**

Around four, we would find somewhere to camp. One of us would go off to fetch water while the other prepared noodles. Sometimes we would talk, but mostly we existed in a kind of companionable silence. By six o'clock, dark, cold and weariness would force us to our tents. Katz went to sleep instantly as far as I could tell. I would read until my shoulders and arms grew chilly. So I would put myself in darkness and lie there listening to the peculiarly clear, articulated sounds of the forest at night.

Adapted from *A Walk in the Woods* by Bill Bryson

A And so we walked – up mountains, through forgotten hollows, along ridges and through mile after mile of dark, deep, silent woods, on a trail about half a metre wide.

B In consequence, you get to know your fellow hikers quite well if you meet them at the shelters. Even at busy times, however, the woods are great providers of solitude, and I encountered long periods of perfect aloneness, when I didn't see another soul for hours.

C So woods are spooky. Quite apart from the thought that they may be hiding wild beasts, there is something sinister about them that makes you sense an atmosphere of doom with every step, and leaves you profoundly aware that you ought to keep your ears pricked.

D The American woods have been unnerving people like this for 300 years. Henry Thoreau thought nature was splendid, but when he experienced this real wilderness, he was unnerved to the core. This wasn't the tame world of overgrown orchards that passed for wilderness in suburban Massachusetts, but a forbidding country that was 'wild and savage'. Apparently, the experience left him, 'almost hysterical'.

E There is a strange frozen violence in a forest out of season. Fallen trees lay across the path every fifty or sixty yards, often with great bomb craters of dirt around their roots. Dozens more lay rotting on the slopes, and every third or fourth tree, it seemed, was leaning on a neighbour. It was as if the trees couldn't wait to fall over.

F When the first Europeans arrived in the New World, there were perhaps 950 million acres of woodland in what became the lower forty-eight states. The Chatahoochee National Forest, through which Katz and I now trudged, was part of an immense canopy stretching from Alabama to Canada and beyond.

G Each morning we rose at first light, shivering and rubbing arms, made coffee, broke camp, and set off into the silent woods. We would walk from half past seven to four. We seldom walked together, but every couple of hours I would sit and wait for Katz to catch up.

Speaking | Part 2

1 Answer these questions about Speaking Part 2. Then compare answers with a partner.

  1 How many photos is each candidate given by the examiner?

  2 How many photos does each candidate have to talk about?

  3 How long does each candidate have to speak for?

  4 What happens after each candidate finishes talking about their photos?

2 Read the examiner's instructions and look at the three photos. Write brief notes in answer to the questions below.

> Here are your pictures. They show people doing dangerous jobs. I'd like you to compare two of the pictures and say what the dangers of the jobs might be and why people choose to do jobs like these.

  1 What are the three jobs? (If you don't know the job title, how can you describe it?)

  2 In what way is each job dangerous?

  3 What words might describe the sort of person who chooses each of these jobs?

3 Work in pairs. Take turns to compare two of the three photos. You should each talk for about a minute. Time your partner, but don't interrupt while he/she is speaking.

4 ▶ **14** Listen to a student speaking about the photos.

  1 Which two is he comparing?

  2 Why does he use these words and phrases?

almost certainly	obviously	I suppose	It must be
he seems to be	probably	I'd say	perhaps

- What are the dangers of these jobs?
- Why do people choose to do jobs like these?

5 Now read these examiner's instructions and look at another set of three photos.

> Here are your pictures. They show people doing dangerous activities. I'd like you to compare two of the pictures and say what skills and personal qualities each activity involves, and how these activities make people feel.

Before you start the task, consider the two questions you have to answer and decide which of these words/phrases are most suited to each question.

adrenalin rush   concentration   control   courage
daring   excitement   exhausted   exhilarated   fit
proud   satisfaction   self-confident   stamina
steady nerves   a sense of achievement   strength
terrified   thrill

6 Work in pairs.

Student A: Choose photos 1 and 2.
Student B: Choose photo 1 or 2 and photo 3.

Now prepare what you are going to say about your two photos.

7 Take turns to speak for one minute about your photos. Incorporate some of the words and phrases from Exercises 4 and 5.

8 After your partner has spoken, ask him/her a question related to his/her photos.

Exam advice

- Listen very carefully to the instructions you are given by the examiner, so that you answer the specific questions you are asked rather than talking vaguely or generally about the photos.
- You are asked two questions, which are printed on the page with the photos. Make sure you answer them both.
- Compare the photos in the context of the questions – don't make irrelevant comparisons. Spend about half your time comparing the photos and the other half answering the questions.
- You shouldn't try to describe the photos in detail.
- If you have time before starting to speak, spend a few seconds planning what you want to say.

- What skills and personal qualities does each activity involve?
- How do these activities make people feel?

Writing | Part 2
A proposal

1   Read the writing task below. Then think about who you would choose as your local hero and make a few brief notes.

> You see this notice on the website for your town or city council.
>
> > The Council is planning to honour a local hero connected with our area. The local hero can be someone well known or an ordinary citizen. He/She could be still living or could be someone from history.
> >
> > Residents are invited to send in proposals identifying a deserving person, giving reasons for their choice and suggesting a suitable way in which this hero should be honoured.
>
> Write your **proposal** in 220–260 words.

2   Take turns to tell a partner about the person you would choose. Give at least two reasons for your choice. Answer your partner's questions about your nomination.

3   Read the sample proposal without paying attention to the alternatives in *italics*. Answer these questions.

   1   How well does the writer know his local hero?
   2   What did Helen Keane do?
   3   What does the writer say she could have done instead?
   4   What has Helen Keane shown people?
   5   How does the writer suggest Helen Keane should be honoured ?

In response to your invitation, I am writing, to suggest a local hero who, [1]*in my opinion / I think*, deserves to be honoured. My hero is from my neighbourhood, but not someone I know personally.

My choice

My choice is Helen Keane, who, until recently, was just an ordinary working [2]*mother / mum*. One Friday last August, Helen was driving home, looking forward to a relaxing weekend. Suddenly, a lorry in front of her swerved and crashed into a bridge. Helen immediately stopped and went to help. When she [3]*got to / reached* the lorry, flames were coming from the cab but, without hesitating, Helen opened the door, pulled the unconscious driver out of his lorry and dragged him to safety. Helen herself [4]*was burnt / suffered burns* which kept her in hospital for two weeks.

Reasons for my choice

My main reason for choosing Helen is that she was an ordinary person going about her daily life. She could easily have [5]*gone off / driven home*, leaving the [6]*ambulance / emergency services* to deal with the accident. But instead, she stopped and saved a man's life. My other reason is that Helen has shown us all that special training is not necessarily required to help other people. Anyone can [7]*make a difference / help*.

Honouring my hero

If my choice of local hero is accepted, I suggest that the council should [8]*set up a fund / get together some money* which could be used to fund [9]*an annual prize / a prize every year* for someone who helps other people. This could be known as the Helen Keane Award.

I hope you will consider Helen Keane a suitable nominee who deserves to be honoured.

4 Work in pairs.

  a Read the proposal again and choose the most appropriate words and phrases in *italics*. Compare your choices with a partner and discuss the reasons for your choice.

  b Has the writer of this proposal covered all parts of the task appropriately?

5 Underline the *-ing* forms in the sample proposal. Then work in pairs to discuss how these forms are used, choosing from this list.

  1 as an adjective
  2 as part of a participle clause
  3 as part of a main verb
  4 after a preposition
  5 as a noun

6 ⊙ Most of the following sentences contain one or more mistakes made by exam candidates. Correct all the mistakes you can find.

  1 We think we can solve this problem by opening the museum to the public and charge them an entrance fee.
  2 In addition to keep up with their studies, university students often have to cope on very low budgets.
  3 Within the next few weeks a new sports centre will be opening in the north of the city.
  4 A hardwork committee has recently put forward a set of interested proposals for improve the food and service be offered in the college canteen.
  5 To bring in new health and safety regulations, the government has shown that it is concerned with improving the wellbeing of the whole population.
  6 I knew my decision to work abroad would mean to leave my friends and family.

7 Which of the adjectives in this list could be used to describe a hero? (Some are negative and would not be appropriate.)

cautious courageous creative enthusiastic exceptional extraordinary fearless generous greedy innovative inspiring kind narrow-minded passionate remarkable self-interested significant tireless

8 Use the adverb form of some of the adjectives above to complete these sentences. (In most cases, more than one answer is possible.)

  1 When the fire broke out, he acted quickly and ....
  2 She works .... to promote green issues.
  3 He was an .... gifted leader.
  4 Her work has contributed .... to the welfare of our community.
  5 He has been .... successful in achieving his aims.
  6 He believes .... in what he is doing.
  7 She treats everyone she meets .... and with respect.
  8 He thinks .... about ways of solving social problems.
  9 Residents have responded .... to the idea of naming the park after her.

9 Now plan and write your proposal for the writing task in Exercise 1.

  • Use the example proposal in Exercise 3 as a model.
  • If you cannot think of a real person to write about, your proposal can be fictional.
  • Write in an appropriately formal style.
  • Try to include *-ing* forms to link ideas in your proposal.
  • Use some interesting and appropriate adjectives and adverbs.

➡ page 190 Writing reference: Proposals

Picture yourself

Starting off

1 Work in pairs. *The Times* newspaper and the Tate Gallery in London held a drawing challenge in which they asked young people aged 11–18 to submit a self-portrait. Look at these submissions to the challenge.

- Which picture appeals to you most?
- What impression do you have of each artist's personality?

2 ▶ 6.1 Listen to three of the artists speaking. Which do you think are their self-portraits? Why?

Speaker A: ....
Speaker B: ....
Speaker C: ....

3 Which of these adjectives / adjective phrases did each speaker use?

> a bit self-conscious   aggressive   approachable
> moody   neat   nice to be around   not threatening
> really serious   sincere   thoughtful   unadventurous
> uptight

4 Work in pairs. Describe a photograph of yourself which you like.

- Where are you?
- What are you doing?
- What are you wearing?
- Who are you with?
- What expression do have on your face?
- What impression do you think the photo gives of your personality? If possible, use some of the adjectives from Exercise 3.

Listening | Part 3

1 Work in pairs. You will hear an interview with Mike Byatt, a portrait painter, and his subject, actress Emily Curran. Before you listen, look at these two portraits by other artists.

- In what ways is a portrait is different from a photo?
- Which of these portraits do you prefer? Why?

Helen Mirren by Ishbel Myerscough

PD James by Michael R Taylor

2 Work in pairs. Before you listen, read the multiple-choice questions 1–6 below and underline the main idea in each question (but not in the options A–D).

1 Mike painted the portrait in Emily's home because
   A he wanted to include her things in the portrait.
   B he wanted her to pose as naturally as possible.
   C he believed it would help him understand her personality.
   D he prefers his subjects to choose the background.

2 How did Emily feel at the beginning of the process?
   A unsure how she should pose
   B uncomfortable with so much attention
   C excited to be achieving a dream
   D impatient about the time it would take

3 According to Mike, the main reason why people have their portrait painted is that
   A portraits are more revealing than photos.
   B portraits are more decorative than photos.
   C portraits indicate a person's importance.
   D portraits stay with the family for many years.

4 Why does Mike prefer painting portraits with the sitter in front of him?
   A He can discuss the portrait with the sitter.
   B He can observe the sitter's moods and personality.
   C He can achieve a more exact image.
   D He enjoys the sitter's company.

5 What surprised Emily about the experience?
   A She had to concentrate.
   B She sometimes annoyed the artist.
   C She found it easy to stay still.
   D She was unhappy when it ended.

6 Mike says the personality of the person he paints
   A is revealed in a successful portrait.
   B is mixed with the artist's own in a portrait.
   C is exaggerated in the final result.
   D is interpreted by the portrait's viewers.

3 ▶16 Listen to the interview. For questions 1–6, choose the answer (A, B, C or D) which fits best according to what you hear.

4 Work in pairs.

- Would you prefer to have a painted portrait or a photograph of yourself in your house? Why?
- How big would it be and where would you put it?

Reading and Use of English | Part 5

1 You will read an article about the Tate Times Drawing Challenge. Before you
read, match these words with their definitions from the *Cambridge Advanced
Learner's Dictionary*.

1	grimace	a	to twist the face in an ugly way as an expression of pain or strong dislike
2	misunderstood	b	having the ability to control your fear in a dangerous or difficult situation
3	enliven	c	interested in things
4	courageous	d	to make something more interesting
5	exuberance	e	strong anxiety and unhappiness, especially about personal problems
6	grin	f	an unusual part of someone's personality or an unusual habit
7	angst	g	energy
8	quirk	h	wanting very much to do or have something, especially something interesting or enjoyable
9	engaged	i	having qualities that people do not recognise or appreciate
10	eager	j	a wide smile

2 Read the article quite quickly. What sorts of portraits did the judges generally prefer?

Teenage self-portraits

*When The Times invited anyone aged 11 to 18 to submit
a self-portrait, the response was phenomenal.*

You were interested in how your face and hair looked. We were
interested in honesty, courage and lack of self-consciousness.
And on Monday our mutual concerns met. A panel of judges
that included a professor of drawing, Stephen Farthing; the
Turner Prize-winning artist Grayson Perry; and myself, an art
critic, assembled to assess the entries for the Tate Times Drawing
Challenge. The competition invited anyone from 11 to 18 to pick
up their pencils and submit a self-portrait, the best of which would
be displayed in the Tate. There were more than 1,000 entries.

A self-portrait can be about total honesty. But, equally, it can
be all about ways of deceiving. Artists can rival actors when it
comes to obscuring or making themselves look better. Think of
the difference between that public face that you practise in the
mirror and that embarrassing grimace in the camera snap. The
construction of an image involves dozens of decisions. To study
a self-portrait is to understand how an artist wants to be seen. In
the case of young people it would seem that for every pretty-faced
teenager who would like to imagine themselves as some soft-focus
fashion model, there is another who is keen for the world to know
that they are lurking alone and misunderstood in their rooms.
Despite all the worst intentions, a self-portrait reveals how its sitter
sees the world. The judges were looking for a vision that seemed
enlivening or truthful, courageous or unselfconsciously fresh.
Sometimes the panel burst out laughing at the sheer exuberance
– though that was mostly in the work of the younger entrants,
before the toothy grins gave way to grimacing teenage angst.
There were pictures of young people doing anything from brushing
their teeth, to donning funny hats, to listening to iPods. But the
most interesting images were less self-consciously presented: it was
as if the sitters had been caught unprepared.

The judges tended to prefer the pictures in which the artist had
really tried to look in a mirror rather than copy the surface of a
photograph. 'The best images,' says Stephen Farthing, professor
of drawing at University of the Arts, London, 'are those done by
someone who has spent time drawing from life, not just trying
to make pictures that look as if they are finished.' Most of the
most obviously perfect images were passed over by the panel.
'The distortions and quirks are where the subconscious leaks out,'
Grayson Perry says.

It was notable how many entrants mapped out the spots on their
faces. Clearly this matters a lot to a teenager. Hair was another
obsession, though several got so caught up that their images were
more like advertisements for L'Oréal. They weren't worth it. Most

3 Read the text again and underline where it answers the following six questions. Then work in pairs and summarise your answers in your own words.

1 In the first paragraph, what does the writer say the judges discovered?
2 According to the writer, what do all self-portraits have in common?
3 How did the children's work generally differ from that of the adolescents?
4 How did the judges generally feel about the way the competitors drew their hair?
5 According to the writer, what is the English Martyrs Sixth Form College an example of?
6 In the final paragraph, what does the writer say about contemporary young people from the competition?

judges preferred the bad-hair days of entrants such as 13-year-old Daniel Adkins, in whose self-portrait the hair took on a character all of its own.

Drawing may be unfashionable – and not least in our art colleges – but it was heartening to see not only how naturally talented so many of the entrants were, but also how naturally drawing could be taught. Three of the self-portraits were by pupils of the English Martyrs Sixth Form College, Hartlepool. Where some schools submitted work that seemed identical, here, it seems, is a teacher who knows how to tease out and develop innate talent. And that matters.

Drawing is a means of expression as much as writing and mathematics. It's a tool to be sharpened so that you can take it out when you need it and do whatever you want. But what does this competition tell us about the entrants? It offered a portrait of young people who are engaged, enthusiastic and eager. Once, young people aspired to be bankers and doctors and lawyers. But who wants to go to the office when they could be an artist?

From *The Times*

Exam advice

- First read the text quickly to get a general idea of what it is about.
- Read the first question, find where it is answered in the text and underline the words in the text which answer it.
- Read each of the options A–D carefully and choose the one which matches the meaning of the text.
- Deal with the other questions one by one in the same way.

4 Now, for questions 1–6 below, choose the answer (A, B, C or D) which you think fits best according to the text.

1 In the first paragraph, the writer says the judges discovered that
   A they shared the same objectives as the competitors.
   B both entrants and judges were equally satisfied with the results.
   C the entrants' and the judges' differing objectives were achieved.
   D the winning entries combined good looks with other positive qualities.

2 According to the writer, what do all self-portraits have in common?
   A They reflect exactly what the artist sees in the mirror.
   B They are used to improve the artist's image.
   C They deceive both the artist and the viewer.
   D They reflect the artist's attitudes and concerns.

3 How did the children's work generally differ from that of the adolescents?
   A It was livelier.
   B It was more honest.
   C It was more absurd.
   D It showed more self-awareness.

4 How does the writer feel about the way competitors drew their hair?
   A It suited them better when it was untidy.
   B It deserved more attention from the artists.
   C It was more attractive than their spots.
   D It took up too much time for some artists.

5 The English Martyrs Sixth Form College is an example of
   A how schools can help pupils to develop their natural abilities.
   B why schools should teach unfashionable subjects.
   C how some schools teach all their pupils to draw in the same style.
   D why only naturally gifted pupils should be taught how to draw.

6 In the final paragraph, what impression does the writer have of those who took part in the competition?
   A They suffer from the typical anxieties of teenagers.
   B They are extremely interested in what they are doing.
   C They generally prefer drawing to writing or mathematics.
   D They are more artistically talented than previous generations.

Grammar
Avoiding repetition

1 Look at these extracts from Reading and Use of English Part 5 and write one word in each gap. Then check your answers by looking back at the text.

1 The competition invited anyone from 11 to 18 to submit a self-portrait, the best of .... would be displayed in the Tate. (para 1)

2 For every pretty-faced teenager who would like to imagine .... as some soft-focus fashion model there is .... who is keen for the world to know that they are lurking alone. (para 2)

3 The best images are .... done by someone who has spent time drawing from life, not just trying to make pictures that look as if .... are finished. (para 3)

4 It was notable how many entrants mapped out the spots on their faces. Clearly .... matters a lot to a teenager. (para 4)

5 Most judges preferred the bad-hair days of entrants such as 13-year-old Daniel Adkins, in .... self-portrait the hair took on a character all of its own. (para 4)

6 Here, it seems, is a teacher who knows how to tease out and develop innate talent. And .... matters. (para 5)

page 164 Language reference: Avoiding repetition

2 ⊙ Exam candidates often make mistakes when using pronouns and determiners. Correct the mistake in each of these sentences. In some cases there is more than one possible answer.

1 I wasn't happy about my hotel room. I said it to the receptionist but she didn't do anything about it.

2 There are several umbrellas in the stand in the hall. I'd advise you to take it if you're going for a walk.

3 I'd always wanted a portable DVD player and when I was given it as a birthday present, I thought it was wonderful.

4 Some of the machines broke down quite often, but when things like these happened we just called a technician.

5 The lecturers will give you a detailed explanation of the subject. You may not be able to understand all, but you should be able to get a general idea.

6 There was a long queue at the ice cream parlour because most of the children wanted it.

7 We're looking for a new accountant and it is why I'm writing to you.

8 You should aim to arrive at any time that's convenient for yourself.

3 Rewrite the following to reduce the number of words and avoid repetition.

1 I've been to two exhibitions at the National Gallery this year. The two exhibitions focused on 17th century painters.

I've been to two exhibitions at the National Gallery this year. Both focused on 17th century painters.

2 Fewer and fewer people listen to classical music. The fact that fewer and fewer people listen to classical music means that less classical music is being recorded.

3 I have to read lots of books for my Business Studies course. The books I enjoy most are the books on management theory.

4 I'm hoping to be given a pay rise. Being given a pay rise will mean I can buy a better car.

5 I want Karl, Pau, Ludmila and Mar to come to the meeting. I've told Karl. Can you tell Pau, Ludmila and Mar?

6 Marina doesn't like spending a lot of money on clothes, so she tends to buy second-hand clothes.

7 My mother asked you to help her and she'd have been so happy if you'd helped her.

8 When Raul feels strongly about something, he says he feels strongly about something.

9 She didn't do the shopping because no one asked her to do the shopping.

10 Someone left a message on the answering machine but the person didn't leave the person's name.

Vocabulary
Adjective–noun collocations (2)

1 Look at this sentence from Listening Part 3.

I've done a fair number of portraits that way and it seems to work better.

One of the adjectives below cannot be used with the word *number* to form a collocation. Which one?

fair	large	huge	big	small	limited

2 ⊙ Candidates often make the mistake of using *big* with the nouns in bold in sentences 1–10. Which of the adjectives in the box can be used to form collocations with each noun? (In all cases several answers are possible.)

amazing considerable endless good great
heavy high huge large loud satisfactory
terrible tremendous valuable wide

1 Pascual is very busy: he spends a .... **amount** of time studying.
2 Our local supermarket sells a(n) .... **range** of coffees, so you should find what you're looking for.

3 I found it difficult to concentrate on the conversation because of the .... **noise** coming from the neighbours' television.
4 Your decision about whether to go to art school or study economics is of .... **importance**, so think it over carefully.
5 Magda was very late for the meeting because of the .... **traffic** on the motorway.
6 Meeting such a distinguished artist was a(n) .... **experience** and quite unforgettable.
7 Quite a(n) .... **percentage** of our students go on to become professional artists – in the region of 60%.
8 I think Jaroslaw has made .... **progress** with his drawing and is showing real talent.
9 Colin is a teacher with .... **experience** of teaching both adults and children.
10 The paintings in this gallery show a(n) .... **variety** of different styles.

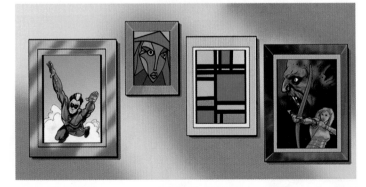

3 Work in pairs. Where there was more than one possibility in Exercise 2, do the different alternatives change the meaning of the sentence? If so, how?

Reading and Use of English | Part 2

1 You will read a text about art in offices. Read the text quite quickly without paying attention to the gaps. According to the text, what are the benefits of having art in the workplace?

2 For questions 1–8, read the text again and think of the word which best fits each gap. Use only one word in each gap.

Art for offices

(0) ....As............ a professional photographer and environmental psychologist, Wayne Hill knows (1) .... needs to be done with bland-coloured offices and windowless conference rooms: hang art on the walls. It cuts (2) .... on stress and raises productivity and creative thinking. 'Our best memories are often of a magic moment in (3) .... of the world's beautiful places. We can be taken back to them with realistic landscape photographs.'

(4) .... questioned, most employees say they are more likely to be inspired by good art than by (5) .... endless supply of the finest coffee. Most workers want some form of art at work. More surprisingly, perhaps, nearly two-thirds of office workers say they have never been consulted (6) .... the décor in their office. However, attitudes are changing. The kind of image companies now try to project through art is no (7) .... just aimed at customers. Now art is spread throughout the building (8) .... the benefit of employees.

Adapted from *The Observer*

3 Use these clues to check your answers to Exercise 2.
  1 a word which means 'the thing which'
  2 part of a phrasal verb which means 'reduce'
  3 a word which indicates that it's a particular place
  4 part of a time phrase or conditional phrase
  5 *supply* is a countable noun – what word is needed before it?
  6 a preposition used with *consult*
  7 part of a phrase that means 'not any more'
  8 a preposition

4 Work in small groups. Imagine you work together in the same bland-coloured office. Your office manager has asked how you think the office can be made a more pleasant place to work. Below are some of her suggestions.

> **Manager's suggestions**
> - some indoor plants
> - our holiday photos on the walls
> - an aquarium
> - our kids' drawings on the walls
> - some original art

1 Discuss how her suggestions would improve the office atmosphere.
2 Discuss which two would be most suitable.

5 Read this text quickly without paying attention to the gaps. Does the writer think graffiti is art or vandalism?

Graffiti: art or vandalism?

(0) ....Until.......... recently, spray-painting a wall would land you in jail, but these days even politicians are associating with graffiti artists in an effort to gain popularity and internationally acclaimed artist Banksy, (1) .... works of art make millions, has transformed the way the community views street art. However, many still see (2) .... as a crime, especially as the cost of removing grafitti from walls runs (3) .... millions of euros every year. Last May, members of a gang which had left a six-year trail of destruction on trains as (4) .... apart as Australia and Japan were jailed for eight months (5) .... pleading guilty to conspiracy to commit criminal damage. (6) .... other form of art has ever divided people so strongly, even (7) .... the custom of leaving paintings on walls goes back to the days of cave art. No one would imagine scraping cave drawings off the walls of a cave, and a thousand years from now children may find (8) .... studying street artists in school.

adapted from *The Olive Press*

6 For questions 1–8, read the text and think of the word which best fits each gap. Use only one word in each gap.

7 Work in small groups. What do you think: is graffiti art or vandalism?

> **Exam advice**
> - Read the text quite quickly to get a general idea of what it is about.
> - Look at the words before and after the space and decide what type of word you need (an article, pronoun, preposition, etc.).
> - Check whether the word you need refers to some other part of the text.
> - Words may be part of fixed phrases or phrasal verbs, e.g. *instead of*, *go along with*, etc.

Speaking | Part 3

1 ▶ 17 Work in pairs. Read the examiner's instruction below and look at the task. Then listen to extracts from two pairs of students doing the task and tick the correct box for each question.

> Now I'd like you to talk about something together for about two minutes. Here are some ways of encouraging young people to spend more time reading and a question for you to discuss. Talk to each other about how successful each of these experiences might be in encouraging young people to read more for pleasure.

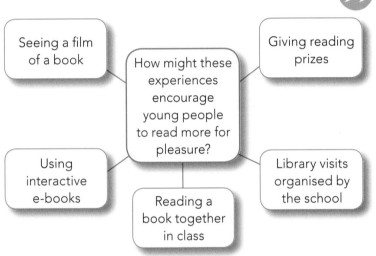

- Seeing a film of a book
- Giving reading prizes
- How might these experiences encourage young people to read more for pleasure?
- Using interactive e-books
- Reading a book together in class
- Library visits organised by the school

Which pair   Pair A   Pair B   Both

1 doesn't start working on the task immediately? ☐ ☐ ☐
2 deals with each suggestion on the task sheet in order? ☐ ☐ ☐
3 spends a lot of time on one or two suggestions, so probably won't have time for all of them? ☐ ☐ ☐
4 relates the suggestions to themselves personally? ☐ ☐ ☐
5 shows most interest in their partner's reactions to the suggestions? ☐ ☐ ☐

2 Work in pairs.
1 Which pair do you think deals with the task better? Why?
2 How do you think each pair could improve their performance?

3 You will get higher marks in the exam if you use advanced vocabulary appropriately when speaking. Work in pairs. In what context did the candidates use each of these phrases? (You need not remember the exact words.)

1 they give me pleasure
2 the high point of the week
3 made me determined
4 I found it rather tedious
5 communicate her enthusiasm
6 out of obligation
7 get more involved
8 get distracted
9 picked up a reading habit
10 just another chore

4 Work in pairs. Do the task in Exercise 1, following the examiner's instructions. Try to use some phrases from Exercise 3.

5 Work in pairs. Look at the examiner's instruction for the second part of Speaking Part 3 and the list of strategies below. Then decide together which strategies would be good for this part of the task. Write *Yes* or *No* for each strategy and give a reason.

> Now you have about a minute to decide which experience you think would be the most successful in encouraging young people to read more.

Strategies
1 Go over each of the options in turn again.
   No. There isn't time – you need to reach a decision in one minute.
2 Suggest an option, give a reason and ask your partner's opinion.
3 Agree with the first option your partner suggests.
4 Disagree with the first option your partner suggests, give a reason, then suggest another option and give a reason.
5 Agree with the first option your partner suggests but then suggest an alternative and give a reason.
6 Disagree with everything your partner says in order to fill the time.

6 **18** Listen to Ivan and Anna doing the second part of the task. Which strategies do they use?

7 Work in pairs. Follow the examiner's instruction in Exercise 5, using one or two of the strategies from Exercise 5.

8 Work in pairs.

1 Read the examiner's instruction below. Then do the first part of the Speaking task.

> Now I'd like you to talk about something together for about two minutes. Here are some creative or artistic activities which young people can study at school and a question for you to discuss. Talk to each other about how young people might benefit from doing each of these activities.

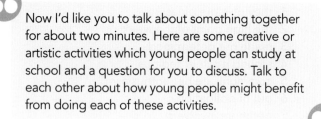

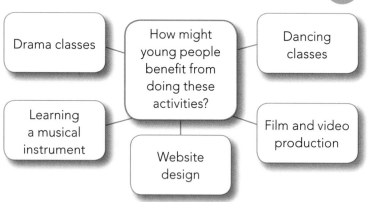

2 Read the examiner's next instruction and do the second part of the Speaking task.

> Now you have a minute to decide which activity it is most important for young people to study at school.

Writing | Part 2
A review

1 Read the writing task below and underline the key points you must deal with.

> You have seen this announcement in an international magazine.
>
> > We receive a lot of letters from readers asking us to recommend novels to read. We believe that they should read novels that they will find interesting and we'd like to publish reviews of novels which other readers have particularly enjoyed. Send us a review which describes the novel, says what you liked about it and explains why you recommend it.
>
> Write your **review**.

2 Work in pairs. Decide which of these elements you should include in your review.

a biographical information about the author
b a summary of the whole plot
c a general synopsis of the plot and characters and why they're interesting
d a description of the type of book, the setting and what it's about
e a mention of things you particularly like
f a recommendation for your readers and reasons for it
g a criticism of things you didn't like
h suggestions for other books that you think your readers would enjoy

3 Read the review of *Cold Mountain* without paying attention to the highlighting. Complete the paragraph plan for this review.

Plan

Para 1: ....*type of novel, setting, outline of story*.........
Para 2: ....
Para 3: ....

4 Does the review give you a clear idea of what *Cold Mountain* is about? Having read the review, do you think you would enjoy the novel? Why (not)?

Cold Mountain by Charles Frazier

● ●

Cold Mountain is a historical novel set in North Carolina during the American Civil War. It tells the story of the main characters, Inman and Ada. Inman is a deserter from the army who makes a hazardous journey across the country to join Ada, the woman he loves. The novel switches between Inman's journey and Ada's life on her farm, where she struggles to survive after her father's death.

The novel contains a gallery of interesting characters. Inman is the thoughtful, observant hero who is desperate to escape the war and stay alive. He is motivated by love, but also capable of extreme violence. Ada, the heroine, comes from a well-off, sheltered background and at first seems incapable of surviving in harsh conditions, but as the novel progresses she becomes self-sufficient and decisive. She is helped by Ruby, a tough but lovable country girl. Also, during his journey, Inman meets many extraordinary minor characters who are trying to stay alive in unusual ways in wild, remote places.

I was fascinated by the vivid descriptions of American rural life at the time. I was also caught up in the suspense of each dangerous situation that Inman and Ada encounter during the story. If you enjoy historical novels, you will really love this book with its wonderful dialogues and its detailed observations and descriptions of life in nineteenth-century America. You will be transported into a world where love and kindness contrast with horror and cruelty to create a novel which is unlike any novel you have ever read before.

4 You will score higher marks in the exam if you use a range of appropriate advanced vocabulary. Match the highlighted adjectives in the review with their synonym or definition from the *Cambridge Advanced Learner's Dictionary*.

   1 able to provide everything you need without help from other people
   2 carefully considering things
   3 producing clear, powerful, detailed images in the mind
   4 dangerous
   5 different from
   6 feeling that you have no hope and are ready to do anything to change the bad situation you are in
   7 good or quick at noticing things
   8 protected too much
   9 rich
   10 strong
   11 unpleasantly hard and demanding
   12 a long way from any towns or cities

5 Work in pairs. Which novel could each of you write about? Tell each other a little about

   • the type of novel, the setting and what it's about
   • the plot and characters
   • what you particularly liked – why you would recommend it.

6 Plan and write your own answer to the task in Exercise 1.

 page 189 Writing reference: Reviews

Exam information and advice

Writing a review tests your ability to describe and give your opinions about something you have experienced (e.g. a book, a film, a café or restaurant, a language course) and to tell your readers whether or not you recommnend it. You may be asked to compare two things of the same type in your review.

When writing a review

■ consider what information will be of interest to your readers (e.g. where is the language course? What are the teachers like? Is it good value for money?)

■ express your opinions of the different elements you decide to include in your review, so that your readers have a clear idea whether or not you are recommending what you are reviewing.

Vocabulary and grammar review Unit 5

Vocabulary

1 Read the text below and decide which answer (A, B, C or D) best fits each gap.

A night to remember

Anna had never been one to **(1)** .... unnecessary risks, but that evening was different. She knew there was a certain **(2)** .... of danger in her plan, but she felt quietly confident. She knew that if she succeeded in getting there by daybreak, she would experience a great **(3)** .... of achievement. She'd been **(4)** .... an eye on the weather all week, so it wasn't simply a question of keeping her fingers **(5)** .... and hoping for the best.

She picked up her overnight bag, left the house and got into her car. In no time, she'd covered fifty kilometres, and was still feeling good about her adventure. Then, without any warning, the car lurched to the right and left the road. The last thing she remembers was her head hitting the steering wheel. When she **(6)** .... round, she heard the sirens and saw the flashing lights of the **(7)** .... services as they arrived.

1	A make	B experience	C take	D feel
2	A element	B factor	C aspect	D component
3	A perception	B sense	C sensation	D recognition
4	A having	B watching	C putting	D keeping
5	A together	B crossed	C folded	D closed
6	A turned	B came	C woke	D went
7	A emergency	B health	C urgent	D safety

Grammar

2 Complete the second sentence so that it has a similar meaning to the first sentence, using the word given. Do not change this word. Use three to six words including the word given.

1 I can't wait to start my new job.
   FORWARD
   I'm really .... my new job.

2 Thank goodness we avoided the floods.
   LUCKY
   We .... the floods.

3 I wish I hadn't phoned my sister.
   REGRET
   I .... that phone call to my sister.

4 We can't buy a new car – we don't have enough money.
   AFFORD
   We .... a new car.

5 He says he's never seen her before.
   DENIES
   He .... her before.

6 We paid our hotel bill when we checked out.
   SETTLED
   It wasn't until .... our hotel bill.

3 Complete these texts with the infinitive or *-ing* form of the verbs in brackets. One verb is in the passive.

Three of the people trapped on the third floor managed [1]........................... (climb) out onto the roof of the hotel, where they jumped to safety. The other two refused [2]........................... (leave) their room and waited [3]........................... (rescue). The manager admitted [4]........................... (wait) for 20 minutes before [5]........................... (phone) the fire brigade. He claimed that he had attempted [6]........................... (put out) the fire himself before [7]........................... (realise) the seriousness of the situation. He apologised to his colleagues for [8]........................... (put) their lives at risk.

The climbers refused [9]........................... (take) the weather forecast seriously and ended up [10]........................... (get) lost when it started [11]........................... (snow). Despite this, they went on [12]........................... (climb), but were eventually forced [13]........................... (admit) defeat. It was then that they tried [14]........................... (phone) mountain rescue [15]........................... (ask) for help. However, because there was no phone signal on the mountain, they could not [16]........................... (contact) the team and spent the night on the mountain, [17]........................... (regret) their decision [18]........................... (ignore) the forecast.

Vocabulary and grammar review Unit 6

Vocabulary

1 In each of the sentences below, cross out the adjective in *italics* which does not collocate with the noun in **bold**.

1 A *high / big / significant* **percentage** of accident victims coming to hospital have been doing DIY at home.

2 For me, visiting Paris is always a *great / wide / tremendous* **experience** – it really is my favourite city.

3 Giovanni attaches *considerable / great / large* **importance** to the way he dresses, so he always gets up extra early.

4 If you want to do a gap year before going to university, there is a(n) *endless / huge / deep* **range** of possibilities for you to choose from.

5 Martina is showing a lot of promise and she's made *high / considerable / satisfactory* **progress** with her English this term.

6 My brother has spent a *huge / heavy / considerable* **amount** of money renovating an old farmhouse – I don't know how he can afford it.

7 They're doing road works in the street and the **noise** is so *loud / terrible / big* that I can hardly hear myself think!

8 One of the attractions of this job is the *endless / high / wide* **variety** of different tasks I have to perform.

Grammar

2 Rewrite the following sentences in order to avoid repetition of words and phrases.

1 'Do you think you'll get a holiday in July?' 'I hope I get a holiday in July!'
'Do you think you'll get a holiday in July?' 'I hope so!'

2 When a child feels unhappy, the child will ask for the child's mother more often than the child will ask for the child's father.

3 Gustav bought a large house by the sea about ten years ago. Buying a large house by the sea turned out to be a good investment.

4 Leonardo lived in Canada as a child. The fact that he lived in Canada is the reason why he speaks such fluent English.

5 Svetlana spent several months trying to decide which car to buy and she finally bought a car last week.

6 Matthew likes reading novels. Matthew especially likes reading romantic novels.

7 Violeta bought apples in the market. Violeta put some of the apples in the fruit bowl. Violeta used the other apples to make an apple pie.

8 Narayan has had two jobs. The two jobs were in a bank. Unfortunately the two jobs were not well paid.

9 There are five official languages in Spain and Manolo speaks all of the five official languages of Spain.

10 Pete had never spoken to Ann, although Pete had often wanted to speak to Ann.

3 Complete the second sentence so that it has a similar meaning to the first sentence, using the word given. Do not change the word given. You must use between three and six words, including the word given.

1 The photo and the portrait look identical to me.
DIFFERENCE
I can't see .... the photo and the portrait.

2 The judges were generally less keen on portraits painted from photos than portraits painted from life.
TENDED
The judges .... on portraits painted from life than portraits painted from photos.

3 This painting does not appear to be finished.
LOOK
This painting .... is finished.

4 Several of the applicants were not considered because of their age.
PASSED
Several of the applicants .... to their age.

5 For many teenagers, their looks are their highest priority.
MATTERS
Appearance is .... many teenagers.

6 It's encouraging to discover that the group is both talented and enthusiastic.
ONLY
It's encouraging to discover that the group shows .... as well.

Starting off

1 What do you enjoy doing in your free time? Choose which of these types of activities you prefer and give examples of specific activities you enjoy. Then compare your preferences with other students.

Activity types	
• indoor	• outdoor
• competitive sports or games	• non-competitive sports or games
• lone activities	• social activities (with other people)
• active: being creative or productive	• passive: watching others doing things
• using electronic technology	• without technology of any kind

2 Discuss these questions.

 1 How have people's leisure activities changed over the last fifty years? What can people of your generation do that your parents and grandparents couldn't do?

 2 Do you combine work or study with leisure? For example, do you listen to music, text friends, or spend time on social networking sites while you are working or studying?

 3 How, when and where do you listen to music?

Listening | Part 4

1 ▶ 19 You are going to hear ten snippets of music. Listen and match each with one of the types of music in the box. Which of these types of music do you enjoy listening to?

classical disco folk jazz Latin opera pop
rap rock

2 What is it that you particularly like about the music you listen to? Exchange ideas with a partner.

3 You will hear five short extracts in which people are talking about an aspect of music which is important to them.

 1 Before you listen, look at the photos and discuss what the people are doing.

 2 Read through Tasks One and Two in Exercise 4. Can you match the people listed in Task One (A–H) with any of the photos?

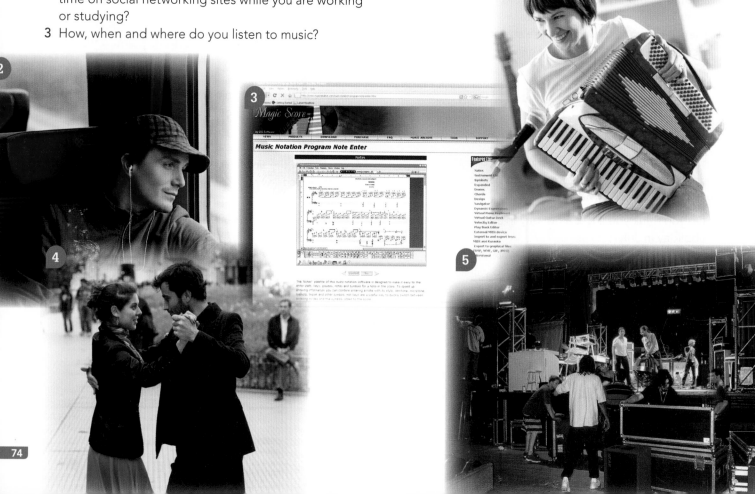

4 ▶20 Listen to the five speakers and do Tasks One and Two.

TASK ONE
For questions **1–5**, choose from the list (**A–H**) the person who is speaking.

A   a composer
B   a festival worker
C   an orchestra member
D   a folk musician
E   someone with varied musical tastes
F   a rock musician
G   a trombone player
H   a novice dancer

Speaker 1 ☐ 1
Speaker 2 ☐ 2
Speaker 3 ☐ 3
Speaker 4 ☐ 4
Speaker 5 ☐ 5

TASK TWO
For questions **6–10**, choose from the list (**A–H**) the feelings expressed by the speakers.

A   gratitude for an invention
B   disappointment at a failure
C   cautious optimism about an ambitious project
D   gratitude to musicians
E   satisfaction in having contributed to a successful event
F   relief that a project has succeeded
G   enthusiasm for a new interest
H   pride in a tradition

Speaker 1 ☐ 6
Speaker 2 ☐ 7
Speaker 3 ☐ 8
Speaker 4 ☐ 9
Speaker 5 ☐ 10

5 ▶20 In each of these sentences, which word did the speaker use? When you have chosen, listen to the recording again to check your answers.

1 He sang at family *assemblies / gatherings / meetings*.
2 The rhythm was so *conspicuous / defective / infectious* that some of the audience got up and bopped about.
3 I have it with me all the time, whether I'm *commuting / computing / conducting* to work, exercising or just chilling.
4 We're planning to make a recording, but the *linguistics / logistics / statistics* are a nightmare.
5 I've just come back from Womad in Singapore – it was *awful / awesome / fearsome*.

Vocabulary
Complex prepositions

1 Some prepositions are phrases of three words, for example:

I've travelled all over the world and played *in front of* audiences of thousands.
As well as the kind of instruments I was familiar with …

Complete these sentences with the correct prepositions.

1 Last night's concert was performed .... aid .... a charitable trust.
2 These remarkable sounds were produced .... means .... magnetic waves.
3 She's bought an electric guitar .... place .... her old acoustic one.
4 We couldn't sleep .... account .... the bright light outside our window.
5 .... behalf .... the whole family, I'd like to thank you for being with us today.
6 I am writing to you .... regard .... your recent enquiry.
7 His grandfather played music very much .... keeping .... folk traditions.
8 We worked for five hours a day .... exchange .... meals and accommodation.

2 Match each three-word phrase from Exercise 1 with the correct meaning.

a because of
b fitting appropriately with
c on the subject of
d in order to help
e in return for
f representing
g as a substitute for
h by using

Reading and Use of English | Part 7

1 Work in pairs. You are going to read an article about virtual online worlds.

   1 What do you know about virtual worlds?

   2 Why do you think people create avatars in virtual worlds? (An avatar is an image or virtual representation of a person.)

2 Read the main part of the article (but not the missing paragraphs A–G).

   1 When did the first virtual world games appear?

   2 Why did Second Life become less popular?

   3 How does the writer expect virtual worlds to develop in the future?

3 Read paragraphs A–G. Note down a phrase that summarises the main idea of each paragraph.

Example:
Para A: what users can do in Second Life

4 Now choose from the paragraphs A–G the one which fits each gap in the text. There is one extra paragraph which you do not need to use.

Your guide to virtual worlds

Virtual worlds are online three-dimensional spaces where you can interact with other people, collect items and build structures, and communicate via a virtual representative of yourself called an avatar. They have been influenced by various science fiction writers, along with the movie *The Matrix*.

1

The origin of virtual worlds goes back to early games such as Maze War, which was developed in the early 1970s. The game included eyeballs as avatars, there were maps showing the levels, and it was one of the first games played on linked computers and eventually on a forerunner of the Internet.

2

In a research paper they wrote: 'At the core of our vision is the idea that cyberspace is a multiple-participant environment. It seems to us that the things that are important to the inhabitants of such an environment are the capabilities available to them, the characteristics of the other people they encounter there, and the ways in which these various participants can affect one another.'

3

Most early virtual worlds like these faded because the hardware and bandwidth requirements were too stringent, and they never established hardcore user bases as dot-com funding dried up at the turn of the millennium.

4

It was this range of creative possibilities that grabbed the attention of the media and marketers, who saw it as a new way of communicating and selling online. *BusinessWeek* ran a cover story called *My Virtual Life*, explaining breathlessly that 'big advertisers are taking notice'. *Wired* magazine ran a special travel guide to Second Life, while Reuters assigned a full-time reporter to cover news that unfolded there.

5

The fact is that even though computer hardware and bandwidth have improved over the years, Second Life still requires sophisticated computer systems and a lot of practice to master the interface. The number of registered avatars is misleading: many people simply try it out and give up, while others have multiple avatars. A more representative number for regular users is the number who have logged in during the past seven days, which is quite low.

6

Despite these difficulties, media companies are still fascinated with virtual worlds and continue to develop them. For example, MTV created a whole range of virtual worlds based on the content of its original television shows and other companies have created worlds for students and teens. Even if today's Second Life doesn't satisfy the mass market, dozens of other virtual worlds will certainly spring up, designed to cater for specific tastes and interests.

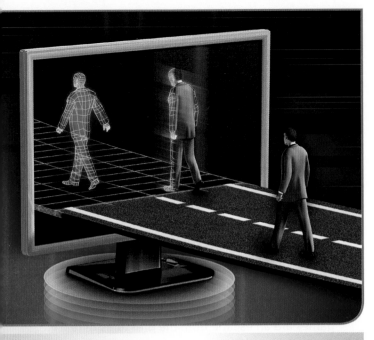

5 Work in pairs. What do you think the phrases in *italics* from the article mean? What clues did you use to guess the meanings?

1 These worlds differ from *multi-player online games*.
2 … eventually a *forerunner of the Internet*.
3 … as long as they couldn't *hack into the system*.
4 The Palace was a more *chat-oriented world*.
5 The *media buzz* led many more people to explore virtual worlds.
6 These business spent money … but then *got little payoff*.
7 … making it difficult for companies to get their attention *en masse*.

6 Discuss these questions.

1 What kind of new online virtual world would attract you?
2 What would your avatar be like?

Exam advice

- First, read the main body of the text carefully to familiarise yourself with the contents of each paragraph and how the whole text is structured.
- Then read each of the missing paragraphs one by one. Pay close attention to the content and place each paragraph in a gap after you have read it.

A However, while other worlds were withering, Linden Labs was developing their new virtual world, Second Life, which still exists today. Here you can create your own objects and buildings, and you have ownership rights over them. 'Linden dollars' are a currency which you can trade with real dollars. Real-world businesses can sell just about anything you could possibly want in the virtual world. Universities offer courses through Second Life, and bands play live shows and chat with fans in special in-world venues.

B That presents a problem for the many marketers such as Coca-Cola and Adidas who set up virtual spaces in Second Life, only to have them largely vacant. These businesses spent money – in the tens of thousands of dollars – to build a virtual island as an experiment, but then got little payoff. Residents are dispersed throughout the virtual world, making it hard for companies to get their attention en masse, and there's a limit to the number of people who can congregate in one place without crashing Linden's servers.

C Later, with the rise of the web, virtual worlds started booming. The Active Worlds platform allowed people to join for free or pay a monthly fee for premium features, while The Palace was a more chat-oriented world that became popular in entertainment circles.

D Second Life is built from user-generated content: its software provides the tools to design a dress, construct a building or carry out a range of other real-world activities. Its population includes a pet manufacturer, a nightclub owner, a car maker, a fashion designer, an architect, a tour guide and a property speculator.

E The media buzz led many more people to explore virtual worlds for the first time and Linden claims to have registered nearly 10 million avatars for Second Life since its inception. But many users ended up disappointed.

F The next stage was when Lucas Film Games, a video game publisher, developed Habitat, a more two-dimensional environment that included humanoid avatars, and people could access the game through an early online service called Quantum Link. Developers Morningstar and Farmer, who still maintain a blog about their experience, say they generally allow Habitat residents to set their own rules governing the world – as long as they couldn't hack into the system.

G These worlds differ from massive multi-player online games (MMOGs) because they don't offer battles against monsters or have an overriding mission for players. For example, a resident of the virtual world Second Life might spend time in that space accumulating virtual land, rather than striving to complete quests as they would in many popular MMOGs.

Grammar
Linking ideas: relative and participle clauses

1 Complete these extracts from Reading and Use of English Part 7 with a word or phrase from the list.

based   explaining   in which   making   played   that   where   which   who

1 Virtual worlds are online three-dimensional spaces .... you can interact with other people.
2 The origin of virtual worlds goes back to early games such as Maze War, ... was developed in the early 1970s.
3 It was one of the first games .... on linked computers.
4 The things that are important are the ways .... these various participants can affect one another.
5 Residents are dispersed throughout the virtual world, ... it difficult for companies to get their attention.
6 'Linden dollars' are a currency .... you can trade with real dollars.
7 It grabbed the attention of the media and marketers, ... saw it as a new way of communicating.
8 *Business Week* ran a story called *My Virtual Life*, ... breathlessly that 'big advertisers are taking notice'.
9 MTV created a range of virtual worlds .... on the content of its original television shows.

2 Discuss these questions on the sentences in Exercise 1.
1 a Which sentences contain a relative clause?
  b Which of these are defining clauses (containing essential information)?
  c Which are non-defining clauses (containing additional, non-essential information)?
2 a Which sentences contain a participle clause?
  b Which of these use a present participle and which use a past participle?
  c In which sentences does the participle clause replace a relative clause?
  d In which sentences does the participle clause link two actions which happen at the same time?
3 In which of the sentences could the relative pronoun be left out? Why?

→ page 171 Language reference: Linking ideas

3 Complete these sentences with relative pronouns. You may also have to include a preposition.
1 Farmville, ... is a popular online game, is usually played through Facebook.
2 Players have a 'home' farm and several themed farms .... they can grow a range of crops.
3 The main way .... a player earns money is by harvesting crops or visiting neighbours.
4 People .... I know quite well spend several hours a day playing Farmville.
5 Anyone .... has experienced it knows all too well – video game addiction is real.
6 There are some people .... lives have been changed forever by their addiction to video games.
7 There are many adults and children .... video games are an escape from the pressures of real life.
8 A self-confessed addict, ... has been hooked on Second Life for years, admits it causes him problems.

Are there any sentences in which the relative pronoun can be left out?

4 Choose the correct participles in these sentences.
1 We came out of the cinema *quivered / quivering* with fright.
2 We'd seen a film *based / having based* on a science fiction short story.
3 *Reading / Having read* the story, I was interested to see how they would turn it into a film.
4 It was only the second film *made / having been made* by this director.
5 I'd read a review of the film in a magazine *specialising / specialised* in science fiction stories.

Linking ideas: apposition

5 It is often possible to link information about someone/something by putting two nouns or noun phrases next to each other, with no relative pronoun.

The next stage was when <u>Lucas Film Games</u>, <u>a video game publisher</u>, developed <u>Habitat</u>, <u>a more two-dimensional environment</u>.

Join these sentences using phrases in apposition.
1 *The Matrix* came out in 1999. It is a science fiction film.
2 Thomas Anderson is the central character. He is a computer programmer and a hacker.
3 The star of the film is Keanu Reeves. Keanu Reeves is a famous American actor.
4 The film popularised 'bullet time'. Bullet time is an effect which allows actions to be filmed at different speeds.

Reading and Use of English | Part 1

1 Work in pairs.

    1 What is your favourite type of film?

    2 What is the best film you've seen in the last twelve months?

    3 How is going to the cinema different from watching a film on your television or computer at home?

    4 What do you know about Bollywood films? How are they different from Hollywood films?

2 Quickly read the article about Bollywood films. Does it confirm or contradict any of the ideas you have just discussed?

3 For questions 1–8, read the article again and decide which answer (A, B, C or D) best fits each gap. There is an example at the beginning (0).

Exam advice

- First read the title and the whole text quickly to get a general idea of what it is about.
- Study the gapped sentences one by one, reading carefully before and after the gap.
- The four words you have to choose from will be similar in meaning but only one will fit correctly into the gap. You should consider dependent prepositions and other grammatical structures.
- If you are not sure which option is correct, discard the options you think are wrong and choose from the others.

4 Discuss these questions.

    1 How would you explain the enduring popularity of musicals?

    2 How do you feel about romantic films and fiction in general?

    3 How important are traditional themes in films in your country?

The changing face of Bollywood

Bollywood is the name (0) ......C...... to popular Mumbai-based Indian films. Bollywood films are generally musicals and contain catchy song-and-dance numbers, and a film's success often depends on the quality of such musical numbers. Indeed, a film's music is often (1) .... before the movie itself, as a way of generating advance publicity. Indian audiences expect value for money from their films, which must include a famous actor in the (2) ....

The (3) .... of Bollywood films have tended to be melodramatic, employing formulaic ingredients such as star-crossed lovers, angry parents, family (4) .... , corrupt politicians, and siblings (5) .... by fate. There have always been Indian films with more sophisticated stories, inside and outside the Bollywood tradition, but these often lose out at the box office to movies with more mass (6) .... Bollywood conventions are changing, however. Large Indian (7) .... in English-speaking countries and increased Western influence at home have made Bollywood films more like Hollywood films. Plots often feature westernised urbanites dating and dancing in discos, rather than the traditional (8) .... marriages.

0 A handed	B donated	C given	D conferred
1 A emitted	B issued	C released	D announced
2 A crew	B characters	C team	D cast
3 A accounts	B plots	C scenes	D plays
4 A feuds	B wars	C hostilities	D complaints
5 A segregated	B separated	C lost	D detached
6 A popularity	B appeal	C attraction	D lure
7 A people	B residents	C populations	D inhabitants
8 A arranged	B coordinated	C orchestrated	D set up

Vocabulary
Money words

1 Complete these sentences with the correct form of the verbs in the box.

> borrow   buy   earn   hire   lend   pay
> rent   sell

1 We're .... a holiday cottage in the south of France for three weeks in the summer.
2 Thousands of people .... their living by .... and .... things online.
3 They're .... a dance band for their daughter's wedding in August.
4 I've asked my parents if they would .... me some money to buy a car. I'll .... it back when I can.
5 People say you shouldn't .... money from friends, but I don't agree.

2 Complete the questions below with ten of the verbs from the box. Then discuss the questions in pairs.

> afford   borrow   burn   buy   cost   cover
> make   meet   pay   raise   sell   shop
> take out

1 If you went for a job interview, how would you try to .... yourself?
2 What would you do if you wanted to .... a quick buck?
3 Do you believe that money can .... happiness?
4 When you go shopping, for example for clothes, how do you .... – in cash or by card?
5 Is there anything you can't .... to buy because it .... a fortune?
6 If you were short of money, what would you do to make ends ....?
7 Would you like to be able to .... a loan to buy a house or flat one day? Why (not)?
8 What is the first thing you would buy if you had money to .... ?
9 How would you .... money for a charity you wanted to support?

They're rolling in money.

He's paid peanuts.

3 Complete the money idioms in these sentences by choosing the correct noun in *italics*. Then discuss in pairs what each idiom means. The idioms are in **bold**.

1 They say they want to help the disabled, but they should **put their money where their** *mouth / pocket* **is**.
2 You need to be a bit more careful with your money. **Money doesn't grow on** *bushes / trees*, you know.
3 The shop wouldn't accept a cheque or a credit card. They insisted on **hard** *cash / money*.
4 Hotels are always expensive but we had to **pay through the** *hand / nose* for the room we wanted.
5 I always prefer to **pay my own** *road / way*, so you pay your bill and I'll pay mine.
6 I've no idea where he gets it from, but Martin's been **spending money like** *air / water* recently.
7 It's the local council that has to decide whether to build a new school. It **holds the** *purse / wallet* **strings**.
8 We couldn't afford a new car – I'm afraid it would **break the** *savings / bank*.

4 ⊙ Each of these sentences contains one or more errors made by exam candidates. Correct the mistakes.

1 I'm sure you'll enjoy the job – and don't forget, you'll be gaining good money.
2 As you will be using your own car and staying in hotels, the company will afford all your expenses and spend you a daily meal allowance.
3 You can pay your ticket here or on the bus.
4 I can borrow you some money, but please give it back tomorrow.
5 You can rent all the books you need from the college library – at no cost.
6 Save time and money if you buy more than $200.
7 In the last month we have earned over £2,000 for charity – most of it from public donations.

Speaking | Part 4

1 Work in pairs. Read the examiner's instruction and the written prompts for a Part 3 task. Discuss the question with your partner.

Here are some team-building activities which have been suggested for new members of a social club. Talk to each other about how effective these activities would be in helping people to get to know each other better.

Playing a team sport

How effective would each of these activities be in helping people to get to know each other better?

Raising funds for a club

Rock climbing

Teaching others a new skill

Playing computer games in teams

2 Read these Part 4 questions that might follow the Part 3 task above. Which of the six questions would you most like to answer? Which would you find the most difficult to answer? Briefly exchange ideas in pairs.

1 Some people say that team-building activities are a waste of time. Do you agree?
2 What qualities does a person need to be a good team member?
3 What can managers do make sure their teams of employees work well together on a day-to-day basis?
4 Large clubs and organisations are more likely than small ones to organise team-building activities. Why do you think this is?
5 What problems can arise if individuals in a large organisation feel isolated or undervalued?
6 Is it always best to for people to avoid conflict with others? Why (not)?

3 ▶21 Listen to two extracts from a Part 4 exam.

1 Which two questions from Exercise 2 are the candidates answering?
2 In each dialogue, what is the first speaker's main point?
3 Does the second speaker agree, partly agree or disagree?
4 What opinion would you give?

4 Now take turns with a partner to answer the questions in Exercise 2. After your turn, ask your partner's opinion about the question you have answered. Use some of the words in the box.

Nouns: achievement   a common goal   cooperation   incentive

Verbs: appreciate   compete   contribute   cooperate   share   support   respect

Adjectives: constructive   creative   productive   supportive   worthwhile

Exam advice

- Listen carefully to all the examiner's questions – you may be asked the same question as your partner.
- Listen to your partner's answers to questions, as you may have to respond to these.
- Try to use a range of expressions to express and justify opinions and to agree and disagree.

Writing | Part 2
An informal letter

1 Answer these questions individually. Then compare your answers with a partner.

1 How often do you write letters (not including emails)?
2 Why and when might you write a letter rather than sending a text or writing an email?

2 Read the extracts A–E from five letters. Number them 1–5 according to how formal they are (1 = very informal, 5 = very formal).

1 What is the purpose of the letter each extract is taken from?
2 What can you deduce about the writers and recipients of each letter?
3 What features of informal language does each extract include?

3 Rewrite these formal expressions in more informal English. The first six expressions are from extracts B and E.

1 We can now confirm that
2 your forthcoming vacation
3 will be debited from your credit card
4 the week following your departure
5 Please accept my apologies for this
6 We do make every effort
7 Firstly, I raised the issue of
8 Should you wish me to act on your behalf
9 There is another factor that needs to be taken into account
10 I am not in a position to provide advice on this matter

→ page 192 Writing reference: Emails and letters

4 Rewrite these openings to letters replying to extracts A and C. Use more appropriate language.

A Thank you for your enquiry about accommodation for five days in November. Unfortunately, our rooms are fully booked during this period and I am therefore unable to comply with your request.

C With reference to your letter of 24 May, I wish to express my appreciation of your invitation to attend the college function on 15 June and to inform you that I shall be very happy to attend.

A
... so am looking for a family of masochists to put me up for a few days. As you seemed sorry we didn't manage to meet up last time I was over, I thought I'd give you first option this time. I'll be around from 7–11 November. Don't worry if it's inconvenient, there are loads of other people I can ask, but it'd be good to see you all.

B
We can now confirm that we have taken 1,490 euros from your credit card account, that being the total cost of your forthcoming vacation. Any agreed deductions for extras, breakages, cleaning, etc. will be debited from your credit card the week following your departure.

C
Secondly, we would like to try to get everyone together before they start their summer break – we're asking all the trainees and course tutors over for a barbecue in Junko's garden on 15 June. It's a Friday evening, so hopefully people shouldn't be going to work or doing anything too serious the next day.

D
Just a short note to thank you for the music on Saturday. Everyone seemed to have an excellent time and we have had some nice emails and notes back. Everyone really liked the dancing as well – I thought it set the evening up very nicely.

E
Please accept my apologies for this. We do make every effort to pack the CDs well and always use the best available courier company. Unfortunately, the CD cases themselves are quite fragile and it only needs one employee in any of the various depots across the country to drop one of the boxes or to throw it into the back of a van and the whole batch can be damaged.

5 Work in pairs. Read the following writing task, then discuss and list some indoor and outdoor activities in your town that you could suggest in reply to the letter.

An Australian friend of yours is attending a language course in your town next month. This is an extract from a letter that he/she has written to you.

> Classes are on weekday mornings, so my afternoons and weekends are free. It would be great if you could suggest how I could spend my free time. Perhaps you can suggest a few indoor as well as outdoor activities? Don't forget, I'm not keen on sport!

Write a **letter** in reply to your friend.

6 Discuss the beginning and end of your letter. Which of these ideas would you include at the beginning and which at the end?

- say you're looking forward to seeing your friend
- comment on the fact that your friend is planning to learn your language
- give some general information about your town
- suggest meeting during your friend's stay
- ask about the language course your friend is attending

7 Look at expressions 1–10 for making suggestions. Which of these are followed by

a an infinitive without *to*?   b *to* + infinitive?
c the *-ing* form?

In one expression there are two possible answers.

1 It might be an idea …
2 What would you think about …?
3 Another possibility would be …
4 I suggest that you should …
5 What about …?
6 I'd say you ought …
7 You could consider …
8 You might feel like …
9 What I think you should do is …
10 I'd say your best option is …

8 Write your answer to the task in Exercise 5 in 220–260 words. Remember to use informal language.

Exam advice

Before you start to write, think carefully about

- the purpose of the letter (this will be stated in the task instruction)
- who the reader will be and what this person will expect to hear from you
- what exactly the question asks you to include in your letter
- how formal or informal the language should be (this will depend on your relationship with the reader and on the purpose of your letter).

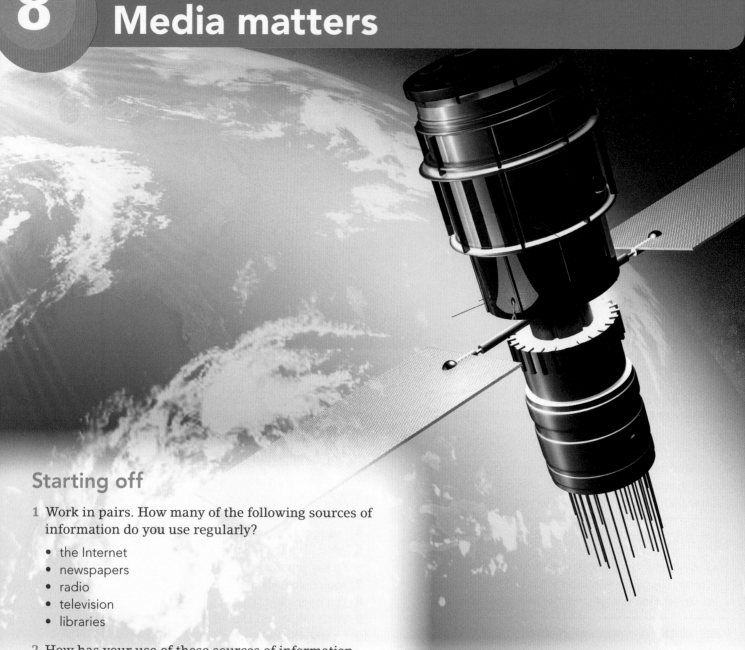

8 Media matters

Starting off

1 Work in pairs. How many of the following sources of information do you use regularly?

- the Internet
- newspapers
- radio
- television
- libraries

2 How has your use of these sources of information changed in recent years? How do you think it will change in the future?

3 Work in pairs. Exchange ideas with you partner.

What are your favourite sources of the following types of information? Try to remember specific examples. If you used the Internet, which websites did you visit?

- a breaking news story about a serious incident in your area
- the result of an important sporting event
- biographical information about someone you are studying or interested in
- information about the side effects of medicine that someone you know is taking
- the departure and arrival times of trains or planes

Listening | Part 3

1 You are going to listen to an interview in which you will hear the phrases in *italics* in the following questions. Before you listen, discuss the questions in pairs.

1 When was television *in its infancy*?
2 If you read an *in-depth analysis* of a news story, would you expect a detailed study or a superficial one?
3 If people *lap something up*, do they enjoy it or not?
4 How do you think *citizen journalism* differs from traditional journalism?

2 ▶02 Now listen to the interview, in which the journalist Harry Cameron talks about how news reporting has developed over the last 60 years. For questions 1–6, choose the answer (A, B, C or D) which fits best according to what you hear.

1 How did Harry feel when he started work as a journalist?
   A important
   B honourable
   C privileged
   D respected

2 Why, according to Harry, has the purpose of newspapers changed?
   A Other news sources are less expensive than newspapers.
   B People don't have time to read newspapers.
   C People prefer to see filmed news reports.
   D There are other more immediately available sources of news.

3 According to Harry, how have the more serious newspapers adapted to the new situation?
   A They concentrate on evaluating news stories.
   B They back up their reports with detailed factual information.
   C They accompany reports with interesting photographs.
   D They keep readers up to date with fashion and sport.

4 What is Harry's view of citizen journalism?
   A He feels sorry for the people involved in it.
   B He resents it for professional reasons.
   C He doesn't consider it to be real journalism.
   D He is broadly in favour of it.

5 Harry believes that internet blogs
   A are less democratic than newspapers.
   B are likely to be more politically biased than newspapers.
   C are as trustworthy as reports written by professionals.
   D are fundamentally unreliable.

6 If Harry were going into journalism now, what would he want to focus on?
   A reporting events as they happen
   B evaluating events knowledgeably
   C being a reliable news source
   D reflecting readers' views

3 Use a word from list A and another from list B to make a phrase matching each definition (1–6). Then make your own sentences using these phrases.

A daily   far-off   in-depth   junior   news   war
B analysis   broadcast   days   newspaper   reporter   zone

1 an inexperienced journalist
2 something you read every day
3 a thorough examination
4 a current affairs programme
5 an area where fighting is taking place
6 a period a long time ago

Exam advice

- Before you listen, read the questions and underline the main idea in each one.
- Read each option carefully and think about its meaning.
- Listen for the general idea of what each speaker is saying.
- Wait until each speaker has finished before choosing an answer.
- Listen for the same ideas to be expressed, not the same words.

Grammar
Reported speech

1 The following are reports of what was said during the interview in Listening Part 3. What were the speakers' actual words?

1 The interviewer asked Harry if he could tell her what being a journalist had been like.
2 Harry said his main memory of those far-off days was the sense of pride he had felt.
3 Harry explained that journalists like him had travelled the world and filed reports.
4 He said he had written his report in his hotel bedroom.
5 Harry said he believed that the function of newspapers had changed.
6 He said that things would never be the same again.

2 ▶03 Now listen and check your answers.

3 What is the difference in meaning between sentences 1 and 2?

1 He said he'd written an article which was going to be in the paper the following day.
2 He said he'd written an article which is going to be in the paper tomorrow.

What do you notice about the tenses in sentence 3?

3 He says he's written an article which is going to be in the paper tomorrow.

4 ▶04 Work in pairs. You are going to listen to four short dialogues between Hazel and Tom.

Student A: Make brief notes about what Tom says.
Student B: Make brief notes about what Hazel says.

5 Convert your notes into reported speech sentences using some of the verbs in the box. Then compare sentences with your partner.

> ask   explain   reply   tell   want to know   wonder

➡ page 174 Language reference: Reported speech

Reading and Use of English | Part 3

1 Work in pairs. Add prefixes to these adjectives to make them negative.

1 .... accurate
2 .... important
3 .... selfish
4 .... legal
5 .... possible
6 .... regular
7 .... similar
8 .... tolerant

Now change each negative adjective into a noun.

2 Add prefixes to these verbs so that they have the meanings given.

1	appear	become invisible	
2	claim	claim back	
3	inform	give the wrong information	
4	judge	judge in advance	
5	react	react more than is necessary	
6	stabilise	make something unstable	
7	state	describe something to make it less important	

Now make your answers into nouns.

3 Add prefixes to these nouns so that they have the meanings given.

1	biography	when a person writes about himself/herself	
2	owner	a joint owner	
3	politician	someone who was a politician in the past	
4	trust	feeling of being unable to trust someone	
5	circle	half a circle	

Now make your answers into adjectives. (One noun does not have a related adjective.)

4 Read the text about attitudes to truth in the media, and answer these questions. (Don't try to fill in the gaps at this stage.)

1 What does the writer accuse universities of?

2 What comparison does he make between television drama and news programmes?

5 Read the text again. For questions 1–8 use the word given in capitals at the end of some of the lines to form a word that fits in the gap in the same line. There is an example at the beginning (0).

6 Discuss these questions in pairs.

1 Do you agree with the view that, from the audience's perspective, there may be 'little difference between an episode of a hospital drama and the main evening news'?

2 How far do you trust TV networks in your country to tell you the truth?

Broadcasters must find ways to regain public trust

The current problems over the truth and (0) ......honesty...... of television programmes are symptomatic of a deep (1) .... suspicion about how such values are judged. In universities, several generations of students in media, cultural studies and even (2) .... have been taught that there is no such thing as truth or (3) .... in television products. These are merely a construction, a 'spectacle', produced for audiences who (4) .... and consume them according to their own tastes. There is little (5) .... between an episode of a hospital drama and the main evening news. I have argued against this approach to understanding media. Yet the depth of the problem for the TV companies is apparent in that there are now (6) .... voices calling for the abandonment of the traditional principle of (7) .... because it is thought impossible to give an accurate account of the full range of positions in a political (8) ....

HONEST

INTELLECT

JOURNAL

ACCURATE

CODE

DIFFER

INSIST

PARTIAL

ARGUE

Adapted from *The Guardian*

Speaking | Part 3

1 Look at the photos and discuss the following questions.

  1 How much do you think people are affected by the influences shown in the photos?
  2 What other powerful influences shape people's ideas? How are people affected by them?

2 Read these written prompts for a Speaking Part 3 task. Briefly consider this task and note down a few ideas.

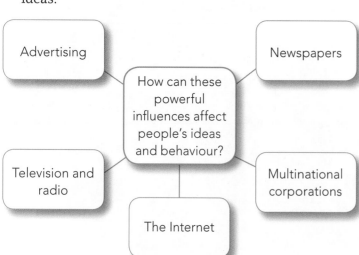

- Advertising
- Newspapers
- How can these powerful influences affect people's ideas and behaviour?
- Television and radio
- Multinational corporations
- The Internet

3 ▶05 Listen to two candidates discussing the prompts, and answer these questions.

  1 Which of the influences do the speakers talk about?
  2 Do they answer the question 'How can these powerful influences affect people's ideas and behaviour?'?
  3 Do they talk about the influences in sufficient depth?
  4 Do they participate equally in the conversation?

4 ▶05 Listen again. Which of these examples of imprecise language do the speakers use? (Imprecise language is used when being accurate is impossible, unnecessary, over-formal or too direct.)

  - *some kind, sort of, stuff, things like that*
  - *two or three, a bit, several, (quite) a few, a lot, lots*
  - *nearly, fairly, pretty, quite, almost, probably*
  - the suffix *-ish*
    Note: *-ish* can be added to words to make them less precise, e.g. *green → greenish* (a shade somewhere between blue and green or grey and green), *thirty → thirtyish* (about 30, between 27 and 33).

5 Work in pairs and do the task in Exercise 2.

  - Make sure you both speak for roughly the same length of time.
  - Use imprecise words and phrases from the list above where appropriate.

6 At the end of Part 3 you and your partner are asked to come to a decision. Follow the examiner's instruction below with your partner.

> Now you have about a minute to decide which two of these influences have the greatest effect on people.

7 ▶06 Listen to the last part of the interview, where the two candidates respond to the instruction above.

  1 Do they make the same choices as you?
  2 How well do they interact to reach their decision?

Exam advice

The most important thing in this part of the exam is to demonstrate good communication skills. This involves

- keeping the conversation going and avoiding long pauses. It may sometimes be necessary to invite your partner to express an opinion.
- listening carefully to what your partner says and responding. Don't just say what you think.

When speaking, look at the person you are talking to.

Vocabulary
'Talking' verbs

1 Complete the gaps in this summary with the verbs in the box in the correct form. In some cases more than one answer is possible.

comment   discuss   say   speak   talk   tell

In Part 3 of the Speaking test the examiner
(1) .... the two candidates that they
have to (2) .... to each other for about
two minutes. In the conversation you listened to,
the candidates (3) .... the comparative
importance of a number of influences on people's
ideas and behaviour. The first candidate started
by (4) .... that TV has a huge influence
on people. They went on to (5) .... on the
influential role played by multinational corporations.
During their conversation the two candidates
(6) .... for about the same length of time.

2 👁 Exam candidates sometimes make mistakes when using 'talking' verbs. Choose the correct verbs in these sentences.

1 Many people believe that the mass media do not always *say / tell* the truth.
2 When I'm in China, I can understand what people are *speaking / saying* to me, but I can hardly *speak / talk* any Chinese myself.
3 This morning's newspaper doesn't even *say / mention* the economic crisis.
4 The spokesperson for the authorities *expressed / spoke* his thanks for people's understanding.
5 There's an article in my newspaper which *says / writes* that people absorb information more quickly from the Internet than from printed material.
6 When asked about the latest rumours, the minister refused to *comment / say*.
7 After Ben had used Wikipedia he *said / told* everyone how great it was. He didn't *mention / tell* the fact that it had taken him an hour to find what he wanted.
8 If you feel strongly about something, you should *express / speak* your mind.

Reading and Use of English | Part 6

1 Discuss these questions in pairs.

1 Which reality TV shows do you watch or have you watched in the past?
2 Which are the best and worst reality TV shows you have seen? Give your reasons.

2 Which of the following reality shows would you watch?

- people with new business ideas competing to win investment money from successful entrepreneurs
- a dance competition featuring celebrities dancing with professional dancers
- celebrities' attempts to survive without luxuries in a jungle environment
- a cooking competition in which amateur cooks are judged by professionals
- teenagers singing in front of judges to win a recording contract
- private detectives investigating people suspected of cheating on their partners

3 Some people object to reality TV for ethical or moral reasons. Why is this? Discuss these ideas:

- the way people are chosen for reality TV shows
- the way people are treated on the shows
- the way the programmes are edited
- the effects on contestants of being in the media spotlight

4 Read texts A–D quickly. What do you understand by the following phrases?

Extract A: **1** *the cult of instant celebrity*
          2 *blatant self-promotion*
          3 *a dumbed-down generation*

Extract B: **4** *operating without scripts*
          5 *cynically manipulated*

Extract C: **6** *social glue*
          7 *'water cooler moments'*
          8 *a cultural imperative*

Extract D: **9** *a meticulous selection process*

5 Decide what each of these sentences means. Choose either a or b.

1 *Reality shows promote the belief that we should aspire to be the reality stars we watch on our televisions.* (Extract A)
  a Reality shows suggest to viewers that the stars of their programmes are role models worth emulating.
  b Reality shows want viewers to believe that they are watching real people.

2 *The unusual settings of shows like* Big Brother *do not reduce the educational value of observing how the contestants cope with their situation.* (Extract B)
  a There is not much that viewers can learn from *Big Brother* and similar shows because contestants are dealing with such unfamiliar situations.
  b Viewers can learn from watching how contestants manage, despite the fact that in *Big Brother* and similar shows they are in unfamiliar surroundings.

3 *The criticism that reality TV shows may corrupt viewers is not sustainable.* (Extract C)
  a Reality TV shows can be justifiably criticised for corrupting viewers.
  b It is impossible to criticise reality TV shows on the grounds that they can corrupt viewers.

4 *This situation is stage-managed by executives who make money by attracting impressionable audiences.* (Extract D)
  a TV managers manipulate this situation and make money because they are able to get naïve viewers to watch their shows.
  b TV managers make money by staging shows which impress viewers.

The ethics of reality TV

Reality TV provokes a range of different reactions among commentators and viewers.

A

Although it's impossible to ignore their popularity, it seems to me that many reality shows send an unfortunate message encouraging a cult of instant celebrity. Many are built around blatant self-promotion and are based on humiliating others for the entertainment of viewers. These programmes suggest that anyone can become famous simply by 'being themselves' on TV, without working hard or displaying any talent. Children who watch these shows may come to believe that they don't need to study conscientiously at school, or train hard for a job. As one commentator points out, 'We tell kids that what matters is being a celebrity and we wonder why some behave as they do. It seems to me that this addiction to celebrity culture is creating a dumbed-down generation.' In pretending to imitate real life, reality shows promote the belief that we should aspire to be the reality stars we watch on our televisions.

B

One of the reasons so many people enjoy reality shows is that they feature real people operating without scripts. The fact that characters have been selected to encourage disagreements or tension and then cynically manipulated does not take away from the reality of the programmes; in fact it adds to it. The unusual settings of shows like *Big Brother* do not reduce the educational value of observing how the contestants cope with their situation. In fact, without such shows, most people would have little concept of how a group of strangers would be able to survive, co-operate and develop in such environments. As *Time Magazine* describes it, 'They provoke and offend, but at least they are trying to do something besides helping you get to sleep.' This insight therefore into the human condition is invaluable, and it is little surprise that so many viewers are eager to watch these programmes.

6 Now do the exam task. For questions 1–4, choose from the extracts A–D. The extracts may be chosen more than once.

Which writer

shares writer C's view of the social value of reality TV?	1 ☐
expresses a different view from the others about the popularity of reality TV?	2 ☐
takes a similar view to B about the way participants are controlled in reality TV shows?	3 ☐
expresses a different opinion from the others about the authenticity of reality TV shows?	4 ☐

Exam advice

- Read the four texts and make sure you understand what they are about. Pay particular attention to any opinions and attitudes expressed. Identify any similarities or differences of opinion which are immediately obvious.
- Read the questions one at a time and identify the aspect of the topic being focused on.
- To answer the questions, you will need to keep this topic in mind and then scan the texts as often as necessary, looking for the similarities or differences of opinion. You will always have to compare all the texts with each other to find the correct answer.

C

Far from discouraging hard work and education, reality TV programmes help to create a society in which we have shared experiences and a strong sense of community. Despite the fact that they do not reflect reality, they provide an important social glue. In the past, there were only a few television channels, and everybody watched the same programmes. This sense of a shared experience helped to bind people together, giving them common things to talk about at work the next day: so-called 'water cooler moments'. Reality programmes play that role in contemporary society with viewership being almost a cultural imperative, an experience shared simultaneously with friends and family. The criticism that reality TV shows may corrupt viewers is not sustainable. Just as it is possible to empathise with real-life criminals without going on to commit crimes ourselves, there is no reason why viewers should be persuaded to emulate the morality of reality TV programmes.

7 Work in pairs and discuss these questions.

1 Do you agree that some reality TV shows are popular because contestants are humiliated?
2 Do you believe that reality TV shows can have an educational value?
3 Do you think that viewers of TV reality shows are likely to emulate contestants?
4 Is it right that reality shows encourage conflict between contestants?

D

The audience appeal of reality shows is understandable and probably does nobody any serious harm, but we should not suppose that we are being shown real life. Contestants who have undergone a meticulous selection process are placed in a 'reality' they would not normally experience. This situation is then stage-managed by executives who make money by attracting impressionable audiences. In *Survivor*, for example, one of the longest-running reality shows, a group of people who did not know each other were put together on an island and then made to take part in contests. After these, some contestants were voted out. This was clearly done primarily in order to create tensions within the group, thereby adding drama and excitement to the programme. By encouraging conflict, programme makers are provoking behaviour very different from what would happen in real-life survival situations, where conflict would be avoided wherever possible.

Grammar
Transitive verbs

1 Transitive verbs must be followed by an object.

- He persuaded **me** to leave. (*Persuade* is a transitive verb which needs an object.)
- He decided to leave. (*Decide* is an intransitive verb which has no direct object.)

Which of the verbs listed need an object to complete these sentences?

1 *allowed agreed warned instructed refused required arranged*

He ...... to leave at 10 o'clock.

2 *told reminded convinced mentioned admitted informed recalled*

She ...... that she was leaving at 10 o'clock.

2 Many verbs can be used both transitively and intransitively, sometimes with different meanings. Discuss the differences in meaning between the verbs in **bold** in these sentences.

1 a He promised he'd be at home, but he was out when I **called**.
  b I was so annoyed that I **called** him a very rude name.

2 a Tarek **runs** every day before he goes to work.
  b He works in London where he **runs** a small IT company.

3 a I'm fine thanks – I can usually **manage** on my own.
  b I've applied for a job **managing** a bookshop.

4 a We need to **leave** in half an hour.
  b You can't take your bike. You'll have to **leave** it here.

5 a We're planning to **move** next year.
  b My car won't start – could you help me **move** it please?

➡ page 177 Language reference: Transitive verbs

3 👁 Exam candidates often miss out objects after transitive verbs, especially verbs with a complex structure. Correct the mistakes in these sentences.

1 I can assure that we will do everything to resolve your case as quickly as we can.
2 I'd be very grateful if you could tell where to look for the information I need.
3 Do you like my new painting? Maria gave to me.
4 We have been taught special techniques that will allow to do well in our exams.
5 I didn't know anyone at Jo's party, so she introduced to some of her friends.
6 Your new job starts on Monday, doesn't it? We all wish the best of luck.

Writing | Part 2
A proposal

1 Read this writing task. What would you propose as the content for programmes about your region?

A television station is planning a series of documentary programmes about life in your region and is inviting proposals from interested members of the public.

The series producer invites you to send a proposal outlining ideas for some of these programmes, which should be of interest to general audiences as well to people who live in the region. You should give reasons for your suggestions and say why you believe people unfamiliar with the region would find the programmes interesting.

Write your **proposal**.

2 Read the sample answer on page 93 and discuss these questions.

1 Has the writer followed the task instructions fully?
2 Is the style appropriately formal?
3 How could the writer sound more persuasive?

3 How could you change these sentences to make them more appropriate for a formal proposal?

1 Maybe the company could think about making a programme about wildlife in the region.
2 This might possibly include a feature on animals native to the region.
3 I should think viewers would probably find this quite interesting.
4 Most people really like watching programmes about animals.
5 Apparently lots of young people would like to watch a programme like this.

➡ page 190 Writing reference: Proposals

I am sure that your decision to make a series of programmes on our region will be warmly welcomed by viewers who live here. I suggest that the series should look at the region today from the points of view of the following different groups of people.

A family

The first programme could perhaps focus on an 'ordinary' family from the region. I would suggest a young couple with two children. The programme might be able to highlight aspects of their everyday life with which many viewers can probably identify: school, travelling, shopping and preferred leisure activities could be covered. It may be important to make it clear from the outset that the series is reflecting the lifestyle of typical residents.

Students

This programme should provide the perspective of young people who have grown up in our region and who will shortly be deciding whether to stay or to move elsewhere. Participants could talk about the advantages and disadvantages of living here in comparison with other places they know. They could also be asked to say whether they intend to stay or move away after the completion of their studies.

Tourist information officer

Finally, a programme featuring a representative of the local tourist information office could inform viewers about significant historical and cultural features of the region, as well as mentioning regular events. Hopefully, this would encourage viewers to visit the region.

In my opinion, these programme proposals would be of interest to people outside our region as well as those who live here. If successful, the series may well be the beginning of a regular magazine programme.

4 The following sentences contain verbs that may be useful for writing a proposal. Complete them with the correct prepositions.

1 It might **benefit** .... further investigation.
2 Members of the public will **contribute** .... the programme.
3 The series will **appeal** .... people of all ages.
4 They should **focus** .... local issues.
5 We should **provide** viewers .... situations they can **identify** ....
6 It will be interesting to see how audiences **respond** .... the series.
7 If the series **succeeds** .... making an impact, this could **result** .... a new series.

5 Read this writing task and make notes in the plan.

> A national TV channel is planning a series of documentary programmes about unusual hobbies and is looking for people and their hobbies to feature in the programmes.
>
> The series producer invites you to send a proposal outlining ideas for two of these programmes. which should be aimed at general audiences rather than other people doing these hobbies. Your proposal should suggest hobbies of different types and give reasons why you think they would make successful TV programmes.
>
> Write your **proposal**.

Plan

Para 1: Introduction: ....
Para 2: Heading: ....
        First idea: ....
        Reasons: ....
Para 3: Heading: ....
        Second idea: ....
        Reasons: ....
Para 4: Conclusion: ....

6 Write your proposal in 220–260 words. Try to use some of the verbs + prepositions from Exercise 4.

Exam advice

- Think about who will read the proposal and how formal you need your writing style to be.
- If you decide to divide the report into sections, think about what sections you need and what section headings are appropriate.
- In a proposal you are trying to persuade someone about an idea or plan you believe in, so your language should be persuasive.

Vocabulary and grammar review Unit 7

Vocabulary

1 Complete these sentences with the correct form of the 'money verbs' in the box.

> afford   cost   earn   hire   make   pay   rent   sell   spend

1 I'd love to own a sports car, but I can't .... one.
2 I'll be working in Prague for two years. Hopefully we'll .... a flat near the city centre.
3 My brother works in a fast-food restaurant. He only .... £120 a week.
4 I've decided to .... my motorbike and get a car.
5 We've .... a jazz band to play at the party on Saturday.
6 Do you know what police officers .... when they finish their training?
7 Those jeans .... a fortune, but it's really the designer label you're .... for.
8 It's amazing how much people .... on birthday presents for their boyfriends or girlfriends.

2 For questions 1–8, read the text below and decide which answer (A, B, C or D) best fits each gap.

> For 70 years now the radio programme *Desert Island Discs* has managed that **(0)** ......C...... feat – to be both enduring and relevant. By choosing as **(1)** .... on the programme the biggest names of the **(2)** .... in science, business, politics, showbiz, sport and the arts, it **(3)** .... a cross-sectional snapshot of the times in which we **(4)** .... As the decades have passed, the programme has kept **(5)** .... : never frozen in time yet always, somehow, comfortingly the same.
>
> *Desert Island Discs* has recently **(6)** .... its 70th birthday. Since its inception in January 1942, nearly 3,000 distinguished people from all **(7)** .... of life have been stranded on the imaginary island, accompanied only by their eight favourite records. This new book, by the programme's **(8)** .... presenter, chronicles the story of one of British radio's favourite programmes.

0 A occasional	B odd	C rare	D scarce
1 A visitors	B guests	C friends	D performers
2 A day	B time	C generation	D date
3 A shows	B displays	C represents	D presents
4 A exist	B are	C live	D survive
5 A pace	B step	C speed	D time
6 A observed	B celebrated	C honoured	D memorised
7 A ways	B types	C kinds	D walks
8 A current	B existing	C living	D contemporary

Grammar

3 Combine sentences in the following extracts from film reviews, using these ways of linking ideas:

- relative clauses
- participle clauses
- apposition

1 Libero
A boy tries to understand his family. He tries to stop it from breaking apart. At the same time he has to deal with his mother's absence. He finds all this very difficult. The boy is only eleven years old.

2 Be Kind Rewind
A man unintentionally destroys every tape in a video store. The man's name is Black. His brain becomes magnetised. The store is owned by Black's best friend. Black and his friend feel sorry for the store's most loyal customer. This customer is an elderly woman. She is losing her memory. The two men set out to remake the lost films. These films include *The Lion King* and *RoboCop*.

3 I Am Legend
A military scientist is left completely alone in New York. The city is deserted. A virus has wiped out the human race. The scientist is played by Will Smith. The film is based on a sci-fi novel by Richard Matheson.

Vocabulary and grammar review Unit 8

Vocabulary

1 Complete these words to match the definitions.

1 ex-..................... (n)   someone who used to work in politics.

2 mis.................... (v)   have doubts about someone's honesty

3 il..................... (adj)   against the law

4 dis.................... (v)   become invisible

5 auto.................... (n)   a life story written by the person him/herself

6 re..................... (n)   the act of claiming something back

7 pre.................... (v)   have an opinion before knowing all the facts

8 de.................... (v)   make unstable

2 Complete the table with the related words. In some cases there is more than one possible answer.

1 ethics (n)	adjective:
2 entertain (v)	noun: adjective:
3 cooperate (v)	noun: adjective:
4 production (n)	verb: adjective:
5 consider (v)	noun: adjective:
6 creative (adj)	verb: noun:

Grammar

3 Rewrite the following quotes in reported speech.

1 'You mustn't tell anyone what you've seen.' (Roland to Joanna)

2 'It was a surprise seeing Tom last week. I hadn't seen him since we were at school together.' (Clare)

3 'Shall I do the shopping this afternoon?' (Ben to Jerry)

4 'You must stop smoking if you want to get rid of your cough.' (doctor to me)

5 'How many languages can you speak?' (Bogdan to me)

4 Rewrite the following as direct quotes.

1 The police officer wanted to know what I was doing out so late.

2 She asked if I had any plans for the following evening.

3 I said that was the worst programme I'd ever seen.

4 I promised I'd phone her as soon as I got home.

5 Jerry said he hoped he'd be going there the following day.

5 Complete the second sentence so that it has a similar meaning to the first sentence, using the word given. Do not change the word given. You must use between three and six words, including the word given.

1 Maria said, 'I'll never do that again.'
PROMISED
Maria .... do that again.

2 'I think you should apply for this job,' Alexei said to me.
ADVISED
Alexei .... job.

3 Simon said, 'Have you ever thought of starting your own business?'
ASKED
Simon .... ever thought of starting my own business.

4 'Let's meet tomorrow,' said Svetlana.
SUGGESTED
Svetlana .... day.

5 'Don't drink if you're driving,' the police officer said to the motorist.
WARNED
The police officer .... if he was driving.

6 Tom and Alexis said, 'We're getting married in May.'
ANNOUNCED
Tom and Alexis .... in May.

At top speed

Starting off

Work in pairs. Discuss these questions.

1 Each of these photos shows a situation where speed is important. Why is speed important in each case?
2 When is it important not to hurry? If you had to choose photos of four situations where it's important not to hurry, which would you choose? Why?
3 Do you enjoy speed? Why (not)?

Listening | Part 1

1 You will hear three extracts where people talk about speed. Extract One is about trains in the 19th century. Before you listen: how do you think the invention of trains changed the way people lived?

2 ▶07 Now listen to Extract One. For questions 1 and 2 choose the answer (A, B or C) which fits best according to what you hear.

Extract One

You hear part of a panel discussion on 19th century travel.

1 According to the woman, people in the early 19th century were concerned about how rail travel would affect
   A the landscape.
   B the human body.
   C their way of life.
2 According to the man, how did rail travel change people's attitude to the natural world?
   A They felt they could dominate it.
   B They understood their need to be part of it.
   C They became more interested in painting it.

3 Work in pairs. The man says, 'I doubt if any other invention has had such a profound influence on the human psyche.' Do you agree?

4 In Extract Two you will hear two people discussing the limits to human ability in Olympic sports. Before you listen: do you think athletes will continue to break records or is there a limit to their improvement?

5 ▶08 Now listen to Extract Two. For questions 3 and 4 choose the answer (A, B or C) which fits best.

Extract Two

You hear two people discussing the future of Olympic sports.

3 The man says that in future new Olympic records will
   A improve only slightly on previous records.
   B become increasingly frequent as athletes improve.
   C attract less attention from the news media.

4 The two speakers agree about
   A the effect of professionalism on sporting achievement.
   B the need for more specialised sports equipment.
   C the prospects for genetic engineering in sports.

6 Work in small groups. Do you think people should devote so much effort to breaking world records? Why (not)?

7 In Extract Three you will hear two scientists talking about travelling in spaceships to other stars. Before you listen,
   • would you like to go on a journey like this?
   • what problems do you think this sort of journey would pose for the spaceship's crew?

8 ▶09 Now listen to Extract Three. For questions 5 and 6 choose the answer (A, B or C) which fits best.

Extract Three

You hear two scientists discussing travel to other planets near other stars.

5 What does the woman say is the main obstacle to using nuclear propulsion for spaceships?
   A the danger to Earth
   B international agreements
   C the technology involved

6 What does the man think would be the main difficulty of using a conventional spaceship?
   A persuading people to travel in it
   B preventing conflict among the crew
   C giving purpose to the crew's lives

Exam advice

   ▪ Listen to the whole piece before you choose: the answer may depend on the general idea rather than a few words.
   ▪ If you are not sure about the answer after listening the first time, try to decide which answers you think are wrong before you listen the second time.

9 In each of these extracts from the recordings, use a verb from the box in the correct form to form a collocation with the noun in **bold**.

break   embark   engage in   have (x3)   lose
make   undergo

1 People's entire world view .... a profound **transformation**.
2 Over the next hundred years railways .... a radical **impact** on the countryside.
3 This .... a subtle but distinct **effect** on the way people regarded their place in the world.
4 I doubt if any other invention .... such a profound **influence** on the human psyche.
5 Do you think people will .... **interest** in Olympic events when athletes no longer .... records?
6 I can't imagine anyone .... such a **difference** nowadays.
7 Even if there were a couple of hundred people prepared to .... on a **journey** like this, they and their descendants would have to live together on the ship all their lives.
8 What **activities** would they .... during all this time?

Grammar
Time clauses

1 In each of these sentences from Listening Part 1 choose the correct alternative in *italics*.

1 When the steam train *was invented / had been invented*, it completely changed 19th century society, didn't it?

2 Outlying villages which had been quiet, sleepy places before trains *arrived / had arrived* became busy suburbs.

3 Do you think people will lose interest in Olympic events when athletes *no longer break / will no longer break* records?

4 Newspapers and TV will always blow them out of proportion when they *occur / will occur*.

5 The key change occurred when top sports people *had stopped / stopped* being amateurs and devoted themselves full time to their sport.

6 I can imagine the travellers degenerating into barbarism and fighting after they *will have spent / have spent* several generations in space.

→ page 176 Language reference: Time clauses

2 Complete these sentences by putting the verbs into the correct tense, using the active or passive form.

1 When Fayed .... (retire) next year, he'll have been working for this company for forty years.

2 We felt very frustrated because the project was cancelled when we .... (work) on it for almost three years.

3 The government is going to pass a law making it illegal to smoke when you .... (drive).

4 Lots of my friends were waiting for me when I .... (get) back from my trip.

5 I'm not going to take my driving test until I .... (be) sure I can pass.

6 She offered the book to several publishers before it .... (accept).

7 We'll really celebrate when I .... (get) the news that I .... (pass) my exams.

8 When Samya .... (write) the proposal, she checked it through, then emailed it to her boss.

3 For questions 1–4 complete the second sentence so that it has a similar meaning to the first sentence, using the word given. Do not change the word given. You must use between three and six words, including the word given.

1 Melissa will complete the report before leaving work.
UNTIL
Melissa will stay .... finished the report.

2 The waiters couldn't relax until there were no more customers left.
LAST
The waiters were only able to relax once ....
.... left.

3 I will deal with the report immediately after my holiday.
GOT
I will deal with the report as ....
from my holiday.

4 He did not stop at the filling station until he had almost no fuel left.
RUN
He stopped at the filling station when he ....
.... fuel.

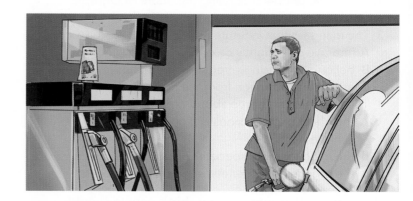

Prepositions in time expressions

4 ⊙ Exam candidates often make mistakes with prepositions in time expressions. Correct the mistakes in these sentences.

1 Mariano likes to watch football at Friday night, but he doesn't often get the chance.

2 Could you give us some advice about where to go or what to do at the evening?

3 I was able to visit the United States for the first time of my life.

4 I would recommend going on that tour in the beginning of summer.

5 The other event of May was a swimming gala.

6 The games contain some violence, but in the same time you have to use your brain.

7 They've met in many occasions but they've never become friends.

8 Unfortunately, we are overloaded with printing jobs in busy times of the day, so you cannot count on your order being dealt with immediately.

9 We have some suggestions about what to do if the weather is bad in the day of the boat trip.

10 You'll have to sit an exam in the end of this course.

➡ page 174 Language reference: Prepositions in time expressions

Vocabulary
action, activity, event and *programme*

1 The words *action, activity, event* and *programme* each have two or three meanings. Match the four words with their definitions (a–i) from the *Cambridge Advanced Learner's Dictionary*.

1 action 2 activity 3 event 4 programme

a a broadcast on television or radio

b a particular thing that happens, especially something important or unusual

c something intentionally done to deal with a problem or difficulty

d a situation in which a lot of things are happening or people are moving around

e a physical movement

f a plan of activities to be done or things to be achieved

g a thin book or piece of paper giving information about a play or musical or sports event, usually bought at the theatre or place where the event happens

h one of a set of races or competitions

i something that is done for enjoyment, especially something organised such as a sport or hobby

2 Complete these sentences from Listening Part 1 with *action, event, programme* or *activity* in the correct form. Then decide which definition (a–i) in Exercise 1 corresponds with the word in each sentence.

1 They began to believe they were no longer totally at the mercy of natural ....

2 They could take .... to harness these phenomena.

3 Will people lose interest in Olympic .... when athletes no longer break records?

4 There are treaties which prohibit nuclear explosions from being used in space ....

5 What .... would they engage in during all this time?

3 For questions 1–12, write *action, event, programme* or *activity* in each gap. Most of the sentences are from the *Cambridge Advanced Learner's Dictionary*.

1 After weeks of frenetic .... , the job was finally finished.

2 I looked in the .... to find out the actor's name.

3 It only needs a small wrist .... to start the process.

4 Our special guest on the .... tonight is Daniel Day Lewis.

5 She wrote a strong letter to the paper complaining about the council's .... in closing the town centre to traffic during the festival.

6 Susannah's party was the social .... of the year.

7 Tennis is a very relaxing spare-time ....

8 The school offers an exciting and varied .... of social events.

9 The women's 200-metre .... will be followed by the men's 100 metres.

10 There was a sudden flurry of .... when the director walked in.

11 This problem calls for swift .... from the government.

12 We had expected to arrive an hour late, but in the .... we were early.

4 Look back at Exercise 3 and note any collocations you can find with *action, event, programme* or *activity*, for example, *frenetic activity*.

Reading and Use of English | Part 7

1 Work in pairs. You are going to read an article about a very fast car. Before you read:

1 How important are cars in your life?

2 What things do/would you consider when choosing a car?

2 Six paragraphs have been removed from the article below. Read the article (but not the paragraphs which have been removed).

- Note down in a few words what each paragraph in the article is about.
- Underline any words and phrases that link the text together, which will help you to place the missing paragraphs when you read them.

Bugatti Veyron

by Jeremy Clarkson

Utterly, stunningly, jaw-droppingly brilliant

When you push a car past 300 km/h, the world actually becomes blurred, like an early Queen pop video. The speed causes a terrifying vibration that rattles your optic nerves, causing double vision. This is not good when you're covering 90 metres a second. Happily, stopping distances become irrelevant because you won't see the obstacle in the first place. By the time you know it was there, you'll have gone through the windscreen.

1	

But once you go past 320 km/h, the biggest problem is the air. At 160 km/h it's relaxed. At 240 km/h it's a breeze. But at 320 km/h it has sufficient power to lift a jumbo jet off the ground. So getting a car to behave itself in conditions like these is tough.

2	

You might point out at this juncture that the McLaren Formula One car can top 390 km/h, but at that speed it is pretty much out of control. And anyway the Bugatti is way, way faster than anything else the roads have seen, but when you look at the history of its development you'll discover it's rather more than just a car.

3	

His engineers were horrified. But they set to work anyway, mating two Audi V8s to create an 8-litre W16 engine with four turbochargers. Needless to say, the end result produced about as much power as the Earth's core, which is fine. Then things got tricky because the power had to be harnessed.

4	

When this had been done, the Veyron was shipped to Sauber's F1 wind tunnel where it quickly became apparent that while the magic 1000 bhp* figure had been achieved, they were miles off the target top speed of 400 km/h. The body of the car just wasn't aerodynamic enough. The bods at Sauber threw up their hands, saying they only had experience of aerodynamics up to maybe 360 km/h, which is the effective top speed in Formula One. Beyond this point Bugatti was on its own.

5	

After some public failures, fires and accidents, they hit on the idea of a car that automatically changes shape depending on what speed you're going. And that means you can top 400 km/h. That's 113m a second.

6	

I didn't care. On a recent drive across Europe I desperately wanted to reach the top speed but I ran out of road when the needle hit 386 km/h. Where, astonishingly, it felt totally and utterly rock steady. It felt sublime. From behind the wheel of a Veyron, France is the size of a small coconut. I cannot tell you how good this car is. I just don't have the vocabulary.

From *The Times*

*Brake horsepower – a measure of the power of a vehicle's engine

3 Choose from the paragraphs A–G the one which fits each gap (1–6). There is one extra paragraph which you do not need to use.

A At those speeds the front of the car starts to lift. As a result you start to lose your steering, so you can't even steer round whatever it is you can't see because of the vibrations. Make no mistake, 320 km/h is at the limit of what man can do right now. Which is why the new Bugatti Veyron is special. Because it can do 406 km/h.

B For this, Volkswagen went to Ricardo, a British company that makes gearboxes for various Formula One teams. 'It was hard,' said one of the engineers. 'The gearbox in an F1 car only has to last a few hours, but the Veyron's has to last 10 or 20 years.'

C It has always been thus. When Louis Rigolly broke the 160 km/h barrier in 1904, the vibration would have been terrifying. And I dare say that driving a Jaguar E-type at 240 km/h in 1966 must have been a bit sporty as well.

D It all started when Ferdinand Piëch, the former boss of Volkswagen, bought Bugatti and had someone design a concept car. 'This,' he said, 'is what the next Bugatti will look like. And it will have an engine that develops 1000 horsepower and it will be capable of 400 km/h.'

E Somehow they had to find an extra 30 km/h, but each extra 1km/h increase in speed requires an extra 8bhp from the power plant. An extra 30 km/h then would need an extra 240 bhp. That was not possible.

F This car cannot be judged in the same way that we judge other cars. It meets noise and emission regulations and it can be driven by someone whose only qualification is an ability to reverse round corners and do an emergency stop. So technically it is a car. And yet it just isn't.

G You might want to ponder that for a moment. Covering the length of a football pitch, in a second, in a car. If you stamp on the middle pedal hard, you will pull up from 400 km/h in just 10 sec. Sounds good, but in those 10 sec you'll have covered 500 metres. That's five football pitches to stop.

4 Work in pairs.

1 Would you like to drive a car like this? Why (not)?
2 Should roads have speed limits and should cars be built that can break speed limits? Why (not)?

Speaking | Part 2

1 Work in pairs. Look at the photos and the examiner's instructions. Which of these phrases would you associate with each photo?

> clear up leaves   cover large areas
> deal with infringements   find suitable pastures
> give somebody a fine   have a criminal record
> keep public spaces tidy   protect from predators
> round up the flock   traffic/parking offences
> check identity   conserve energy

Here are your pictures. They show people using different machines or devices. I'd like you to compare two of the pictures and say what problems the people might have with their jobs and how the machines or devices might help the people to do their jobs better.

• What problems might the people have in their jobs?
• How might the machines or devices help these people to do their work better?

2 Now take turns to do the task in Exercise 1.

3 ▶10 Listen to Anna and Daniel doing the same speaking task. Which of these does Anna do? Write *Yes* or *No*.

1 Although she's not sure, she guesses what the policeman's device is.
2 She explains what the device is and what it can be used for.
3 She suggests just one way in which the policeman could be using the device.
4 She knows exactly what to call the man in the second picture.
5 She corrects herself when she realises she hasn't used the best word for something.
6 She tries to use phrases she's not sure about in order to express herself more clearly.
7 She deals with all parts of the task.

4 ▶10 Complete each of these phrases by writing two words in each space. Then check your answers by listening again.

1 … using what I think ………………………………… a tablet computer …
2 The other picture shows – ………………………………… you call the person? – a cowboy or a shepherd, I'm not sure.
3 He's rounding up his herd, ………………………………… his flock of sheep.
4 He can check information in – ………………………………… the phrase? – in real time.
5 By using a – I'm not ………………………………… the name of the vehicle, is it a quad bike? – he doesn't have to walk or use a horse all day.

5 In which sentence(s) in Exercise 4 does Anna

a correct herself?
b say she's guessing what something is?
c say she's not sure what the correct word is?

6 Work in pairs. Look at the six photos. Which of these phrases would you associate with each photo?

backbreaking work   become disorientated
combat the cold   deep in the woods   deep-sea diver
deep underground   handed down from father to son
hard physical labour   the heat and noise   lack of oxygen
lose your way   plough a field   skilled craftsmanship
take pride in your work   take strict safety precautions
underwater archaeology

7 Work in pairs.

▶ 11 **Student A:** Look at photos 1–3 in Set A, listen to the examiner's instructions and do the task.

Set A

- Why might the people have chosen to do these activities in such remote places?
- What might be the dangers of doing each of them?

▶ 12 **Student B:** When Student A has finished, look at photos 4–6 in Set B, listen to the examiner's instructions and do the task.

Set B

- Why might the people be doing these activities in a traditional way?
- How difficult might it be to do these activities?

Exam advice

- Be ready to speculate or guess about what the photos show.
- If you notice you've made a mistake, correct it – don't pretend it hasn't happened!
- If you don't know a word, don't avoid the problem. Explain the idea using other words.

Reading and Use of English | Part 4

1 Correct the mistakes in these Part 4 answers.

1 You will get home from work to find I have cooked supper.
TIME
I will have supper cooked by ....~~the time you will get~~.... home from work.

2 I am driving faster than ever before.
AS
It's the first time I ....~~drive so fast~~............ as this.

3 They tested the car on a race track when they had solved the problem.
TRIED
With ....~~solving the problem, they tried~~.... the car on a race track.

2 For questions 1–6, complete the second sentence so that it has a similar meaning to the first sentence, using the word given. Do not change the word given. You must use between three and six words, including the word given.

1 It's pointless to go to the station by taxi in such heavy traffic.
POINT
The traffic is so heavy that .... a taxi to the station.

2 Karl didn't consult anyone before starting the project.
AHEAD
Karl went .... consulting anyone.

3 The accident was caused by ice on the road.
BLAME
Ice on the road .... the accident.

4 We had no idea the journey would take nearly so long.
FAR
The journey .... we expected.

5 We didn't get to the party until all the food had been eaten.
TIME
There was no food .... to the party.

6 Our view of the world has certainly been affected by new technology.
IMPACT
New technology has certainly .... we view the world.

Exam advice

Read the original sentence, the word given and the sentence with the gap. Think about

- whether you need an expression, e.g. *it's not worth*
- whether you need a phrasal verb, e.g. *turn out*
- what grammar you will need, e.g. do you need to change a verb from active to passive, put something into reported speech, use a verb + *-ing*?

Writing | Part 1
An essay

1 Read the writing task and underline the key points.

Your class has participated in a discussion on the following proposition: *Technological progress makes us live faster, but it also means we have less time for the important things in life, such as relationships.*

You have made the notes below.

> **Some areas to cover**
>
> - entertainment
> - working life
> - health

Some opinions expressed during the discussion:

'In the past, large amounts of time were spent on chores.'

'Our great-grandparents could not have imagined the opportunities open to us today.'

'Technology allows us to communicate with more people.'

Write an essay on the proposition above. Discuss **two** of the areas in your notes, **expressing your own opinions** and **giving reasons** to support them.

You may, if you wish, make use of the opinions expressed during the discussion, but you should use your own words as far as possible.

2 Work in small groups. Discuss these questions and note down your opinions and ideas.

1 In what ways does technological progress make us live faster? Think of examples.

2 Do you agree that we have less time for the important things in life, such as relationships? Why (not)?

3 Work in pairs.

1 Read the essay below without paying attention to the gaps. Which ideas and examples were also mentioned during your discussion?
2 Which opinions from the essay task did the writer use? Did she express them using the same words or her own words?
3 Do you agree with the writer's conclusions? Why (not)?

Technological progress

Many people worry that we no longer have time for the important things in life, such as relationships and thinking about ourselves and our place in the universe. This may be true ¹.......................... but I think that in broad terms this argument is flawed.

In my great-grandparents' time technology was slower than it is at present. Most people travelled to work on foot or by public transport and may perhaps have had more time to think about things when they were travelling. They did not have the distractions of television, the Internet or all the other technological marvels which compete for our attention today. ².......................... , they probably spent more time together in conversation.

³.......................... , I doubt if their relationships or the quality of their lives were really better. ⁴.......................... , they had to work much longer hours, both in their jobs and in routine household tasks, because labour-saving technological devices did not exist. ⁵.......................... , they did not have the financial resources or the technology to enjoy their leisure time like we do now. While they were perhaps not so stressed, ⁶.......................... , they could not learn, travel and relate to people from all over the world with the ease that we do.

⁷.......................... , I do not agree that we have less time for the important things in life. ⁸.......................... , I believe we have far greater opportunities to take advantage of the enormous variety of good things life has to offer.

4 Complete the essay by writing a phrase from the box in each of the gaps.

as a result   however   in conclusion   to some extent
what is more   in contrast   to ourselves   in general
on the contrary

5 Work in pairs. Which paragraph in the essay

1 explains in what ways the statement is not true?
2 explains to what extent the statement is true?
3 summarises the writer's argument?
4 tells us what point of view the writer is going to argue?

 page 186 Writing reference: Essays

6 Read this writing task. How far do you agree with the proposition? Note down your ideas and opinions.

> Your class has participated in a discussion on the following proposition: *People in the modern world have become too reliant on information technology.* You have made the notes below.
>
> > **Some areas to cover**
> >
> > - working life
> > - studying
> > - leisure time
>
> > **Some opinions expressed during the discussion:**
> >
> > 'Most people spend too long using social media instead of seeing real people.'
> >
> > 'Instead of thinking about things carefully, most people just look for quick solutions on the Internet.'
> >
> > 'Information technology allows us to deal with so many things more quickly and efficiently.'
>
> Write an essay on the proposition above. Discuss **two** of the areas in your notes, **expressing your own opinions** and **giving reasons** to support them.
>
> You may, if you wish, make use of the opinions expressed during the discussion, but you should use your own words as far as possible.

7 Write an essay plan with a similar structure to the sample essay in Exercise 3. Note down the ideas and opinions you will express in each paragraph.

8 Write your essay.

Exam advice

- Use a formal, academic style when you write an essay.
- Write a structured argument and link your ideas with phrases such as *for example, in conclusion, in contrast.*
- Show that you are aware of counter-arguments.
- Make sure that your opinion on the subject is clearly expressed.

Starting off

1 Work in pairs.

1 Look at the photos of different educational establishments. How many of these have you attended? Which did you enjoy most? Why?

2 Tell each other about your education to date. What do/ did you most like and dislike about the process?

3 In some countries, children start school at the age of four, while in others the age is seven. When did you start? What do you think is the most appropriate age?

4 What do you think is the optimum number of students in a class at primary, secondary and higher education levels?

2 How far do you agree or disagree with these opinions about education?
Tick the boxes (1 = strongly agree; 5 = strongly disagree).

	1	2	3	4	5
a Parents should have the choice of sending children to school or educating them themselves at home.					
b An education system which does not teach young people how to think for themselves is a failure.					
c My country's education systems encourage conformity and discourage originality and creativity.					
d A teacher's main job is to help pupils or students to pass examinations.					
e The main purpose of education is to equip young people with the practical skills they need for work.					
f The purpose of a university education is to produce future generations of leaders.					

3 Compare ideas with your partner and discuss any points of disagreement.

Listening | Part 2

1 Work in pairs.

1 Would you like to study abroad? Why (not)?
2 Which country/countries would you choose? Why?
3 What difficulties might you experience?
4 What difficulties might a foreign student experience in your country?
5 How do you think a period of study abroad would change you?

2 You will hear a British student talking about her daily life in Abu Dhabi, where she is currently spending a year studying. Which of these aspects of her life there do you think she might comment on?

climate food accommodation clothes language
transport lessons teaching staff exams social life

3 ▶ 13 Listen to the recording to find out if any of your ideas are mentioned.

4 Now read the sentences below. Can you guess what word or phrase is missing from each sentence?

The speaker chose to study Arabic because one of the teachers had a **(1)** .... for the subject.

The language spoken in the city where she is studying is a **(2)** .... which people understand across the region.

The fact that students were a **(3)** .... who were not married meant that they were not allowed to stay at the first hotel.

One member of the group returned home soon after arriving because he was suffering from **(4)** ....

The **(5)** .... is located in a shopping area.

In the **(6)** .... they do with their teacher Ingy, the students learn how to shop for food.

Arabic pronunciation is not easy for the speaker because the back **(7)** .... has to be used to produce some sounds.

The speaker and her friends spend their weekends at a **(8)** .... where they can swim and lie by the pool.

5 ▶ 13 Listen to the recording again. For questions 1–8 in Exercise 4 complete the sentences with a word or short phrase.

Exam advice

■ Read the gapped sentences before you listen. This will show you how the recording is organised and give you an idea of the topic. The gaps in the sentences should provide a clear idea of what information you are listening for.
■ Fill in the gaps with the actual words you hear, without changing them in any way.
■ Check that your completed sentences are grammatically correct.
■ Answer every question even if you are not sure.

6 Work in pairs.

1 Imagine you had the chance to study any language in the world.
  • Which language would you choose?
  • Where would you choose to learn it?
2 Do you think single-sex groups learn better than mixed-sex groups?
3 How influential do you think teachers are in students' choice of subjects?

Reading and Use of English | Part 1

1 You are going to read a short article describing the importance of training in the workplace. Before you read, do the exercise in the Exam round-up box.

2 Write your own definitions for these phrases, which appear in the article.

lifelong learning   retraining
upgrade (your) skills

3 Work in pairs. Compare your definitions, then discuss these questions.

1 Why do some adults want to learn something new?
2 How is learning as an adult different from learning as a younger person?
3 Why do you think the idea of lifelong learning has become so popular in recent years?

4 Read the article *Why do we need lifelong learning?*. Does the writer mention any of the ideas you discussed?

5 Read the article again. For questions 1–8, decide which answer (A, B, C or D) best fits each gap. There is an example at the beginning (0).

Why do we need lifelong learning?

Incentives play an important (0) .....C..... in our decisions to learn. As we age, the outcomes of (1) .... in learning are not the same as when we were younger. The type of work-related learning we do also changes as we get older. Most workers over 45 participate in learning (2) .... directly related to their function. By contrast, young workers are more likely to regard training as an (3) .... in their future careers.

Organisations want to continually renew their skills base and until recently have (4) .... this largely through a steady inflow of newly qualified young people onto the labour (5) .... Traditionally, we have had a mix of those young people, who bring new skills to the workplace, and a proportion of older workers, who (6) .... their experience. We are now seeing a decreasing proportion of young people entering the workforce and an increase in the proportion of older people. So unless we change the (7) .... of our learning across life, we will see a (8) .... in these new skills in the working population.

0 A focus	B game	C role	D feature
1 A participation	B joining	C attendance	D activity
2 A actions	B activities	C acts	D modules
3 A interest	B investment	C investigation	D inspiration
4 A affected	B fulfilled	C achieved	D succeeded
5 A workforce	B employment	C staff	D market
6 A donate	B supply	C contribute	D sell
7 A way	B method	C means	D nature
8 A decline	B cutback	C fall	D lessening

Speaking | Part 4

1 Work in pairs. Discuss these written prompts for a Speaking Part 3 task.

Self-study

A class of 20–30 with a teacher

For what purposes are these approaches to learning suited?

Group work without a teacher

One-to-one: a teacher with a student

A lecture to many people

2 Questions 1–6 below are some possible Part 4 questions which might follow on from the written prompts you have been discussing. Which questions

a ask you to choose between two options?
b ask for an explanation of an established fact?
c ask whether you agree with something or not?
d ask for a number of different ideas?

1 Why do you think lectures are a more common as a form of teaching in universities than in schools?
2 What are the advantages and disadvantages of one-to-one teaching from a student's point of view?
3 Some people think that individual study is the least effective way of learning. Do you share this view? Why (not)?
4 Do you think project work is an approach more suited to older or younger students? Why?
5 Which do you think is more important from a student's point of view: a good teacher or a small class? Why?
6 Do you think that exams are the best and fairest means of assessing students? Why (not)?

3 How would you answer questions 1–6 in Exercise 2? Make brief notes.

4 ▶ 14 Listen to two exam candidates discussing two of these questions. Which questions do they discuss? Do they express any ideas that are similar to yours?

5 Look at the following words and phrases from the recording. Which ones could you use to answer questions 1–6 in Exercise 2?

academic study   class teaching   individual student
learning style   pair or group work   primary school
programme of study   range of abilities
secondary school

give clear instructions   manage one's own learning
work independently

effective   (in)formal   motivated   motivating
time-consuming

6 Work in pairs. Answer the questions in Exercise 2, taking turns to start the discussion. Use some of the language from Exercise 5 in your discussion.

Exam advice

- Listen very carefully to the question you are asked, but also to your partner because you may be asked to respond to something he/she says.
- Express your opinions clearly and be prepared to justify or explain what you say, or to suggest a range of possible ideas to answer the question.
- Remember that fluency is important, so make sure you give full answers.

Reading and Use of English | Part 8

1 Imagine you are about to apply for a university course. Which of these factors would be most important to you in choosing which course to apply for?

- the location of the university
- the quality of teaching
- the reputation of the university
- the cost of tuition
- the number of students in each class/lecture
- the quality of student accommodation
- the help and support provided for applicants
- the atmosphere on the university campus
- the opportunities for socialising
- the non-academic facilities, e.g. for sports, entertainment, shopping

2 Which of the universities shown in the photos most appeals to you? Why? Compare your answers to this and Exercise 1 with other students.

3 You are going to read comments from five students explaining why they chose their university. First read questions 1–10 and underline the key ideas.

Which student

chose a university which sold itself more convincingly than others he/she had seen?	1
feels as if he/she really belongs to the university he/she chose?	2
is doing a degree course which precedes a course of professional training?	3
is hoping to pass on knowledge to others?	4
chose not to live in student accommodation even though he/she was impressed by it?	5
initially thought that the location of the campus was a negative feature?	6
was impressed by the teachers' enthusiasm for their subjects?	7
was very impressed by how knowledgeable the people he/she met on open day were?	8
was won over by the friendly welcome he/she received?	9
will leave university with a dual qualification?	10

4 Now read the texts. For questions 1–10, choose from the texts (A–E). The texts may be chosen more than once.

5 Work in small groups.

1 Discuss what measures could be taken to improve education in your country. Think about all levels, from nursery school to university.

2 Make a list of five suggestions to present to the rest of the class.

Exam advice

- The questions or statements precede the text(s) in this part of the exam. Study these carefully before you read the text(s).
- Read the text(s) carefully, looking for the information referred to in the ten questions or statements.
- Many of the sections may say similar things, so you will have to read carefully to decide which section answers the question exactly.

Choosing a university

A JASON

I decided right from the word go that I wanted to be about an hour away from home – close, but not too close. As luck would have it, my first open day was at this university – and I knew immediately that it would take a lot of beating. It was the whole package. Everyone I spoke to about the course was very clued up about their subjects, and seemed genuinely interested in teaching students, something that wasn't true everywhere. Although I liked the compact campus, the fact that the university is a fair way from the town centre put me off a bit to start with, because it meant I couldn't pop into town to do my shopping during my breaks, but I've got used to that.

B MARIA

When the time came to select the university I wanted to go to, I was in a bit of a quandary. I'd spent weeks poring over the glossy brochures and I had eventually narrowed down my options to just three possibilities, but I still could not decide between them. So it was time to schedule campus tours to find out how the reality measured up to the hype. Every campus was different and of course they all had their advantages, but this place instantly appealed to me. It's difficult to put my finger on exactly why but for one thing, as soon as I arrived, I was struck by the smiles and greetings everyone gave me. I knew that this place had everything I wanted: a wide range of subjects, opportunities to become involved in student life, and staff who would have my best interests at heart. What I value most here is the feeling that I am part of a supportive community.

C OSVALDO

One of the reasons I chose this university was because of the effort that they put into organising the open day. The course representatives, including lecturers and current students, went to great lengths to provide an honest and enthusiastic overview of their courses and of life in the city. This was in marked contrast to other universities I visited which, although considered more prestigious, seemed content to let their reputation do the talking and put little effort into making us feel welcome or valued.

The location of the main campus, in the centre of a city with a thriving student population, was point two in this university's favour. Although I chose not to live on campus, the rooms there seemed comfortable and very reasonably priced.

D KAZUMI

My main reason for coming here was the Human Rights course. When I was at school I couldn't decide whether I wanted to be a doctor or a lawyer, but having decided to be a lawyer, I then had to choose which first degree I should take before starting law school in a different city. I've always wanted to help people and I figured that taking Human Rights would allow me to learn about how I can make a real difference in the world. The course lecturers were inspirational and passionate about their subjects – this has been evident in all of their lectures. I also decided to come here because it is a remarkable city. I had been here before and just fell in love with the city and its culture.

E VLADIMIR

The main reason I chose this university was its Engineering course. I am one of those people who just love maths, and I have always known that maths would be part of my career. I was torn between two possibilities: I could become an engineer and apply maths at a practical level, using it to solve problems and hopefully to change the world one day. Or I could combine my love of maths with my desire to help others by becoming a maths teacher. That way I knew I'd be changing the world one student at a time.

I needn't have worried because in the end I didn't have to choose! I got everything I wanted thanks to this course, which will qualify me to be a high school teacher while gaining a general engineering degree at the same time. So I'll be able to start teaching as soon as I qualify.

Grammar
Expressing ability, possibility and obligation

1 Discuss these questions about extracts a–g from Reading and Use of English Part 8.

　1 Which extracts express ability, which possibility and which obligation?

　2 Do the extracts refer to the past, the present or the future?

　a It meant I couldn't pop into town to do my shopping.

　b I had narrowed down my options to just three possibilities, but I still could not decide between them.

　c I then had to choose which first degree I should take before starting law school.

　d I could become an engineer and apply maths at a practical level.

　e I needn't have worried …

　f … because in the end I didn't have to choose!

　g I'll be able to start teaching as soon as I qualify.

2 Read these pairs of sentences and decide if both in each pair are correct. If both are correct, discuss the difference in meaning between them.

　1 a I have to finish this essay, so I can't go out.
　　b I must finish this essay. I really want to do well.

　2 a I didn't need to catch a taxi home from the airport. My brother picked me up.
　　b I needn't have caught a taxi home from the airport. My brother would have picked me up.

　3 a You don't have to go to the lecture this afternoon. It's optional.
　　b You mustn't go to the lecture this afternoon. It's only for first-year students.

　4 a After a lot of effort, I could finally start the car engine.
　　b After a lot of effort, I finally managed to start the car engine.

　5 a He can stay for up to 90 days with this kind of visa if he wants to.
　　b He could stay for up to 90 days with this kind of visa if he wanted to.

　6 a In the future, we might not study in classrooms with other students.
　　b In the future, we could not study in classrooms with other students.

➡ page 168 Language reference: Expressing ability, possibility and obligation

3 👁 Exam candidates often make mistakes with modal verbs. Find and correct the mistakes in the sentences below.

　1 He must have correct his work before he gave it to the teacher.

　2 The students at the back of the lecture hall became frustrated because they can't hear very well.

　3 I think they might lie to you when you bought the TV last week.

　4 I'm happy to tell you that we could offer you a place on the degree course.

　5 Could you tell me the name of the manager, so I would be able to contact him in the future?

　6 If we afford the fees, our daughter will apply to this college.

4 Work in pairs. Tell each other about the following.

　• things you can do that you're proud of
　• something you couldn't do for a long time but eventually managed to do
　• something you'd like to be able to do
　• things you have to / don't have to do as part of your job or studies
　• something you needn't have worried about
　• something you really must do in the next few days

Vocabulary

chance, occasion, opportunity and possibility

1 Read these definitions. Then circle the correct alternatives in *italics* in the sentences below.

> *occasion*
>
> a particular time when something happens
>
> *My sister's wedding was a very special **occasion**.*
>
> Collocations
>
> Adjectives *formal, historic, memorable, rare, solemn, special, unique*
>
> Verbs **mark** *an occasion,* **rise** *to the occasion*
>
> Use **on** *one occasion, the occasion* **when** *+ clause*

> *opportunity*
>
> a situation in which it is possible to do something you want to do
>
> *I'm going to work in Hong Kong for a year. It's a great **opportunity**.*
>
> Collocations
>
> Adjectives *equal, excellent, golden, perfect, tremendous, welcome*
>
> Verbs *have, lose, miss, seize, take + the opportunity, opportunity + arise/occur*
>
> Use *the opportunity* **to do** *something, the opportunity* **for** *+ noun*

> *possibility*
>
> a situation where something may or may not happen
>
> *There's a definite **possibility** of a strike by train drivers next week.*
>
> Collocations
>
> Adjectives *definite, distinct, real, remote, serious, slight, strong*
>
> Verbs *face, accept, rule out, recognise, ignore + the possibility*
>
> Use *the possibility* **of doing** *something [not* possibility to do*], the possibility* **that** *+ clause*

1 Schools try to ensure that all students have an equal *opportunity / possibility* to succeed.
2 On several *occasions / opportunities* recently the university has made changes to the syllabus without consulting students.
3 If you study abroad, you should take every *occasion / opportunity* to learn the language.
4 There's a strong *opportunity / possibility* that you will win one of the three available scholarships.
5 Our graduation ceremony next week will be a very special *opportunity / occasion*.
6 According to the weather forecast, there's a distinct *possibility / occasion* of rain tomorrow.

2 *Chance* can mean *possibility* or *opportunity*, but is generally used less formally. Read these definitions and complete the sentences below with *chance, occasion, opportunity* or *possibility*. Sometimes two answers are possible.

> *chance*
>
> 1 an occasion which allows something to be done; an opportunity
>
> *I'm afraid I didn't get the **chance** to tell him the good news.*
>
> Collocations
>
> Adjectives *good, ideal, last, second, unexpected*
>
> Verbs *get, have, deserve, welcome, give someone, take, turn down + the chance*
>
> Use *the chance* **to do** *something*
>
> 2 likelihood; the level of possibility that something will happen
>
> *There's an outside **chance** that I'll have to go to Japan next week.*
>
> Collocations
>
> Adjectives *fair, outside, realistic, reasonable, slim*
>
> Verbs *be in with a chance / stand a chance of + -ing*
>
> Use *the chance* **of doing** *something, there's a chance* **that** *+ clause, by any chance, on the off chance, No chance!*

1 If you don't do well in your exams, you'll have the .... to retake them next summer.
2 Our education system is based on the principle of equal ....
3 Have you ever considered the .... of training to be a teacher?
4 If you go on working hard, you stand a good .... of getting into Harvard.
5 Your exams start on Monday, so this weekend is the last .... you'll have to revise.
6 I think there's a real .... that I'll get the grades I need.
7 We're having a party to celebrate the end of our exams – it'll be a great ....
8 Is there any .... that you could help me with my homework?

3 Complete these sentences with your own words, then compare ideas with a partner.

1 I hope one day I'll have the opportunity …
2 Next year there's a possibility that I'll …
3 Unfortunately, I have very little chance of ever …
4 I hope the occasion never arises when I …

Writing | Part 2
A report

1 Read the writing task and consider the facilities in a school or college that you know. How would you rate them, from your point of view as a student? Think about the following areas listed below and give each one a star rating (★★★ = excellent, ★★ = adequate, ★ = inadequate).

- classrooms
- study areas
- technological equipment
- food and drink
- leisure or sports facilities
- car parking

A committee is looking into ways of improving facilities in your place of study. The committee chairperson has asked you to write a report on the current situation and make suggestions for improvements. Address the interests of these three groups of people:

- students
- staff members: teachers and administrative staff
- visitors: prospective future students and others.

Write your **report** in 220–260 words.

2 Work in pairs and compare your ratings, giving reasons. Where you agree about facilities that are not adequate, discuss ways in which they could be improved.

3 Read this sample report without paying attention to the missing headings. Does the writer make any points that are similar to ones you and your partner have made?

Report on improving college facilities

(1) ....

The purpose of this report is to suggest ways in which college facilities could be improved for students, staff and visitors. The report is based on comments from these three groups and on my own observations.

(2) ....

Both students and staff commented on the need for increased provision of computers. Students would welcome more study areas equipped with computers, while staff felt strongly that they would also be able to work more efficiently if they had their own computer programmes.

(3) ....

Staff expressed the view that the cost of food in the canteen was unnecessarily high and recommended a reduction. Students did not mention price, but would appreciate a wider choice of food.

(4) ....

Dissatisfaction with car parking facilities was expressed by staff and visitors. Staff would like reserved spaces away from other parking areas, while visitors would be grateful for extra spaces to be made available to them, especially on certain weekday mornings. Visitors also said they would like key places, like the main reception, to be more clearly signposted from parking areas.

(5) ....

Students suggested that the gym and other sports facilities should be enlarged to take account of the increase in student numbers in recent years.

(6) ....

I would recommend implementing all the suggestions listed above with the exception of providing more car parking spaces. It is clear from past experience that demand for parking is never satisfied. I would suggest urging drivers to make alternative travel arrangements.

4 Choose the correct alternative in each of these statements about headings in a report.

a Headings *need / don't need* to be brief.
b They *are / are not* usually in the form of a full sentence.
c They should cover *all the ideas / the main topic* in the paragraph that follows.

Now think of suitable headings for the sample report.

5 Discuss these questions.

1 Apart from the title, how can you tell that the sample text is a report?
2 What structures are used with the verbs *recommend* and *suggest*?
3 What reporting verbs are used instead of *said*?
4 What verbs and phrases are used to mean *would like*?

6 Look at these phrases and think of more formal equivalents, which you might want to use in your report.

1 families students stay with
2 learning with the help of a computer
3 mix with people
4 more chance to speak
5 pick up (a language)
6 teachers who know what they're doing
7 the number of students in a class
8 things to do in your free time
9 ways of teaching
10 working on your own

 page 191 Writing reference: Reports

7 Read the writing task below.

1 Who will read the report you write?
2 How many sections will you include in your report?
3 What headings will you give these sections?

> Numbers of foreign students attending a language school in your town have been falling recently and a governors' committee has been established to increase future numbers.
>
> The school principal has asked you to write a report for this committee on the current situation and to recommend how more students could be attracted to the school. Your report should address the following:
>
> • what attracts foreigners to your town
> • new teaching methods and facilities that could be offered
> • how leisure facilities and opportunities for socialising could be improved.
>
> Write your **report** in 220-260 words.

8 Write your report, making use of the following:

• the verbs *suggest* and *recommend*
• a variety of reporting verbs
• a variety of words and phrases meaning the same as *would like*.

Exam advice

■ Read the instructions carefully to identify who will read the report amd what its purpose is.
■ Deal with all the information in the input material.
■ Give factual information and, if required, make recommendations.
■ Organise your report clearly. You may want to divide it into sections with headings.

Vocabulary and grammar review Unit 9

Vocabulary

1 Complete the sentences below by writing the correct word, *action, activity, event* or *programme*, in the gaps.

1 The stadium is a hive of .... , with workers hurrying to get it finished before the games.
2 The authorities have asked the police to take .... against anyone caught scrawling graffiti on the town hall.
3 The sporting .... I most enjoy doing is sailing.
4 Can you look on the .... to see when the interval is?
5 For me, one of the most exciting and historic .... of the last century was the fall of the Berlin Wall.
6 The final .... of this weekend's festival of Irish culture will be a traditional folk dance.
7 Thanks to prompt .... by the fire service, the school fire was prevented from spreading to the neighbouring houses.
8 The government plans to unveil its electoral .... later today.

2 For questions 1–8 read the text below. Use the word given in capitals at the end of some of the lines to form a word that fits in the gap in the same line. There is an example at the beginning (0).

Commuters on bikes

Cyclists who commute readily make the
(0) ....admission........ that part of the reason for   ADMIT
riding a bike is to beat the traffic. There is a
thrill in weaving around (1) ....   APPEAR
stationary cars. Also, without licence plates any
traffic (2) .... they commit is virtually   OFFEND
untraceable. 'It's really exciting to look at your
speedometer and see that you're going at 30
miles an hour,' said one (3) ....   INTERVIEW
in our survey. Many cyclists now record their
(4) .... journeys to work with a   DAY
camera mounted on their helmet and post them
online to show the trip in (5) ....   GRAPH
detail. There are now cyclists who also record
(6) .... or dangerous driving and post   CONSIDER
it online to shame the drivers.

What the speed of bikes and their mass
(7) .... have done is foster an   AVAILABLE
attitude of moral (8) .... : that   SUPERIOR
because cyclists are so vulnerable, it is everyone
else who should be on the lookout for them.

Grammar

3 Circle the correct alternative in *italics* in each of the following sentences.

1 Sonia will call you as soon as she *will finish / has finished* lunch.
2 I'll do the cooking tonight when everyone else *works / is working*.
3 It wasn't until the match *was / had* been over that he realised he'd strained a muscle.
4 I haven't seen him at all since he *is working / has been working* there.
5 In future, please don't call me while *I will have / I'm having* my supper.
6 Rory learnt to speak Arabic perfectly when he *was working / had worked* in Cairo.
7 As soon as the teacher *has arrived / arrived*, we started work.
8 Tracey and Pierre performed together in perfect harmony and while she *played / was playing* the piano, he sang in a high tenor voice.

Vocabulary and grammar review Unit 10

Vocabulary

1 Circle the correct alternatives in *italics* in each of these sentences.

1 The system aims to give everyone *an equal / a same* opportunity at the beginning of their lives.
2 Friday is the *last / late* chance we'll have to enter the competition.
3 The swearing-in of the first woman president was a *historic / historical* occasion.
4 There's a *slight / little* possibility that I won't be back in time for tomorrow's meeting.
5 Don't *lose / miss* this *gold / golden* opportunity to win a two-week holiday in the south of France.
6 There seems to be a *factual / real* possibility that the party will lose at the next election.
7 The funeral of the firefighters who died in the blaze was a very *depressed / solemn* occasion.
8 In my opinion, everyone deserves a *next / second* chance in life.

2 For questions 1–8, read the text below. Use the word given in capitals at the end of some of the lines to form a word that fits in the gap in the same line. There is an example at the beginning.

Adult learners have many (0) ....*characteristics*.... that distinguish them from school or college learners. Firstly, they come to courses with experiences and (1) .... in diverse areas. They often prefer practical learning (2) .... that enable them to draw on the skills and experience they have acquired. In the main, adults have (3) .... aims and have (4) .... insights into what is likely to be successful. In addition to this, they are (5) .... able to relate new facts to past experiences and enjoy having their talents explored in (6) .... situations. Adults have established opinions and beliefs, which have been formed over time through their experience of families, work, community, or politics.	CHARACTER KNOW ACT REAL VALUE READY LEARN
A (7) .... of adults also have intrinsic motivation and their effort increases because of their desire to learn. They are also motivated by the (8) .... of the material to be addressed, and learn better when material is related to their own needs and interests.	MAJOR RELEVANT

Grammar

3 Complete these sentences with the correct form of *must, need* or *have to*. In some cases more than one answer is possible.

1 My new job starts next Monday. Hopefully, I .... work such long hours as I do now.
2 I .... make sure I wake up in time for my first lecture. Yesterday, I didn't have any lectures, so I .... get up at all.
3 Our lecturers have told us that we .... send them our assignments by email, otherwise they won't mark them. This means we .... have our own email.
4 Take it easy! Today's lecture's been cancelled, so you .... hurry.
5 You .... smoke in here. Didn't you see the sign? If you want a cigarette, you .... go outside.
6 I .... get some cash out before the weekend – otherwise I'm going to run out.

4 Four of these sentences have mistakes with modal verbs. Correct the mistakes.

1 It's a complicated route – I hope I could find my way back.
2 You can find all the information you'll ever need on Wikipedia.
3 We're delighted to inform you that we could offer you the post of manager.
4 At the fourth attempt I could pass my driving test. The first three times, I failed spectacularly.
5 If you were a fast reader, you could be able to finish that novel in one evening.

11 Being somewhere else

Starting off

1 Work in pairs. The photos show different types of travel experience. Choose two of the photos and think of vocabulary, phrases, expressions and topics which are relevant to the photos.

Example
Photo 1: hardship, proving themselves, a voyage into the unknown, rapids, waterfalls, mosquitoes, exploration, chilly, remote wilderness, inhospitable countryside

2 Write two questions asking for someone's opinions on topics arising from the photos you chose.

Example
Some people think you can learn a lot about yourself from travel involving hardship. Do you agree?

3 Ask several different people in the class the questions you have written.

4 When you have finished, work with your original partner and compare the answers you heard.

Listening | Part 1

1 Before you start Listening Part 1, do the exercise in the Exam round-up box.

2 You will hear three different extracts. Before you listen, underline the key idea in each question.

Extract one

You hear a conversation between a man and a woman who are travelling on a river.
1 What complaint does the man make about the journey?
 A He would prefer something more exciting.
 B He would like protection from insects.
 C He would prefer healthier surroundings.

2 How does the woman react to what the man says?
 A She takes offence at being criticised.
 B She suggests alternative activities.
 C She reprimands him for his attitude.

Extract Two

You hear a woman and a man planning a sponsored walk.
3 The man insists the journey should go ahead because
 A they will not be affected by bad weather.
 B they have plenty of time to complete it.
 C they have promised that they would do it.

4 What do they agree will happen if they don't reach their objective?
 A They will suffer economically.
 B They will be less well regarded.
 C They will have to try again later.

Extract Three

You hear a conversation between a man and a woman who have both visited the same country.
5 The man thinks travellers gain more from their visit to the country if they
 A avoid hasty judgments about what they encounter.
 B are ready to try new experiences when they arise.
 C prepare for potential problems in advance.

6 How does the woman feel about her journey now?
 A relieved that she completed it safely
 B surprised by the conditions she encountered
 C grateful to her travelling companions

3 ▶ 15 Listen and for questions 1–6, choose the answer (A, B or C) which fits best according to what you hear.

4 Work in pairs. What's the hardest journey you've ever made?

Vocabulary
Phrasal verbs

1 ▶15 Listen again to the recording for Listening Part 1 and match these phrasal verbs with their definitions from the *Cambridge Advanced Learner's Dictionary*.

1 count on something
2 sign up (for something)
3 let someone down
4 put something off
5 set off (on something)
6 go through with something
7 never live something down
8 pay up
9 come up

a do something unpleasant or difficult that has already been agreed or promised
b agree to become involved in an organised activity
c be unable to stop feeling embarrassed about something you have done
d decide or arrange to delay an event or activity until a later time or date
e disappoint someone by failing to do what you agreed to do or were expected to do
f expect something to happen and make plans based on it
g give someone the money that you owe them
h happen, usually unexpectedly
i start a journey

2 Complete these sentences by writing one of the phrasal verbs in the correct form in each gap.

1 All sorts of unexpected things can .... if you travel without a detailed programme or plan.
2 I've .... to help with the sponsored walk on Sunday and I hope I haven't taken on too much.
3 Marie made some rather foolish remarks and now she feels she'll ....
4 Martina didn't want to .... her friends .... by not turning up to their party.
5 Sasha .... the start of the climb till he'd got over the injury to his ankle.
6 Unless you .... , I won't have enough money to go on holiday this year.
7 We were late .... and that's why we were late arriving.
8 You'll need to take some waterproof clothes because you can't .... the weather being good at this time of year.
9 He threatened to leave the expedition, but I never expected him to .... it.

Grammar
Conditionals

1 Work in pairs. Look at the ten sentences a–j from Listening Part 1. Which sentences refer to

1 past time?
2 past and present time?
3 just present time?
4 future time?
5 any time because the speaker is making a general point?

a If I'd known about the mosquitoes, I'd never have signed up for this.
b If only you would put on some repellent!
c If you would please just stop moaning for a while, perhaps we could start enjoying ourselves a bit.
d Even if we had stayed at home, it would be better because I would be relaxing in front of the telly right now instead of paddling up this miserable river.
e So, what will we do if the weather breaks?
f Look, if things start looking really bad, we can always put the walk off for a while and set off a bit later.
g If we don't do it, we'll never live it down.
h Still, I guess they'd pay up anyway even if we didn't make it, wouldn't they?
i If you leave yourself open to whatever comes up, it can be very rewarding.
j It could all have been quite dull otherwise, you know.

2 Read these sentences and answer the questions about them.

Even if we had stayed at home, it would be better because I <u>would be relaxing</u> in front of the telly right now instead of paddling up this miserable river.
1 Why is the underlined verb in the continuous?

If it <u>hadn't been snowing</u> while we were waiting for the bus, we wouldn't have got so cold.
2 Do the verbs in this sentence refer to present or past time?
3 Why does the speaker say 'hadn't been snowing', not 'hadn't snowed'?

Terry <u>wouldn't have insisted</u> on climbing to the top of the mountain if he <u>wasn't</u> so stubborn.

4 Which underlined verb refers to past time?
5 How would the meaning change if we said, 'If he hadn't been so stubborn.'?

→ page 165 Language reference: Conditionals

3 Put the verbs in brackets into the correct form. You will need to decide on the correct conditional form and whether the verb should be simple or continuous.

1 If you .... (not leave) the map at home, we .... (not wander) around this forest right now, looking for somewhere to spend the night.

2 Innsbruck is a lovely city and if I .... (not rush) to catch a train just now, I .... (be) happy to show you around a bit.

3 Kamal always thinks he knows best, and if he .... (not be) such an obstinate man, we .... (probably reach) the hotel by now instead of being stuck in this traffic jam.

4 'What do you do when you fall ill on holiday?' 'Well, it hasn't happened to me yet, but I guess I .... (try) to find a local doctor who spoke some English. If I .... (be) seriously ill, I .... (have) to get help from the consulate.'

5 If I .... (be) you, I .... (carry) my money in a money belt.

6 It was your own fault. The accident .... (not happen) if you .... (concentrate) properly at the time.

7 Karen is an intrepid traveller and I don't imagine she .... (ever abandon) a journey unless she .... (travel) somewhere really unpleasant or dangerous.

8 If you .... (like) to come with me, I .... (show) you to your room.

4 👁 These sentences each contain one mistake made by exam candidates. Correct the mistakes.

1 If you eat so much chocolate, you wouldn't enjoy the delicious cake I've made.
2 I would be grateful if you send me a reply at your earliest convenience.
3 If you do not give me a refund, I am obliged to write to the local council.
4 If you had followed all my instructions, you would now stand in front of the cathedral.
5 In my country few people smoke, so if I were you, I won't smoke at all.
6 If I was able to travel back in history and I had the chance to choose where exactly to go, then I would have travelled four centuries into the past.

5 For questions 1–6, complete the second sentence so that it has a similar meaning to the first sentence, using the word given. Do not change the word given. You must use between three and six words, including the word given.

1 As long as I know you'll support me, I won't worry about money.
COUNT
Provided I .... support me, I won't worry about money.

2 I don't think we'll miss the train if we leave home on time.
LONG
We should manage to catch the train .... off from home on time.

3 Martin is only working late tonight because he has to finish an urgent job.
UNLESS
Martin would not .... he had to finish an urgent job.

4 Ellie was given a trophy by her school because she had worked so hard.
PRESENTED
Ellie's school .... a trophy if she had not worked so hard.

5 Could you please cancel my appointment?
GRATEFUL
I .... cancel my appointment.

6 If it had not been for some unexpected difficulties, we would not be feeling so stressed.
COME
If some unexpected difficulties .... , we would not be feeling so stressed.

Reading and Use of English | Part 5

1 Before starting Reading and Use of English Part 5, do the exercise in the Exam round-up box.

2 Work in pairs. You will read an extract from a book by Paul Theroux about a journey he made through Africa. Before you read, look at the photos here and on the next page.

1 Which aspects of your daily life and routine would you like to escape from by making a journey?
2 What things do you think a man in his 60s would want to escape from? Why? Do you think they are the same or different from the things young people want to escape from when they travel?

3 Read the text quickly. Why did the writer choose to travel in Africa again?

Disappearing into Africa

I wanted the pleasure of being in Africa again. Feeling that the place was so large it contained many untold tales and some hope and comedy and sweetness too, I aimed to reinsert myself in the bundu, as we used to call the bush, and to wander the antique hinterland. There I had lived and worked, happily, almost forty years ago, in the heart of the greenest continent.

In those old undramatic days of my school teaching in the bundu, folks lived their lives on bush paths at the
10 end of unpaved roads of red clay, in villages of grass-roofed huts. They had a new national flag, they had just gotten the vote, some had bikes, many talked about buying their first pair of shoes. They were hopeful, and so was I, a schoolteacher living near a settlement of mud huts among dusty trees and parched fields – children shrieking at play; and women bent double – most with infants slung on their backs – hoeing the corn and beans; and the men sitting in the shade.

The Swahili word safari means 'journey', it has nothing
20 to do with animals, someone 'on safari' is just away and unobtainable and out of touch. Out of touch in Africa was where I wanted to be. The wish to disappear sends many travellers away. If you are thoroughly sick of being kept waiting at home or at work, travel is perfect: let other people wait for a change. Travel is a sort of revenge for having been put on hold, or having to leave messages on answering machines, not knowing your party's extension, being kept waiting all your working life – the homebound writer's irritants. But also being kept
30 waiting is the human condition.

Travel in the African bush can also be a sort of revenge on mobile phones and email, on telephones and the daily paper, on the creepier aspects of globalisation that allow anyone who chooses to get their insinuating hands on you. I desired to be unobtainable. I was going to Africa for the best of reasons – in a spirit of discovery; and for the pettiest – simply to disappear, to light out, with a suggestion of I dare you to try to find me.

Home had become a routine, and routines make time pass quickly. I was a sitting duck in this predictable routine: people knew when to call me, they knew when I would be at my desk. I was in such regular touch it was like having a job, a mode of life I hated. I was sick of being called up and importuned, asked for favors, hit up for money. You stick around too long and people begin to impose their own deadlines on you.

Everyone always available at any time in the totally accessible world seemed to me pure horror. It made me want to find a place that was not accessible at all … no phones, no Internet, not even mail delivery, the wonderful old world of being out of touch; in short, of being far away.

All I had to do was remove myself. I loved not having to ask permission, and in fact in my domestic life things had begun to get a little predictable, too – Mr Paul at home every evening when Mrs Paul came home from work. 'I made spaghetti sauce … I seared some tuna … I'm scrubbing some potatoes …' The writer in his apron, perspiring over his béchamel sauce, always within earshot of the telephone. You have to pick it up because it is ringing in your ear.

A morbid aspect of my departure for Africa was that people began offering condolences. Say you're leaving for a dangerous place and your friends call sympathetically, as though you've caught a serious illness that might prove fatal. Yet I found these messages unexpectedly stimulating, a heartening preview of what my own demise would be like. Lots of tears! Lots of mourners! But also, undoubtedly, many people boasting solemnly, 'I told him not to do it. I was one of the last people to talk to him.'

From *Dark Star Safari* by Paul Theroux

4 For questions 1–6, choose the answer (A, B, C or D) which you think fits best according to the text.

1 What did Paul expect from his journey?
   A to have a variety of enjoyable experiences
   B to see how Africa had changed
   C to meet some old friends
   D to see impressive scenery

2 Forty years ago, how did Paul feel about the future of the country where he was living?
   A Little was likely to change.
   B People's aspirations were too limited.
   C Women would do most of the work.
   D Things were likely to improve.

3 In paragraph 3, what reason does Paul give for wanting to travel to Africa?
   A He wanted people to be unable to contact him.
   B He wanted a change of activity.
   C His health was suffering from staying at home.
   D He had been waiting to return to Africa for many years.

4 Paul says 'I was a sitting duck' in paragraph 5 to show that
   A he was bored.
   B he was easy to find.
   C he had a fixed lifestyle.
   D he was always lending money.

5 Paul mentions his cooking activities
   A to show he can look after himself.
   B to explain why the phone was within earshot.
   C to show how he was a good husband.
   D to show why he felt trapped.

6 In the final paragraph, what is Paul's reaction to his friends' messages?
   A sadness about leaving them
   B surprise at their excitement
   C pleasure at their concern
   D annoyance at their seriousness

5 Work in small groups.

   1 Would you be happy to be out of touch on a journey?
   2 What can be the benefits/drawbacks of travelling to a place with a very different culture from your own?

Vocabulary

at, *in* and *on* to express location

1 Complete the sentences below with *at*, *in* or *on*. Then check your answers by looking again at the text in Reading and Use of English Part 5.

1 I wanted the pleasure of being .... Africa again.
2 There I had lived and worked, ... the heart of the greenest continent.
3 Folks lived their lives .... bush paths .... the end of unpaved roads of red clay, ... villages of grass-roofed huts.
4 ... women bent double – most with infants slung .... their backs.
5 If you are thoroughly sick of being kept waiting .... home or .... work, travel is perfect.
6 People knew when to call me, they knew when I would be .... my desk.
7 Everyone always available at any time .... the totally accessible world seemed to me pure horror.

2 Work in pairs. Which preposition, *at*, *in* or *on*, is used to talk about the following? Find examples for each rule in Exercise 1.

a a position which is thought of as a point, not an area   at (3, 6)
b a position in contact with a surface
c a position along a border or boundary (e.g. the coast, the ocean) or along something which connects two places (e.g. a road, a river)
d a position within a larger area or space

➡ page 163 Language reference: *at*, *in* and *on* to express location

3 👁 Each of these sentences contains a mistake with prepositions made by exam candidates. Correct the mistakes.

1 I come from Mendoza, a town of Argentina.
2 I'd like to introduce you to my boss, whose office is at the 5th floor.
3 Portugal is one of the most beautiful countries of the world.
4 Public phones are available at almost every large square.
5 She spends far too long talking at her mobile phone.
6 There's a garage at the left and I live just two doors along from it.
7 We waited at a queue for more than twenty minutes.
8 You will find a youth hostel in almost every island.
9 You'll find a large shopping centre at the outskirts of the city.
10 She decided to go and live for a year to Italy.

Reading and Use of English | Part 2

1 Before doing Reading and Use of English Part 2, answer the questions in the Exam round-up box.

Exam round-up

Work in pairs. How much do you remember about Reading and Use of English Part 2? Discuss these questions.

1 How many questions are there in this part?
2 What should you do before you start filling the gaps?
3 If you can't think of a word for a gap, what should you do?
4 How important is correct spelling?
5 What should you do when you have finished?

2 Work in pairs. Some people suggest that in the future virtual travel using computer and internet technology may replace real travel.

1 What advantages would virtual travel have over real travel?
2 Would you prefer it?

3 You will read a short article about two people who were searching for an island. Read the article quickly, without paying attention to the gaps, to find out how they found the island.

Island wanted

A few years ago, Ben Keene and Mark James launched Tribewanted (0) ....in.......... in a torrent of media coverage. (1) .... they had had was a simple idea with potentially enormous consequences for tourism: the creation of an eco-friendly sustainable community existing simultaneously in the virtual world of the Internet and (2) .... an actual desert island.

How do you go (3) .... finding an island? Where (4) .... would you look but on the Internet? Ben and Mark could have bought islands anywhere in the world (5) .... that they had been able to pay the typical starting price of one million dollars. They were not having much luck (6) .... their searches finally led them to a specialist island broker who pointed them towards Vorovoro, off the wild north coast of Fiji. With just (7) .... money on Ben's credit card for two return tickets, they decided to have a look. No (8) .... had they seen it than they decided to buy it.

Adapted from *The Guardian*

4 Work in pairs. For questions 1–8, read the article again and think of the word which best fits each gap. Use only one word in each gap. There is an example at the beginning (0).

5 Work in pairs.

1 Would you be interested in spending time on a small Pacific island? Why (not)?

2 What do you think is meant by *eco-tourism* and why is it important?

6 Read the text below and think of the word which best fits each gap. Use only one word in each gap.

Paradise found

My atlas index shows eight entries for 'Paradise'. There is **(0)** ....one........... missing, though: Paraíso in the Dominican Republic. **(1)** .... you look carefully at a detailed map of the country, you are unlikely to notice its name there, because this particular paradise with its stunning beaches, situated **(2)** .... a virgin coastline of jungle-clad mountains, has so **(3)** .... escaped the indexers, as well as most of the four million tourists who visit the island annually. As the majority head for the resorts of the east and north coasts, they miss **(4)** .... entirely on the gorgeous southwestern triangle that dips deep into the Caribbean and embraces Paraíso. And it is incredible **(5)** .... they miss! The resort offers the **(6)** .... enchanting combination of scenery, wildlife and good food you can imagine and this bounty has **(7)** .... only inspired a handful of independent lodges but also earned the region its status **(8)** .... the Dominican Republic's only biosphere reserve, which is not a bad setting for Paraíso.

Adapted from *The Independent*

Speaking | Part 1

1 Work in pairs. Which of the questions below could you answer using conditional verb forms?

1 If you could travel anywhere in the world, where would you choose to go? Why?

2 If some friends from abroad were visiting your region, which places would you take them to see? Why?

3 What things do you most enjoy doing when travelling on holiday? Why?

4 Do you find it's useful that you can speak English when you travel? Why?

5 What's the best time of year for people to visit your country? Why?

6 Would you enjoy going on an adventurous, possibly dangerous journey? Why (not)?

7 What is the most interesting place you have ever travelled to? Why?

8 If you could choose something completely different from your usual type of holiday, what would you choose? Why?

9 Would you enjoy working with tourists? Why?

10 Would you prefer to spend a year travelling or to spend a year working? Why?

2 ▶ 16 Listen to three people, Laura, Daniel and Marta, answering questions from the list 1–10 above.

1 Which question is each of them answering?

2 Which speakers use conditional forms in their answers?

3 Do they use conditional verb forms all the time? Why (not)?

4 Who sounds most enthusiastic in their answer? What words do they use which show enthusiasm? What other way do they have of showing enthusiasm?

5 Do the speakers repeat the words of the questions, or do they express the ideas using their own vocabulary? Why is this a good idea in the exam?

3 Take turns to ask each other the questions in Exercise 1.

Student A: Ask your partner questions 1, 3, 5, 7 and 9.

Student B: Ask your partner questions 2, 4, 6, 8 and 10.

Exam advice

- Before going to the Speaking test, make sure you can speak about your work, your studies, your family, the area where you live and your free-time interests.
- Expand your answers with reasons, examples and extra information.

Writing | Part 2
A review

1 Read this writing task and underline the points you must deal with in your answer.

You see the announcement below on a website called travelfortravellers.com.

> ### HOTELS NEAR ME
> We'd like to know what local people think of different hotels in their area, so we're opening a section written by local people to help visitors to choose the hotel which suits them best.
>
> Send us a review which recommends two hotels in your area for two different types of visitor and says what sort of visitor each hotel would suit and why.

Write your **review** in 220–260 words.

2 Work in pairs. Make notes on the following points.

- the two types of visitor you could write for
- what things each type of visitor would want to know about when reading a review

3 Discuss: Which of these do you think would be the best plan for the review?

Plan A

Para 1: Introduction: why different types of hotel suit different visitors

Paras 2 and 3: Features of hotel 1

Paras 4 and 5: Features of hotel 2

Para 6: Conclusion: the type of visitor each hotel would suit and why

Plan B

Para 1: Introduction: the range of hotels available in your area, which two you have chosen to review and why

Para 2: Comparison of rooms and prices in each hotel

Paras 3 and 4: Comparison of other features in each hotel, e.g. business facilities, restaurant, gym

Para 5: Conclusion: the type of visitor each hotel would suit and why

Plan C

If you don't like either Plan A or Plan B, discuss and write your own plan for the review.

4 Read this review without paying attention to the gaps. Which plan, A, B or C, does it follow? If the answer is C, write the plan.

Two hotels in St Petersburg

St Petersburg is an important business as well as tourist destination. [1]................................. , business people often don't like sharing their hotels with tour groups and require different facilities. [2]................................. , holidaymakers want a break from the serious atmosphere of a business hotel. Each of the hotels I recommend caters for a different type of visitor.

Situated on Nevski Prospect not far from the Hermitage Museum, Nevinski Hostel is a compact, moderately-priced hotel which would suit backpackers and tourists on a tight budget. The rooms are clean and airy, [3]................................. quite basic, with twin beds and en-suite bathrooms.

Nevski Prospect is the main shopping street, so it wouldn't suit light sleepers [4]................................. you should expect some noise [5]................................. from the constant

traffic and perhaps from other boisterous guests. Unfortunately, the hotel lacks a restaurant, so you'll have to find your own breakfast in one of the many cafés nearby. However, the staff are friendly and helpful. 6................................. the hotel has bicycles available for its guests to explore this beautiful city at their leisure.

Peter the Great Hotel is an elegant, moderately-sized business hotel situated in a converted neoclassical palace not far from the statue of the Bronze Horseman, with fabulous views across the Neva River. 7................................. its five stars indicate, the hotel offers luxurious, spacious rooms at a price. It contains a range of well-equipped conference rooms 8................................. a gourmet restaurant allowing business people to entertain clients in style. The management and staff are competent and professional, as you'd expect, and will organise trips and events to make your stay 9................................. productive but pleasurable too.

Whichever hotel you stay at, St Petersburg won't fail to delight you.

5 Complete the review in Exercise 4 by writing one of these linking words/phrases in each gap.

> an added attraction is that   as (x2)
> both   equally   however   not only
> though   together with

6 Read the review again and note down adjectives used to describe

1 the hotels in general
2 the rooms
3 the staff.

7 Work in pairs.

1 How would you describe the style of the review? Choose a, b or c and give reasons for your choice.
   a very colloquial and informal
   b informative, but with some informal features; it addresses the reader personally
   c formal and academic
2 The style in which the exam task is written often indicates the style in which the answer can be written. Which two style features of the task in Exercise 1 are also used in the sample review?

8 Prepare to write your own review.

- Make any changes you want to your plan in Exercise 3.
- Consider whether you want to use any of the adjectives you noted in Exercise 6.
- Underline any other words and phrases you would like to use from Exercises 4 and 5.

9 Write your review.

→ page 189 Writing reference: Reviews

Exam advice

You will often have to compare two things in your review.

- Think about your target readers and what information they need.
- Write a plan thinking about each of the things you want to describe and in what order.
- Decide what recommendation(s) you are going to make and include them in your answer.

The living world

Starting off

1 Work in pairs. Look at the newspaper headlines and photos, and discuss these questions.

  1 Which headlines do the two photographs illustrate?
  2 What environmental issues do the headlines relate to?
  3 Which headlines suggest an optimistic view of the future?

A **China to build wind power complex**

B **U.S. Fish and Wildlife Service to Consider Black-footed Albatross for Protection**

C **Pollutant linked to bronchitis in toddlers**

D **Britons top table of carbon emissions from planes**

E **Is the bio fuel dream over?**

F **Arctic Melt Opens Northwest Passage**

2 Which environmental issue do you consider to be the most important at the present time, in your country or internationally? When you have decided, write a headline to draw attention to this issue.

Listening | Part 2

1 Before you start Listening Part 2, do the exercise in the Exam round-up box.

Exam round-up

Say if the following statements are true (T) or false (F). If a statement is false, rewrite it to make it true.

In Listening Part 2
1 you have to complete six sentences
2 no more than two words will be missing from each sentence
3 the sentences are not identical to sentences on the recording
4 you should read the gapped sentences after you have listened
5 if you are not sure of an answer, leave it blank.

2 You are going to listen to a radio talk about the effects of climate change on the Inuit people of the Arctic. Before you listen, look at the photo on page 129 and discuss these questions.

  1 What natural resources do you think the Inuit have traditionally depended on?
  2 How do you think climate change is affecting the Inuit?
  3 What information would you like to find out about the Inuit people?

3 ▶17 Listen to the brief introduction to the talk about the Inuit people. What information does the speaker give about the natural resources you discussed in Exercise 2?

4 ▶18 Now listen to a professor of anthropology talking about problems facing the Inuit people. For questions 1–8, complete the sentences with a short word or phrase.

Professor Moore believes that the majority of (1) .... are likely to be familiar with the concept of global warming.

The Inuit are alarmed by the damage which is occurring to their (2) .... , which is characterised by such phenomena as melting ice sheets.

A ring around the moon was one of the (3) .... which the Inuit people used to rely on.

Elderly Inuit people give (4) .... of wildlife suffering as a result of climate change.

The belief of the Inuit people that the Arctic is melting is now supported by (5) ....

Warning signs include the erosion of (6) .... and the disappearance of lakes.

George Hobson believes the Inuit people have survived because they have a (7) .... of their environment.

The elderly Inuit woman believes that her people may be unable to (8) .... to what is happening to the environment.

---

5 Discuss these questions.

1 Are there other groups of people who are suffering directly from climate change? What can be done to help groups like this?
2 What 'traditional knowledge' is associated with your culture? How do people view this knowledge today?

Vocabulary
Prepositions following verbs

1 Circle the correct prepositions in *italics* in these sentences.

1 The daily weather markers *on / for* which they have relied for thousands of years are becoming less predictable.
2 The Inuit elders and hunters who depend *of / on* the land are also disturbed.
3 These feelings are not simply based *on / to* Inuit superstition.
4 Scientists are now paying attention to what the Inuit are reporting, and are incorporating it *into / on* their research
5 They have adapted *for / to* the cold climate.
6 She doesn't try to blame anyone *for / on* the change in her environment.

2 ⊙ Exam candidates sometimes use the wrong prepositions after verbs. Correct the mistakes in these sentences.

1 Many people firmly believe to the traditional wisdom of their ancestors.
2 It is difficult to concentrate in your work if there is loud music playing.
3 I recently participated on a charity event at my college.
4 The company is insisting in the use of low-energy light bulbs in their offices.
5 The government will double the amount it spends in the environment.
6 Every flight you take contributes with global warming.
7 Many TV documentaries are now focusing in environmental issues.
8 The new energy-saving laws apply for all factories and offices.

➡ page 167 Language reference: Dependent prepositions

Reading and Use of English | Part 7

1 Do the exercise in the Exam round-up box.

Exam round-up

Circle the correct alternative in *italics* for each of the statements below.

In Reading and Use of English Part 7

1 the text has *six / seven* gaps where missing paragraphs belong
2 there *is one / are two* extra paragraph(s) that you do not need to use
3 you should start this task by reading the *gapped text / missing paragraphs*
4 you should concentrate on *the structure of the text / finding words common to the gapped text and the missing paragraphs.*

2 You are going to read an article about a speaking parrot. Before you read, discuss these questions.

  a How do you think parrots learn to speak?
  b When a parrot speaks, do you think it understands what it is saying?
  c Which other animals could be taught to speak, do you think?

3 Read the main part of the article (but not the missing paragraphs A–G).

  1 How does the article answer the three questions you have been discussing?
  2 What do the photos show?

4 Now choose from the paragraphs A–G the one which fits each gap in the text. There is one extra paragraph which you do not need to use.

Alex the African Grey

Science's best-known parrot dies, aged 31

THE last time Irene Pepperberg saw Alex, she said goodnight as usual. 'You be good,' said Alex. 'I love you.' 'I love you, too.' 'You'll be in tomorrow?' 'Yes, I'll be in tomorrow.' But sadly, Alex, whose name is supposedly an acronym of Avian Learning Experiment, died in his cage that night. This brought to an end a life spent learning complex tasks which, it had originally been thought, only primates could master.

1

Even then, the researchers remained human-centric. Their assumption was that chimpanzees might be able to understand and use human sign language because they are humanity's nearest living relatives. It took a brilliant insight to turn this human-centricity on its head and look at the capabilities of a species only distantly related to humanity, but which can, nevertheless, speak the words people speak: the parrot.

2

Dr Pepperberg and Alex last shared a common ancestor more than 300 million years ago. But Alex, unlike a chimpanzee, learned to speak words easily. The question was, was Alex merely 'parroting' Dr Pepperberg? Or would that pejorative term have to be redefined? Do parrots actually understand what they are saying?

3

The reason why primates have evolved intelligence, according to Dr Humphrey, is that they generally live in groups. And, just as group living promotes intelligence, so intelligence allows larger groups to function, providing a spur for the evolution of yet more intelligence. If Dr Humphrey is right, only social animals can be intelligent – and so far this has been borne out.

4

An additional relevant factor is that, like primates, parrots live long enough to make the time-consuming process of learning worthwhile. Alex lived to the age of 31. Combined with his ability to speak, or at least 'vocalise' words, Alex looked a promising experimental subject.

5

By the end of this process, Alex had the intelligence of a five-year-old child and had not reached his full potential. He had a vocabulary of 150 words. He knew the names of 50 objects and could describe their colours and shapes. He could answer questions about objects' properties, even when he had not seen that particular combination of properties before. He could ask for things, and would reject a proffered item and ask again if it was not what he wanted. He understood the concepts of 'bigger', 'smaller', 'same' and 'different'. And he could count up to six, including the number zero. He even knew when and how to apologise if he annoyed Dr Pepperberg or her colleagues.

6

There are still a few researchers who think Alex's skills were the result of rote learning rather than abstract thought. Alex, though, convinced most in the field that birds as well as mammals can evolve complex and sophisticated cognition, and communicate the results to others.

Adapted from *The Economist*

A And so it proved. Using a training technique now employed on children with learning difficulties, Dr Pepperberg and her collaborators at the University of Arizona began teaching Alex how to describe things, how to make his desires known, and even how to ask questions.

B And the fact that there were a lot of collaborators, even strangers, involved in the project was crucial. Researchers in this area live in perpetual fear of the 'Clever Hans' effect. This is named after a horse that seemed to be able to count, but was actually reacting to unconscious cues from his trainer. Alex would talk to and perform for anyone, not just Dr Pepperberg.

C Dr Pepperberg's reason for suspecting that they might – and thus her second reason for picking a parrot – was that in the mid-1970s evolutionary explanations for behaviour were coming back into vogue. A British researcher called Nicholas Humphrey had proposed that intelligence evolves in response to the social environment rather than the natural one. The more complex the society an animal lives in, the more intelligence it needs to prosper.

D Early studies had concluded that linguistic ability in apes was virtually non-existent. But researchers had made the elementary error of trying to teach their anthropoid subjects to speak. Chimpanzee vocal cords are simply not up to this, and it was not until someone had the idea of teaching chimps sign language that any progress was made.

E However, not all animals which live in groups can be classified in this way. Flocks of, say, starlings or herds of wildebeest do not count as real societies, just protective groupings. But parrots such as Alex live in societies in the wild, in the way that monkeys and apes do, and thus, Dr Pepperberg reasoned, Alex might have evolved advanced cognitive abilities.

F The dictionary definition of *to parrot* is to repeat exactly what someone says without understanding it. It is used about politicians who simply repeat the party line, or schoolchildren who learn facts by heart. Dr Pepperberg's experiments with Alex have helped to demonstrate the validity of this usage.

G This novel approach came to Dr Pepperberg, a theoretical chemist, in 1977. To follow it up, she went to a pet shop and bought an African Grey parrot, which was then just a year old. Thus began one of the best-known double acts in the field of animal-behaviour science.

Grammar
Nouns and articles

1 Work in pairs. Find the following in the text below.

1 two singular countable nouns
2 three plural countable nouns
3 three uncountable nouns
4 two of these three uncountable nouns that could be countable in other contexts
5 two proper nouns (names), apart from Baobab

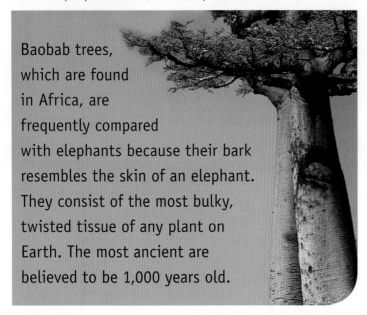

Baobab trees, which are found in Africa, are frequently compared with elephants because their bark resembles the skin of an elephant. They consist of the most bulky, twisted tissue of any plant on Earth. The most ancient are believed to be 1,000 years old.

2 Many words have different meanings depending on whether they are countable or uncountable. What is the difference in meaning between these pairs of sentences?

1 a I like *coffee*.
  b I'd like a *coffee*.
2 a I can't see – my *hair* is in my eyes.
  b I've got a *hair* in my eye.
3 a Most English *cheese* is hard.
  b There are more than 1,000 British *cheeses*.
4 a Anna lost a lot of *weight* when she was ill.
  b Lifting *weights* strengthens your muscles.
5 a Car windscreens are made from toughened *glass*.
  b I only wear *glasses* for reading.
6 a He has no *experience* of living in a cold climate.
  b But he has read about the *experiences* of other people.
7 a *Exercise* is good for you.
  b We've got four *exercises* to do for homework.

➡ **page 166 Language reference:** Countable and uncountable nouns

3 Circle the correct articles in these extracts from Reading and Use of English Part 7 (Ø = no article). Then check your answers by looking back at the text.

1 *A / The* last time Irene Pepperberg saw Alex, she said goodnight as usual.
2 It took *a / the* brilliant insight to turn this human-centricity on its head.
3 This novel approach came to Dr Pepperberg, *a / Ø* theoretical chemist, in 1977.
4 But Alex, unlike *a / Ø* chimpanzee, learned to speak words easily.
5 *Ø / The* birds as well as *Ø / the* mammals can evolve *Ø / a* complex and sophisticated cognition.
6 Dr Pepperberg and her collaborators at *a / the* University of Arizona began teaching Alex.
7 She went to *a / Ø* pet shop and bought an African Grey parrot, which was then just *a / the* year old.
8 … the capabilities of a species only distantly related to humanity: *a / the* parrot.
9 Thus began one of *a / the* best-known double acts in the field of animal-behaviour science.
10 Researchers in this area live in *Ø / a* perpetual fear of the 'Clever Hans' effect. This was named after *a / the* horse that seemed to be able to count.

4 Now match each use of *a/an*, *the* and *Ø* in Exercise 3 with one of these rules for the use of articles.

1 Use the definite article (*the*)
  a when there is only one of something/someone
  b with superlative adjectives and *first, last, only, same*
  c to refer to something/someone that has been mentioned before or that the reader already knows about
  d to refer to all the members of a group or species.

2 Use the indefinite article (*a/an*)
  a to refer to something/someone for the first time
  b in place of the number *one*
  c to refer to something/someone which is not specific (i.e. it doesn't matter which one)
  d to refer to someone's job.

3 Use no article (*Ø*)
  a with uncountable nouns which refer to something general
  b with plural countable nouns which refer to something general.

➡ **page 163 Language reference:** Articles

5 Complete this text with the correct article: *a/an*, *the* or no article (Ø). For some gaps, more than one answer is possible.

(1) .... South China tiger population was estimated to number 4,000 individuals in (2) .... early 1950s, but over (3) .... following 30 years, approximately 3,000 tigers were killed as the subspecies was officially hunted as (4) .... pest. Although (5) .... Chinese government banned (6) .... hunting in 1979, and declared the tiger's survival (7) .... conservation priority, by 1996 (8) .... surviving population was estimated to be less than (9) .... hundred individuals. And, as no tiger has been sighted in (10) .... wild for more than 25 years, (11) .... scientists believe that it is 'functionally extinct'. It is thought that even if (12) .... few individuals remain, the existing protected areas or (13) .... habitat are not sufficiently large or undisturbed to sustain (14) .... viable tiger population.

6 ◉ The following sentences contain mistakes with articles made by exam candidates. There may be more than one mistake in each sentence. Find and correct the mistakes.

1 Make sure you wear suit and tie if it's formal occasion.
2 You should get job even though you haven't got high-level qualifications.
3 This report aims to describe advantages and disadvantages of green taxes.
4 Students can access Internet in their classrooms.
5 Society needs to provide affordable accommodation for homeless.
6 A most important thing is to get people talking about the issues.

7 Tokyo is a capital of Japan.
8 Nowadays the technology is everywhere.
9 I have basic knowledge of French, German and Spanish.
10 Even though he hasn't got the degree, he should find the work in the IT.

7 Work in pairs. First discuss why the words in **bold** are used in the following sentences, and then talk about the subjects themselves.

- **The** first thing you remember
- **The** most frightening or **the** most exciting thing that has happened to you
- **A** job you'd like to do
- **The** advantages and disadvantages of being single (or married)

Vocabulary
Word formation

1 What are the noun forms for each of these verbs from the article about Alex the parrot?

> apologise   communicate   conclude   convince
> describe   perform   propose   prosper   suspect

2 What are the verbs related to these nouns from the article?

> assumption   behaviour   combination   evolution
> explanation   progress   response

3 Some words, like *progress* and *suspect*, can be nouns or verbs.

- If they are used as verbs, the stress is on the second syllable: *Some researchers sus'pect that Alex's abilities are no more than a circus trick.*
- If they are used as nouns, the stress is on the first syllable: *Investigating the case of the strange phone message, police consider a parrot to be the prime 'suspect.*

Make pairs of sentences using these words as verbs and nouns. Then say or read your sentences to a partner, putting the stress in the right place.

> contest   convict   increase   insult   export   present
> produce   progress   protest   rebel   refuse   reject

⮕ page 181 Language reference: Word formation

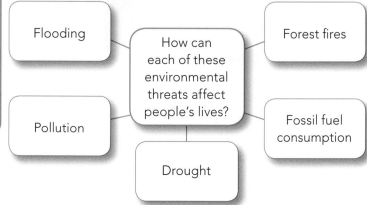

3 Read these Part 3 written prompts and spend a few moments thinking about possible answers.

Flooding

How can each of these environmental threats affect people's lives?

Forest fires

Pollution

Fossil fuel consumption

Drought

Speaking | Part 3

1 Do the exercise in the Exam round-up box.

Exam round-up

Circle the correct alternative in *italics*.

In Speaking Part 3
1 you speak to *your partner* / *the examiner*
2 you will be given a set of *pictures* / *written prompts* to talk about
3 you and your partner will be expected to talk for *three* / *four* minutes
4 communication skills are *more* / *less* important than expressing correct opinions
5 you *must* / *need not* agree with your partner.

2 Look at the three photos showing environmental problems. Discuss these questions.

1 What problems do the photos show? Make a two-word phrase for each photo by choosing words from this list.

air clearance conditions consumption damage
drought fires flood forest fossil fuel pollution
rainforest

2 Use the remaining words in the list to make phrases for three other environmental problems.
3 To what extent are humans to blame for the problems?

4 ▶ 19 Listen to two candidates discussing the prompts in Exercise 3.

1 How well do they describe how the five threats can affect people's lives?
2 How could their discussion be improved?

5 ▶ 20 Now listen to the examiner's final instruction in Part 3 and the discussion that follows. Do the candidates reach agreement?

6 Work in pairs. Discuss the prompts in Exercise 3.

• Try to describe clearly how the threats can affect people's lives.
• Include some of the compound nouns in the list below in your discussions.

• fire risk   fire damage   insurance costs
• desert region   water shortage   crop failure
• rainforest   farmland   cash crops
• exhaust fumes   vehicle emissions   factory chimneys breathing difficulties
• flood water(s)   flood defences   river banks
• oil rig   fuel consumption   fuel shortage(s)

• Finally, try to reach agreement about which environmental problem poses the greatest threat.

Reading and Use of English
Part 3

1 Make as many words as you can from the 'root' words in the box.

> ~~able~~ friend help know live move nation sense

Example

able: ability, inability, disability, enable, disable, unable, disabled, ably

2 Each of these sentences contain at least one word with an incorrect suffix or prefix. Correct the mistakes.

1 Some people find it inpossible to sleep if they drink coffee late at night.
2 Demonstraters are trying to unstabilise the government's environmental policies.
3 I've got terrible backache – that chair was so discomfortable.
4 Be caring with that parcel – the present inside is breakible.
5 Poor service in the restaurant was the main cause of our unsatisfaction.
6 Paul's such a creative person – he's always full of innovatant ideas.
7 Stop trying to mistract me. Can't you see I'm busy?
8 It's not that I disbelieve you, but I hope you know what you're doing – not all mushrooms are edable.

3 Read the text *Species loss accelerating*. For questions 1–8, use the word given in capitals at the end of some of the lines to form a word that fits in the gap in the same line. There is an example at the beginning (0).

Species loss accelerating

An international report has shown that human **(0)** .....activities..... are destroying three animal or plant species every hour. This equals 150 species a day, and between 18,000 and 55,000 species a year. The main **(1)** .... of the report is that we must slow down the worst spate of extinctions since the **(2)** .... of the dinosaurs 65 million years ago. — ACT / FIND / APPEAR

Scientists and **(3)** .... have identified various threats to **(4)** .... and plants as diverse as right whales, Iberian lynxes, wild potatoes and peanuts. Global warming is adding to existing threats such as land **(5)** .... for farms or cities, pollution, and rising human populations. To deal with these challenges, we need to move rapidly, and with more **(6)** .... at all levels – global, **(7)** .... and local. — ENVIRONMENT / CREATE / CLEAR / DETERMINE / NATION

Many experts believe that the world will fail to meet the target, set by political leaders some years ago, of a major **(8)** .... in the rate of loss by next year. Rates of species loss are currently rising by more than a thousand times natural rates. — REDUCE

4 Discuss these questions in pairs or groups.

1 What other species of plants or animals are in danger of becoming extinct?
2 What can international organisations, national governments and individuals do to slow down the rate at which species are becoming extinct?

Writing | Part 2
A proposal

1 Do the exercise in the Exam round-up box.

2 Work in pairs. Read this Part 2 writing task and then follow the instructions below.

> You see this announcement from an environmental agency in a local newspaper.
>
> > We are running a campaign to persuade organisations in our town to use resources more carefully and to reduce waste. The agency invites you to submit a proposal outlining the current situation in an organisation that you know well and to suggest ways in which this situation could be improved. We will provide financial support for approved proposals.
>
> Write your **proposal** in 220–260 words.

1 Think about an organisation you know well. It could be a club, college, office or shop. What kind of resources is this organisation currently wasting? Think of materials, such as paper, and less visible resources, such as electricity.

2 Make a list of things that individual members of this organisation could do to reduce waste. Start with simple things that everyone can do, like turning lights off at night, and then go on to more radical actions, like working from home on one day a week.

3 Read the sample proposal and discuss these questions.

1 Has the writer dealt fully with all parts of the task? Is there factual information as well as suggestions?

2 Is the proposal clearly organised?

Introduction

The purpose of this proposal is to suggest ways in which my college could use resources more carefully and reduce wastage. I will suggest a range of measures to achieve this.

Paper

The college currently uses twice as much printing paper as it did two years ago. This is despite the fact that information is stored on computers. Any unnecessary use of paper affects the environment in two ways: firstly by using valuable resources, and secondly by posing a waste disposal problem. I suggest that in future no documents should be printed unless there is a good reason for doing so, and students should be required to submit assignments electronically.

Electricity

Currently, many lights, heaters and computers are not turned off when no one is in the building. Televisions and other electrical equipment are left on stand-by overnight, adding to the college's energy consumption. Students and staff should be reminded to turn off all lights and equipment when they are not needed.

Travel

It is well known that some students are making unnecessary journeys to college by car or motorbike. This adds to our energy consumption. I recommend that students should be advised not to come to the college unless they have classes, and public transport or bicycles should be used where this is possible. In addition to this, staff might consider working from home on at least one day per week.

Conclusion

I believe that if all the suggested measures were implemented, the college would be able to reduce wastage by at least 20% every year.

4 What do the words and phrases in *italics* refer to in these extracts from the sample proposal?

1 The college currently uses twice as much printing paper as *it* did two years ago.
2 *This* is despite the fact that information is stored on computers.
3 I suggest that in future no documents should be printed unless there is a good reason for *doing so*.
4 Students and staff should be reminded to turn off all lights and equipment when *they* are not needed.
5 *This* adds to our energy consumption.
6 Students should be advised not to come to the college unless *they* have classes.
7 Public transport or bicycles should be used where *this* is possible.

Why are reference words like these used?

5 Work in pairs.

1 Identify all the passive verbs in the sample proposal.
2 Discuss why the passive has been used in preference to the active.
3 Which of the following sentences could be rewritten using passive verbs?
  a We need to encourage people to use the recycling bins.
  b If they replaced the air conditioning system, they would waste less electricity.
  c The problem has become worse over the past year.
  d The builders should have insulated the roof when they constructed the building.
  e I believe all residents will agree with this proposal.
  f At present no one is taking the problem seriously enough.
  g Engineers have been developing more efficient forms of solar heating.
4 Rewrite the sentences you have identified and say why the others cannot be changed.

6 Read this writing task and follow the steps below.

> You see this announcement on the notice board of your local council.
>
> > The Environmental Planning Committee is organising a campaign to make our town more 'green'. You are invited to submit a proposal related to your neighbourhood. Present some factual information about the area, pointing out any relevant environmental issues, and suggest practical measures which individuals and families could take to make the neighbourhood more green.
>
> Write your **proposal** in 220–260 words.

1 Underline the key ideas in the task.
2 Write brief notes under these headings:
  • Facts about the current situation
  • Suggestions for improvements (number these in order of priority)
3 Make a paragraph plan and think of suitable headings.
4 Write your proposal, using passive verbs where appropriate and any phrases from the following list that may be useful.

> buy local produce   dispose of rubbish responsibly
> recycle waste   save energy   share car journeys
> switch to natural energy   use public transport

➡ page 190 Writing reference: Proposals

Vocabulary and grammar review Unit 11

Vocabulary

1 Complete each sentence with the correct form of one of the phrasal verbs from the box.

> call off   call up   drop out   pay up   put off   sign up

1 Helen has a bit of free time and has decided to .... for a cookery course.
2 I tried to .... Francesca .... , but she'd got her phone turned off.
3 The conference has been .... because not enough people are interested in attending.
4 Paul was supposed to come travelling with us but he had to .... at the last minute.
5 Mikhail has had to .... his holiday till next month because he has too much work on at the moment.
6 They owe us a lot of money and unless they .... soon, we'll take them to court.

2 Complete each of the sentences below with a phrase or expression from the box.

> get your hands on   kept waiting   nothing to do with
> out of touch   sick and tired of   the whole point of
> without a trace

1 What I call real travelling has .... the holiday trips that most tourists tend to go on.
2 With smart phones and internet cafés, there's no excuse for being .... when travelling nowadays.
3 I'm a busy man and I hate being .... by people who are late.
4 I'm .... people phoning me to sell me things and interrupting my work.
5 If you travel with a group, you miss .... travelling, which is to have completely new experiences and meet completely new people.
6 He disappeared .... somewhere in the Pacific, some weeks after setting off in a small boat to sail round the world.
7 If you can .... a good grammar book, it should help you a lot with your exam preparation.

3 Complete these sentences by writing *at, in* or *on* in each of the gaps.

1 I'll be waiting .... the news stand when you arrive.
2 Did you see Ferenc .... the conference?
3 Samya is .... her third year .... university.
4 Don't interrupt me while I'm .... the phone!
5 We do all our shopping .... that big new shopping centre .... the outskirts of town.
6 I'd love to spend my holidays .... a Pacific island!

Grammar

4 Complete the second sentence so that it has a similar meaning to the first, using the word given. Do not change the word given. You must use between three and six words, including the word given.

1 Dieter missed the plane because he overslept.
   WOULD
   If Dieter had .... missed the plane.
2 Nelson didn't get the job because when he came to his job interview, he arrived late.
   TIME
   If Nelson .... his job interview, he would have got the job.
3 Eva couldn't apply for the job in IT because she knows that her computer skills aren't good enough.
   BETTER
   Eva knows that if her computer skills .... for the job in IT.
4 Could you please refund my money as soon as possible?
   GRATEFUL
   I .... would refund my money as soon as possible.
5 We would have gone swimming if Bruno hadn't advised us not to.
   FOR
   If it .... , we would have gone swimming.
6 I am only participating in this activity because my teacher asked me to.
   PART
   I .... this activity if my teacher had not asked me to.

Vocabulary and grammar review Unit 12

Vocabulary

1 Use the word given in capitals to form a word that fits in the gap in each of these sentences.

1 I don't know why everyone's being so .... towards me. I've done nothing wrong. FRIEND
2 Global warming is one of the world's most serious .... problems. ENVIRONMENT
3 It can be difficult for people with certain .... to find a job. ABLE
4 She has an extensive .... of French history. KNOW
5 You can tell from his .... that he spends a lot of money on clothes. APPEAR
6 In this job you have to be original and to think .... CREATE
7 I hope my solicitor will be able to .... my legal situation. CLEAR
8 Yesterday there was a sudden downward .... in share prices. MOVE

2 Two of these sentences are correct, but the others contain mistakes with prepositions. Correct the mistakes.

1 Over a hundred thousand people participated with yesterday's marathon.
2 Whether we go skiing or not depends to the weather and the state of the snow.
3 Do you have anything useful to contribute in our discussion?
4 This morning's lecture will focus on Picasso's early work.
5 You needn't fill in that section of the form – it doesn't apply for you.
6 If the CD doesn't play properly, I'd take it back to the shop and insist for a refund.
7 Can you turn the TV down? I can't concentrate to what you're saying.
8 Do you believe in supernatural phenomena?

Grammar

3 Complete this text with *a/an, the* or Ø (no article).

For some years, **(1)** .... global warming, which is the gradual heating of **(2)** .... Earth, was **(3)** .... topic of heated debate in **(4)** .... scientific community, but today the consensus among **(5)** .... researchers is that **(6)** .... phenomenon is real and is caused by **(7)** .... human activity, primarily **(8)** .... burning of fossil fuels that pump **(9)** .... carbon dioxide and **(10)** .... other greenhouse gases into **(11)** .... atmosphere. Scientists have found that the number and severity of **(12)** .... extreme weather events, which include high or low temperatures and intense storms, are **(13)** .... effective measure of **(14)** .... climate change and global warming. Indeed it is now agreed that global warming will have **(15)** .... far-reaching and, in many cases, devastating consequences for **(16)** .... planet.

4 Read the text below and think of the word that best fits each gap. Use only one word in each gap.

What is biofuel?

A biofuel is a hydrocarbon **(0)** ....that.... is made by or from a living organism that humans can use **(1)** .... power something. This definition of a biofuel is rather formal. **(2)** .... practice, any hydrocarbon fuel that is produced from organic matter in a short period of time is considered a biofuel. This contrasts **(3)** .... fossil fuels, which take millions of years to form, and with other types of fuel which are **(4)** .... based on hydrocarbons – nuclear fission, for instance.

What makes biofuels tricky to understand is that they **(5)** .... not be made by a living organism. Biofuels can also be made through chemical reactions, carried **(6)** .... in a laboratory or industrial setting that uses organic matter to make fuel. **(7)** .... only real requirements for a biofuel are that the starting material must be CO_2 that was fixed by a living organism and the final fuel product must be produced quickly **(8)** .... than over millions of years.

Starting off

1 Work in pairs. Use words from the box to describe the health advantages and disadvantages of the following.

1 doing sport or other physical activities
2 having childhood vaccinations
3 living in a rural area
4 living in a city

ache allergy blister bruise contagious disease
fracture immunity infection muscles sprain sting
venomous

2 Discuss these questions.

• Which do you think has a greater influence on someone's health, their lifestyle or their genes?
• What do you do to make sure you stay healthy and fit?

Listening | Part 3

1 Before starting Listening Part 3, do the exercise in the Exam round-up box.

Exam round-up

Circle the correct alternative in *italics* for each of the statements below.

In Listening Part 3
1 you will hear a *monologue / conversation*
2 the recording lasts approximately *two / four* minutes
3 you have to answer *six / eight* multiple-choice questions
4 there are *three / four* alternative answers for each question
5 the correct alternative will *express the same ideas / use the same words* as the recording.
6 you should read the questions *before / after* you listen for the first time
7 you should choose an answer *while the speaker is talking / after the speaker has finished talking*.

2 Work in pairs. You are going to hear a radio phone-in programme on the subject of allergies. Before you listen, discuss questions 1–3 using these words and phrases: *allergen, asthma, immune system, pollen*.

1 Do you think more people suffer from allergies now than in the past?
2 What percentage of the population do you think has an allergy?
3 What aspects of modern life can increase the chance of people suffering from allergies?

3 ▶21 Listen to the recording and check your answers to the questions in Exercise 2.

4 Now read these questions. How many can you already answer?

1 Which of these explanations for the possible increase in allergies does the programme presenter mention in her introduction?

A People are exposed to more pollen and other substances causing allergies than in the past.

B People's resistance to substances which cause allergies is lower than in the past.

C New allergy-causing substances are being released into the atmosphere.

D Higher levels of stress have made people more prone to allergies.

2 Which of these questions does the first caller, Tim, want to know the answer to?

A What is the cause of his allergy?

B Why is he allergic to grass and pollen?

C Will he ever be free of the allergy?

D How can he improve his condition?

3 According to the doctor,

A allergies are most likely to affect the very young.

B allergies often start between the ages of thirteen and twenty.

C allergies can start at any age.

D some elderly people are immune to allergies.

4 Arabella, the caller from Amsterdam,

A thinks she may have passed on her allergy to her children.

B asks how she can minimise the risk of her children having allergies.

C wants to know whether her peanut allergy will persist.

D wants to know if her allergy can be inherited.

5 According to the doctor, if one parent has a particular allergy, that child

A will probably have the same allergy.

B has no higher risk than any other child of developing that allergy.

C could develop a different allergy.

D is at a slightly higher risk of developing an allergy than any other child.

6 According to the doctor, some people believe that the main reason more young children are suffering from asthma is because

A modern buildings are centrally heated or air-conditioned.

B of toxic emissions from cars and other vehicles.

C they spend too much time in hygienic environments.

D of medicines used to treat illnesses.

5 ▶21 Listen to the recording again. For questions 1–6 choose the answer (A, B, C or D) which fits best according to what you hear.

6 Work in pairs.

1 Would you be prepared to do without air conditioning and central heating if you were sure that this would lead to a reduction in allergies?

2 Do you agree that our modern culture is obsessive about cleanliness?

Vocabulary
Prepositions following adjectives

1 Complete these extracts from Listening Part 3 with the correct prepositions.

1 These days we're all too familiar .... the word *allergy*.

2 I'm allergic .... pollen from grass and certain trees.

3 Vaccinations may make children less resistant .... allergens.

4 We are getting better .... diagnosing and treating some allergies.

5 Some experts believe that in this modern age we're obsessed .... cleanliness.

2 👁 Exam candidates often make mistakes with prepositions after adjectives. Seven of the following sentences contain mistakes and one is correct. Correct the mistakes.

1 We sincerely apologise and hope this 10% discount will be acceptable by you.

2 Drivers exceeding the speed limit are responsible for 90% of accidents in the city.

3 I am delighted for your invitation and look forward to seeing you at the event.

4 Living on the outskirts of the city is very convenient to the motorway system.

5 Teachers should try to be sensitive for the needs of their students.

6 That part of the stadium is closed for visitors – it's for athletes only.

7 She is someone who isn't aware with what is going on in the news.

8 I hope you will be capable to putting your plans into practice.

➡ page 167 Language reference: Dependent prepositions

Grammar
Ways of contrasting ideas

1 In these extracts from Listening Part 3, underline words and phrases used to point out a contrast between two facts or ideas.

 1 Someone who was allergic to eggs would find it fairly easy to avoid eating anything containing eggs, whereas you would find it impossible to avoid all contact with pollen.

 2 I have to be really careful about foods which contain peanuts, but what I'd like to know is …

 3 In the case of your child, this would rise to 20%. However, if the child's father also had an allergy, this risk would increase to 40%.

 4 Even though we are getting better at diagnosing and treating some allergies, there is a year-on-year increase in the number of patients with asthma.

 5 Some experts believe we're obsessed with cleanliness, while others believe that vaccinations to protect our children may actually weaken their immune system.

2 Work in pairs. Discuss these questions about the words/phrases you have underlined in Exercise 1.

 1 Which words or phrases contrast facts or ideas in a single sentence?

 2 Of these, which words or phrases must be placed between the two clauses?

 3 Which word is an adverb which contrasts facts or ideas in separate sentences?

 4 What other contrasting words and phrases do you know?

 5 Which words or phrases could replace *whereas* and *even though* in sentences 1 and 4?

➡ page 180 Language reference: Ways of contrasting ideas

3 Complete the following sentences using words from the box.

> although   but   even though   however   whereas

 1 I recognised you as soon as I saw you, ... we'd never met before.

 2 Some people seem to enjoy cold, rainy weather, ... I'm not one of them.

 3 Adults can be slow to learn new skills, ... children pick things up very quickly.

 4 We thought the case was over. .... , new evidence has just come to light.

 5 .... I've been here twice before, I'd forgotten where the post office was.

4 We can also use *despite / in spite of (the fact that)* to express contrast. Which two sentences in Exercise 3 can you change to use one of these, and what other changes would you have to make?

5 ⊙ Exam candidates sometimes make mistakes in their use of link words for contrast. Find and correct the mistakes in each of these sentences. (There are several possible ways of correcting them.)

 1 Despite you are not a mechanic, you should learn to understand how cars work.

 2 There are several kinds of snacks you can have between 9.00 am and 6.00 pm, however hot meals are limited to lunchtime.

 3 However he was usually a very efficient teacher, he wasn't available when I needed this information.

 4 I appreciate being asked to give this talk again. Though I would like to suggest ways of improving this year's event.

 5 We used to have only a few TV channels, where nowadays we have many more choices.

 6 While he left school at the age of sixteen, he went on to become one of the most famous politicians of his generation.

6 Complete these sentences with your own endings.

 1 I don't mind going to the dentist, but …

 2 I realise that it's very important to keep fit. However, …

 3 Whereas most people I know go to the gym at least twice a week, I …

 4 Even though many people eat better food than they did a hundred years ago, …

Speaking | Part 2

1 Do the exercise in the Exam round-up box.

> **Exam round-up**
>
> Say if the following statements are true (T) or false (F). If a statement is false, rewrite it to make it true.
>
> In Speaking Part 2
> 1 you have to speak about three photos
> 2 you have to answer three questions about the photos
> 3 each candidate has to speak for one minute
> 4 you should not try to describe the photos in detail
> 5 you have to answer a question on your partner's photos
> 6 if you notice that you've made a mistake, don't correct it.

2 Work in pairs. Look at the six photos and discuss these questions.

1 What do all six photos have in common?
2 Which of these activities are popular with people in your country? How would you explain this?

3 Work in pairs. Read the examiner's instruction for the photos in Set A.

> Here are your pictures. They show people involved in physical activities. I'd like you to compare two of the activities, and say how effective the activities are as a means of keeping fit, and why they are so popular.

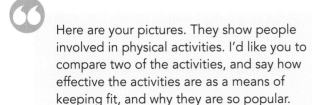

Student A: Talk about two photos for one minute, with Student B listening.

Student B: You then answer this question: *Which groups of people get the most benefit from activities like these?*

Set A

- How effective are these activities as a means of keeping fit?
- Why are the activities so popular?

4 Now read this instruction for the photos in Set B.

> Here are your pictures. They show people involved in demanding physical activities. I'd like you to compare two of the activities, and say what qualities a person needs to succeed in them, and why people want to participate in them.

Student B: Talk about two photos for one minute, with Student A listening.

Student A: You then answer this question: *How are activities like these different from sports like football or basketball?*

5 ▶ 22 Listen to two candidates doing the tasks.

1 Which candidate does the task more successfully?
2 What advice would you give each candidate to help them do better next time?

Set B

- What qualities does a person need to succeed in these activities?
- Why do people want to participate in them?

Reading and Use of English | Part 8

1 Before starting the reading task, do the exercise in the Exam round-up box.

2 Look at the photos of sports and discuss these questions in pairs.

  1 Do you know the names of these sports? What similar sports do you know?
  2 What kinds of sports are they? For teams or individuals? For men, women or both? Where are they played?
  3 What are the most popular sports in your country? Who plays them? Are they mainly amateur or professional?

3 Read questions 1–10 below and underline the key idea in each one.

Which sport

allows players to hit a ball with equipment and parts of their body?	1
is based on a traditional native sport?	2
allows players to use their bodies to obstruct their opponents?	3
makes the wearing of protective equipment optional?	4
disapproves of players looking at what they are doing?	5
often receives funding from business?	6
is not played all the year round?	7
is played mainly for pleasure and relaxation?	8
has a ball which is designed to be picked up easily?	9
involves contestants holding on to part of each other's clothing?	10

4 Now quickly read through the texts about national sports. Are any of the five sports described similar to the ones in the photos you discussed?

5 Read the texts again. For questions 1–10 above, choose the correct sport (A–E). Sports may be chosen more than once.

Unusual national sports

A **Glíma** is by far the oldest form of wrestling in Iceland. The most widespread version of the sport is Brokartök glíma, in which two wrestlers attempt to trip and throw each other by grasping a belt worn around their opponent's waist and thighs. To win, a wrestler must make his opponent touch the ground with a part of his body between the elbow and the knee. Wrestlers have to stand straight and are not allowed to fall on their opponents or to push them down by force. Most importantly, when they are fighting they should always look over each other's shoulders, because it is considered more gentlemanly to wrestle by touch and feel than by sight. This form of glíma has always been a friendly recreational sport, but there are other versions which are played much more violently.

B **Hurling** is an outdoor sport played mainly in Ireland. Players use an axe-shaped wooden stick, called a hurley, to hit a small ball between the other team's goalposts, either over or under the crossbar. Fewer points are scored if the ball goes over the crossbar. The ball can be caught in the hand and carried for no more than four steps, or hit in the air or on the ground with the stick. It can also be kicked or slapped with an open hand. A player who wants to carry the ball further than three steps has to bounce or balance it on the end of the stick. No special clothing or padding is worn by players, but a plastic helmet with a faceguard is recommended.

C The official national sport of Argentina is **Pato**, a game which is played on horseback and combines elements of two other sports: polo and basketball. The sport, which is thought to have begun over four hundred years ago, consists of two teams of four members each. Teams fight for possession of a ball which has six conveniently sized handles, and score by throwing the ball through vertically positioned rings, located at the top of three-metre-high poles. A closed net, extending downwards, holds the ball after goals are scored. The winning team is the one with the most goals scored after six periods of eight minutes. The word *pato* is the Spanish for *duck*, as in the past, instead of using a ball, a live duck was used inside a basket.

D **Lacrosse** is an outdoor team sport in which players use netted sticks to pass and catch a hard rubber ball. The aim is to score goals by propelling the ball into the opponent's goal. The team which scores more goals wins. Lacrosse is Canada's national summer sport and is also becoming more and more popular in the USA. Each team is composed of ten players: three attackers, three midfielders, three defenders and one goaltender. In men's lacrosse, players wear protective equipment on their heads, shoulders, arms and hands, as body-checking is an integral part of the men's game and stick-checks to the arms and hands are considered legal.

E **Tejo** is a Colombian sport in which players hurl a metallic plate weighing around two kilograms through the air to try to hit a clay-filled box with gunpowder in the middle. When the disc hits this target, there is a loud explosion. Whichever team causes more explosions wins. Turmeque, a much more ancient version of the sport, has been played for over 500 years by the indigenous groups living in the different parts of Colombia. The modern game itself is no different from this, except that today players use a metal disc rather than one made of gold or stone. Nowadays in Colombia it is very common to find professional tejo teams in the major cities and towns. Most teams are sponsored by local companies.

6 Which words or phrases in the texts gave you the information you needed to answer the questions?

Example

1 equipment: wooden stick (hurley),
  parts of the body: foot (kicked), hand (slapped with the open hand)

7 Work in pairs. Which of the five sports you have read about would you like to try? Are there any you would refuse to play? Give your reasons.

Grammar
The language of comparison

1 Complete these extracts from Reading and Use of English Part 8. Then check your answers in the texts.

1 Glíma is by .... form of wrestling in Iceland.

2 .... ,when they are fighting, they should always look over each other's shoulders,

3 It is considered .... to wrestle by touch and feel than by sight.

4 There are other versions (of glíma) which are played ....

5 .... are scored if the ball goes over the crossbar.

6 The ball can be caught in the hand and carried for .... four steps,

7 A player who wants to carry the ball .... three steps has to bounce or balance it on the end of stick.

8 The winning team is the one with .... goals scored after six periods of eight minutes.

9 Lacrosse is also becoming .... popular in the USA.

10 The team which scores .... goals wins.

11 Turmeque, a .... version of the sport, …

12 The modern game itself is .... from this.

2 Answer these questions about the language of comparison used in the extracts above.

1 What kinds of words can follow *more* and *most*?

2 *More* has two opposites: *less* and *fewer*. How are these words used differently? What kinds of words can follow each?

3 Look at the negative comparison in sentence 6. Can you think of a way of rephrasing it?

4 What does the phrase *by far* add to the meaning of a superlative adjective? Compare these sentences:
He's **the brightest** student in the class.
He's **by far the brightest** student in the class.

5 How can we add *very* to qualify *different* in this sentence?
The modern game is no different from this.

6 What is the opposite of *much* in this sentence?
I'm feeling **much** better now.

→ page 171 Language reference: The language of comparison

3 Rewrite these sentences, using the words in brackets.

1 Many people don't earn as much money as they did five years ago. (*less*)

2 Finding a new job was easier than I expected it to be. (*difficult*)

3 I've never seen a funnier film than that. (*funniest*)

4 There aren't as many unemployed people today as there were ten years ago. (*fewer*)

5 Working conditions are worse than they used to be. (*good*)

6 Petrol is become increasingly expensive. (*more and*)

4 ⦿ Exam candidates sometimes make mistakes in their use of comparative words. Find and correct the mistakes in these sentences.

1 I think a female boss is far much understanding than a male boss.

2 Actually, eating junk food is even worst for your health than smoking.

3 The other actor wasn't as handsome like James.

4 I noticed that there were less angry people than there had been a year ago.

5 Easily the harder thing about football for me is the training I have to do.

6 If you travel at night, you'll find there is fewer traffic on the roads.

7 This will make the problem of obesity difficult even more.

8 If you learn English, you will have much fewer problems when you travel abroad.

5 Compare the food in these photos in different ways, using words from the box.

Nouns: a balanced diet   calories   cholesterol   fat   fibre   minerals   protein   seafood   vitamins

Adjectives: appetising   fattening   greasy   (un)healthy   low-fat   oily   tasty

Verbs: diet   lose weight

Reading and Use of English
Part 3

1 Do the exercise in the Exam round-up box.

2 Some of the given words in Part 3 tasks are root words to which you have to add a prefix or a suffix or both, e.g. *APPEAR → appearance, disappear, disappearance.* But you have to make more complex changes to other root words, e.g. *DESTROY → destruction, destructive, indestructible.*

Complete this table with words related to the root verbs 1–9. Often more than one word is possible.

verb	noun	adjective	adverb
1 destroy	destruction destroyer	destructive indestructible	destructively
2 intend			
3 apply			
4 explode			
5 advise			
6 know			
7 repeat			
8 include			
9 describe			

3 For questions 1–8, read the text below. Use the word given in capitals at the end of some of the lines to form a word that fits the gap in the same line. There is an example at the beginning.

Why I run

I started running when I was thirteen. I was
(0) ....immediately....... intoxicated with a beginner's   IMMEDIATE
enthusiasm: the special thrill of physical exertion,
and a feeling that my body had **(1)** ....   LIMIT
energy. I tried to maximise every moment on that
first run and then had to hobble around for a week,
almost **(2)** .... of moving. But once the   CAPABLE
(3) .... diminished I was back out there,   SORE
running again. I was hooked.

As with the acquisition of any skill, there were
various stages of **(4)** .... , competence   INVOLVE
and **(5)** .... Now that I've been running   SATISFY
for over 25 years, and have spent a great deal of time
helping others incorporate running into their lives,
I see a similar pattern of **(6)** .... in   EVOLVE
just about all runners. Progress is a matter of
maturing and knowing yourself; one stage leads
(7) .... to the next.   LOGIC

Not everyone has the same aspirations. But
understanding the experience common to most
veteran runners will **(8)** .... you to   ABLE
maximise the gains of your running future.

Adapted from *The Five Stages of a Runner*

4 Discuss these questions in pairs or groups.
1 How much exercise do you do a day or a week? What kind of exercise do you do?
2 What is your main reason for exercising? Do you enjoy it?
3 If you were told you needed to do more regular exercise, what would you do?

Writing | Part 2
A letter

1 Do the exercise in the Exam round-up box.

2 Read this writing task and make brief notes on the three bulleted points as if you were going to write this letter.

> You belong to a small sports club and have been asked by other members to write a letter of complaint to the club manager. Your letter should include the following:
>
> • why club members are not satisfied with the club and the way it is organised
> • how the club could be improved
> • what may happen if improvements are not made
>
> Write your **letter**.

3 Read Marek's letter, without paying attention to the alternatives in *italics*. Does the letter cover all parts of the task?

4 Work in pairs. Look at the structure of the letter. What is the topic of each paragraph?

5 A letter like this should be written in a style which is not too informal. Circle the appropriate words and phrases in *italics* in Marek's letter.

Dear Sir,

I am writing on behalf of a number of members of the sports club who are [1]*concerned about / fed up with* the club and [2]*the way it is being run / how you run it.*

It has been clear to us for [3]*quite a while / some time* that we have a membership problem. The club, which I visit regularly, has been [4]*noticeably less busy / pretty empty* in recent months. In the view of members, there are two possible explanations for this decline. [5]*For a start, / Firstly,* we believe that some members are joining other clubs with more state-of-the-art facilities. Secondly, the cost of membership at the club appears to be high compared with other clubs [6]*in the area / round here.*

As to what action can be taken, our main suggestions are for all the club's gym equipment to be replaced and for management to [7]*change / adjust* the cost of membership. While the charge for adult members could remain the same, reduced fees could be [8]*brought in / introduced* for [9]*old people / retired people*. There could also be a new family rate to encourage parents to come with their children. We also believe that the tennis courts should be resurfaced, because they have been neglected for several years. They are now not fit for purpose.

We believe that if these improvements are not made soon, more members will vote with their feet and move to other clubs on a permanent basis. We trust that you will [10]*think about / consider* our ideas and we would be grateful if you could look into making the improvements we have suggested [11]*as soon as possible / very soon.*

Yours faithfully,

Marek Novák

6 What is the meaning of the expressions in **bold** in these extracts?

1 I am writing **on behalf of** a number of members
2 clubs with more **state-of-the-art** facilities
3 The tennis courts are now **not fit for purpose**.
4 more members will **vote with their feet**

7 Find phrases that are used in Marek's letter to introduce

- explanations for the decline in membership
- suggestions for solving the problem.

8 Read the following writing task and discuss questions 1–3 below.

> It has recently been announced that your area will receive funding for a range of new sports and fitness facilities for young people. Your council is inviting residents from the area to write letters suggesting how the funds should best be spent. Your letter should explain:
>
> - why this funding is to be welcomed
> - what facilities should be provided
> - how the new facilities will make a difference to young people in the area.
>
> Write your **letter**.

1 When you see the phrase 'young people', what age range do you think of?
2 What facilities are currently available for this age group in your area?
3 What facilities are missing? Assuming that there is not enough money for every possible improvement, make a list of the top three new facilities in order of importance.

9 Before you start your letter, make a paragraph plan. Then write your letter using appropriate language. Use some of the language for explanations and suggestions from Exercise 7.

➡ page 192 Writing reference: Emails and letters

14 Moving abroad

Starting off

1 Work in pairs.

1 Why do people migrate? Think of as many reasons as you can.
2 Would you like to migrate? If so, why and where? If not, why not?

2 ▶ 23 You are going to hear six people who have migrated talking about their experiences. Listen and match each person with the aspect of migration (A–H) that they mention. (There are two aspects you do not need.)

Speaker 1 ....   Speaker 4 ....

Speaker 2 ....   Speaker 5 ....

Speaker 3 ....   Speaker 6 ....

A I migrated to fulfil my ambitions.
B I encountered some negative attitudes to start with.
C I've felt homesick since I left.
D I find it difficult to stay in one place for long.
E I moved because of a relationship.
F I wanted a better environment for my children.
G I was fed up with the weather.
H I'm surprised how well my life has turned out.

3 Work in small groups.

1 Do you know anyone whose reasons for emigrating or experiences of emigrating are similar to the ones you've just heard?
2 How can emigration benefit
  • the country people emigrate from?
  • the country people immigrate to?

Grammar
Comment adverbials and intensifying adverbs

1 Look at this extract from Starting off. Which word or phrase in each sentence shows the speaker's attitude or opinion about what he says?

You see, unfortunately I'm one of those typical expatriates who spends two years working in this country and three years working in that. I don't think I could ever go back to my home country because, quite honestly, I just wouldn't fit in.

→ page 165 Language reference: Comment adverbials

2 Rewrite each sentence below, replacing the underlined words with a comment adverbial from the box in each gap.

apparently   fortunately   generally speaking   kindly
obviously   personally   to be honest   undoubtedly

1 <u>It's lucky that</u> she has a very supportive family.
.... , she has a very supportive family.

2 <u>I'm absolutely certain that</u> he's the best player.
He's .... the best player.

3 <u>Most of the time</u> the weather here is pleasant.
.... , the weather here is pleasant.

4 <u>I'm telling you the truth when I say that</u> I found the journey very uncomfortable.
.... , I found the journey very uncomfortable.

5 <u>From what I've heard</u>, Bill is thinking of emigrating to Canada.
.... , Bill is thinking of emigrating to Canada.

6 Anaya's parents have invited me to stay with them, <u>which is very kind of them</u>.
Anaya's parents have .... invited me to stay with them.

7 <u>It's clear that</u> he wasn't happy with the way he was treated.
.... , he wasn't happy with the way he was treated.

8 <u>To give you my opinion</u>, I wouldn't buy that car.
.... , I wouldn't buy that car.

3 ▶23 Listen again to the speakers in Starting off.

absolutely   completely   incredibly   totally   utterly

a Complete the sentences below by writing an intensifying adverb from the box in each gap.
b Say which other adverbs in the box could also be used for each gap.
c Decide how adding an intensifying adverb affects each sentence.

1 We were .... fed up with the crime and feeling of insecurity that surrounded us.
2 I was .... astonished to find that many people looked down on me when I first arrived.
3 I just found the short grey days and the continual rain .... depressing.
4 I'd be .... out of touch.
5 I've been .... lucky, though.

4 Complete these sentences by choosing the alternatives in *italics* which form a collocation. There may be one or two correct answers to each question.

The Japanese drummers' performance was **(1)** *extremely / utterly / absolutely* amazing. We'd never seen anything like it. The audience was **(2)** *absolutely / completely / totally* delighted and applauded for about ten minutes.

For immigrants, finding somewhere to live and work is **(3)** *totally / incredibly / perfectly* simple and presents no problem. The difficulty is integrating into the community because local people are **(4)** *absolutely / utterly / completely* indifferent to foreigners, so many of them end up feeling **(5)** *extremely / incredibly / perfectly* depressed.

Temperatures often rise above 40° C in the summer, so this heat is **(6)** *perfectly / incredibly / absolutely* normal. Many newcomers to this part of the world feel **(7)** *totally / extremely / utterly* exhausted by the end of the day unless they have air conditioning.

You'll need to work hard to learn the language because it's **(8)** *utterly / incredibly / totally* hard. However, if you persist, you'll find it isn't **(9)** *extremely / absolutely / incredibly* impossible and you will make progress.

Listening | Part 4

1 You will hear five short extracts in which people are talking about migrants and migration. Before you listen, do the exercise in the Exam round-up box.

2 ▶24 Listen and complete the two tasks.

TASK ONE

For questions **1–5**, choose from the list (**A–H**) the aspect of migration that each speaker is referring to.

A loss of local culture
B integration in schools
C changing eating habits
D finding accommodation
E mixed marriages
F communication problems
G sending money home
H starting a business

Speaker 1	1
Speaker 2	2
Speaker 3	3
Speaker 4	4
Speaker 5	5

TASK TWO

For questions **6–10**, choose from the list (**A–H**) the thing which has impressed each speaker the most.

A Employment is created.
B Families are divided.
C The quality of life improves.
D The cost of living rises.
E Standards are raised.
F Local people lose their jobs.
G Local people learn something new.
H Attitudes are more diverse.

Speaker 1	6
Speaker 2	7
Speaker 3	8
Speaker 4	9
Speaker 5	10

3 Work in small groups. Take turns to summarise what one of the speakers said. Each student should choose a different speaker.

- Before you speak, spend a minute or two thinking about what you are going to say.
- Try to use some of the comment adverbials from Grammar Exercise 2 on page 151 when you speak.

Vocabulary

learn, find out and *know; provide, offer* and *give*

1 Exam candidates often confuse *learn, find out* and *know*. Match the words with their definitions from the *Cambridge Advanced Learner's Dictionary*.

1 know	2 find out	3 learn

a to get information about something because you want to know more about it, or to acquire a fact or piece of information for the first time
b to get knowledge or skill in a new subject or activity
c to have the information in your mind

2 *Provide, offer* and *give* often have very similar meanings. However, sometimes their meanings are slightly different. When their meanings are different, which word, *provide* or *offer*, means

1 to give someone something they need?
2 to ask someone if they would like to have something or if they would like you to do something?

3 Complete each of these sentences written by exam candidates with *learn, find out, know, provide, offer* or *give* in the correct form.

1 I phoned a taxi company to .... the average rate from the airport to the city centre.
2 We will .... overnight accommodation if you miss the last train.
3 You should go to the information desk to .... where to pick up your luggage.
4 While studying English, you also .... about their customs and traditions.
5 I've checked the timetable to .... the time of the next train to Łódź.
6 The government should make an effort to .... more facilities in rural areas.
7 During the lecture, we .... how Turkish people lived in the past.
8 Comfy Catering Services aims to .... good food for students at low cost.
9 We feel that the authorities should be prepared to .... a solution to those parents who require one.
10 Studying at the Ace School in London will .... you the opportunity to make new friends and meet people.
11 I'm writing to complain about the service you .... during our stay in your hotel last weekend.
12 This watch is important to me because my parents .... it to me for my 18th birthday.

Reading and Use of English | Part 6

1 Do the exercise in the Exam round-up box.

Exam round-up

Answer these questions about Reading and Use of English Part 6.

1 How many texts does it contain and how many questions must you answer?
2 Should you read the questions before or after you read the texts for the first time? Why?
3 What does this part test your ability to do?

2 Work in small groups. You will read four extracts about immigration and cities. Before you read, discuss these questions.

1 How important is each of the areas below in ensuring successful integration of new immigrants?
   • language
   • employment
   • dress
   • adopting the host culture
2 What other areas do you think are important?

3 Read extracts A–D and answer these questions.

1 According to A, how have attitudes and policies to do with immigration changed recently?
2 According to B, how are cities defined and where in a city does successful integration occur?
3 According to C, what should local government's role be in encouraging integration?
4 According to D, what are the advantages and dangers of cultural diversity?

4 Academic texts may contain ideas expressed in complex ways. Decide what each of these sentences means. Choose either a or b.

1 *Successful integration is no coincidence.* (Extract A)
   a Integration can only be successful if it is planned.
   b Successful integration is the result of unlikely events happening at the same time.

2 *Cities and towns were starting to think differently about immigration.* (Extract A)
   a Cities and towns were changing their immigration policies.
   b Cities and towns no longer wished to accept new immigrants.

3 *The untapped potential of immigrants … had long been overlooked.* (Extract A)
   a People ignored immigrants because they were considered to be a nuisance.
   b The authorities did not realise that there were immigrants whose skills were not being used.

4 *There is now global competition for information technology professionals, creative artists and highly skilled individuals upon whom to place our hopes for future prosperity.* (Extract A)
   a Skilled and creative people are taking part in a worldwide competition to win jobs.
   b Countries depend on skilled people for their future wealth and therefore compete to attract them.

5 *More humans than ever now live outside their country of birth.* (Extract B)
   a The majority of people now emigrate.
   b There are more emigrants in the world than ever before.

6 *The well-being of cities depends on whether they can create an inclusive public culture.* (Extract B)
   a Cities will only prosper if they have a culture which encourages all inhabitants to participate.
   b Cities with museums, art galleries and theatres are healthier places to live.

7 *Past experience demonstrates that cultural diversity in itself is not a sufficient condition to bring about the sustained inclusion of the different groups that populate a city.* (Extract D)
   a We know from past experience that a policy of cultural diversity in a city will not always be successful over a long period of time.
   b We know from past experience that different cultural groups do not always wish to form part of a diverse culture and may wish to leave the city.

8 *Managing cultural exchanges among people and organisations, and dealing directly with inequities and discrimination are challenges that cities must face if they are to be socially inclusive and culturally diverse.* (Extract D)
   a Unless cities are socially inclusive and culturally diverse, they won't be able to manage their cultural exchanges or deal directly with inequities or discrimination.
   b Unless cities manage cultural exchanges among people and organisations, and deal directly with inequities and discrimination, cities will not be socially inclusive or culturally diverse.

5 Now do the exam task. For questions 1–4, choose from the extracts A–D. The extracts may be chosen more than once.

Which extract	
shares C's view on the relationship between employment and integration?	1
expresses a different view from the others regarding the possible outcome of immigration?	2
shares B's view concerning the role of public space in integration?	3
expresses a more specific view than the others of the type of people who might immigrate?	4

6 Work in groups.

1 Which of these statements do you agree with more?
   Particular cities thrive because they exemplify cultural diversity.
   Immigrants are attracted to particular cities because they are thriving.
2 The second paragraph of extract A appears to advocate a selective immigration policy. Do you think countries should select who they allow to immigrate?

Cities and immigration

Cities attract immigrants and need to ensure their successful integration.

A "We are rich and happy because we have so many immigrants," explained Wolfgang Schuster, Mayor of Stuttgart. This came as a surprise to the jury of Germany's first national competition on local integration policy. The competition "Successful integration is no coincidence – Strategies for community policy" showed that cities and towns were starting to think differently about immigration. Previously, integration and migration had been viewed as a nuisance, a peripheral issue, and, above all, as a problem. The untapped potential of immigrants and their economic and strategic significance had long been overlooked.

Following a phase of restrictive migration policy in many countries, the last few decades have seen more open immigration policies that focus on skilled labour. There is now global competition for information technology professionals, creative artists and highly skilled individuals upon whom to place our hopes for future prosperity. "Brain gain" rather than "brain drain" is the driving force in today's migration policies.

B "We are living in "the Age of Migration." More humans than ever now live outside their country of birth. More countries than ever are now major senders or receivers of migration flows. And whatever part of the world migrants move to, they overwhelmingly settle in cities.

Cities have always been composed of diverse populations with the interaction between different ethnic groups forming the essence of big city life for 3,000 years. By definition, cities are places that attract outsiders, and which constitute a meeting place between different cultures. On what terms do these different cultures converge in the modern city? The answer is that the well-being of cities now depends on whether they can create an inclusive public culture. Such successful integration may well begin on the street, as accepting diversity implies sharing public space.

C Successful cities are ones which value diversity and where local governments encourage conditions in which immigrants and all residents thrive. Thus as service providers, local governments are responsible for areas that affect our daily lives, such as schools, emergency services, swimming pools and soccer fields, parks and streets, while as democratic institutions, they draw on community input and create opportunities for all residents to participate in transparent and accountable decision-making.

Local governments also drive economic development to ensure that the city prospers. As major employers, they can institute good practices by hiring immigrants and managing a diverse workforce. As major buyers of goods and services, they can ensure that immigrant-owned or immigrant-friendly businesses have a fair chance to compete for public contracts. In these ways, local governments contribute to labour market integration and the success of local businesses across all sectors of the population.

D It has long been recognised that urban areas, especially large cities, are places where cultural diversity flourishes. Cities like New York, Paris, London and Amsterdam, which receive migrants from all over the world, exemplify the cultural, social, and religious diversity that many believe is a fundamental characteristic of places that will thrive –economically and socially – in an era of global interdependence.

Past experience demonstrates, however, that cultural diversity in itself is not a sufficient condition to bring about the sustained inclusion of the different groups that populate a city. The collapse into inter-ethnic conflict of some once relatively harmonious multicultural cities highlights the fragility of cultural diversity. Managing cultural exchanges among people and organisations, and dealing directly with inequities and discrimination are challenges that cities must face if they are to be socially inclusive and culturally diverse.

Speaking | Part 4

1 Do the exercise in the Exam round-up box.

2 Work in pairs. Which of the phrases in the box could you use when answering each of the questions below? (You can use some of the phrases with more than one answer.)

> cover people's basic needs   create cultural diversity
> encourage tolerance towards other ways of life
> help them integrate   live side by side
> open up people's minds   provide housing
> make the transition to a new society
> make society a richer place
> people from different backgrounds with different outlooks

1 What are the benefits of a multicultural society?
2 Should people who go to live in another country adopt the culture of that country? Why (not)?
3 How can governments help immigrants?

3 ▶25 Now check your answers by listening to Laura and Daniel.

4 ▶26 Complete these extracts from Laura and Daniel's answers by writing a modal verb (*can, may, should*, etc.) in each gap. Then check your answers by listening to the extracts.

1 I think it .... open up people's minds to other experiences that they .... not be able to have otherwise.
2 I personally think it .... make society itself richer by having diversity within it.
3 I think people .... be allowed to have some of the elements of their own culture as long as they're not detrimental to the good of the majority.
4 What they .... to do is provide lots of information at the beginning so that people .... make the transition to a new society.
5 Housing is something I think they .... be providing.

5 Work in pairs. Discuss your answers to the three questions in Exercise 2. Try to use some of the phrases from the box in Exercise 2 when you speak.

6 Work in pairs to discuss these questions.

1 Many companies expect their employees to be ready to move to different places and countries to work. Do you think everyone should be ready to move for their job? Why (not)?
2 How has your country changed in recent years as a result of immigration or emigration?
3 Some people suggest that immigrants should be obliged to learn the language of the country they go to. Do you agree?

Grammar
Cleft sentences for emphasis

1 Rewrite each of the sentences below beginning with the words given.

1 It was the climate I couldn't stand any longer.
   I couldn't …
2 What impressed me most was seeing their new in-laws learning how to cook new dishes.
   I was most impressed …
3 It's being away from your children and family that must be the worst thing.
   The worst thing …
4 What we've ended up with is quite a cultural mix in our office.
   We've ended up …
5 It's their ability to work hard that absolutely amazes me.
   I am …

➡ **page 165 Language reference:** Cleft sentences for emphasis

2 Express the ideas below in a more emphatic way by using cleft sentences starting with the words given.

1 I believe that young people benefit from living and working abroad. What I believe …

2 Many people move overseas because they don't like the climate in their own country. It's because …

3 Living in a multicultural society enriches our lives. What enriches …

4 I feel lonely living away from my family. It's living …

5 He doesn't do anything except listen to music in his room. All he does …

6 Franz learnt to speak the language perfectly by living in the country. It was …

7 A good education teaches tolerance. What a good education …

8 I just want to be able to visit my family again. All I want …

Reading and Use of English | Part 4

1 Do the exercise in the Exam round-up box.

Exam round-up

How much do you remember about Reading and Use of English Part 4? Complete the following sentences by writing one word from the list below in each space.

> word   contractions   change   same   number
> given   three   six

- There are (1) .... questions.
- You have to write between (2) .... and six words in each space, using the (3) .... given.
- (4) .... count as two words.
- You must not (5) .... the word given.

Read the question and decide what grammar and vocabulary you need. When you have finished, read your answer and check that

- it means the (6) .... as the original sentence
- you have used the correct (7) .... of words
- you haven't changed the word (8) ....

2 For the Part 4 question below, which is the correct answer: a, b, c or d? Why are the other answers incorrect?

Boris should have contacted us the moment he arrived.
TOUCH
Boris was supposed .... as soon as he arrived.

a getting in touch with us
b to get in touch with us
c to have got in touch with us
d to have made contact with us

3 For questions 1–4, complete the second sentence so that it has a similar meaning to the first sentence, using the word given. Do not change the word given. You must use between three and six words, including the word given. .

1 Could you remind me to phone Charlie on Friday?
GRATEFUL
I'd .... me to phone Charlie on Friday.
Clue: There are two parts to this answer: a request and an indirect question.

2 Mario managed to complete the project without any help.
ALL
Mario succeeded .... himself.
Clue: Use an expression which means 'alone'.

3 You won't get into the national team unless you try much harder.
MAKE
You'll have .... if you're going to get into the national team.
Clue: What noun can we use with 'make' to mean 'try hard'?

4 Fatima still hasn't decided if she'll study in New Zealand next year.
MIND
Fatima hasn't .... to study in New Zealand next year.
Clue: What expression with 'mind' means 'to decide'?

4 Now do this Part 4 task without clues.

1 It's possible that the heavy traffic is delaying Katya.
HOLDING
What may .... the heavy traffic.

2 I wasn't sure who was to blame for the accident.
FAULT
I couldn't tell .... was.

3 After Ranjit had discovered the truth, he reported the facts to the police.
OUT
Having .... , Ranjit reported the facts to the police.

4 Franz didn't get to the office until lunchtime.
NOT
It .... Karl got to the office.

5 Many people were discouraged from emigrating by the idea of crossing the Atlantic.
OFF
What .... the idea of crossing the Atlantic.

6 Many of the emigrants first saw the sea on the day they set sail to America.
TIME
For many emigrants, the day they set sail to America was .... the sea.

Writing | Part 1
An essay

1 Do the exercise in the Exam round-up box.

Exam round-up

How much do you remember about how to approach Writing Part 1? Put the following advice in the correct order (1–8).

a Check what you have written, looking for specific mistakes you know you make. ....

b Organise your notes into a paragraph-by-paragraph plan, including some of the vocabulary you'd like to use. ....

c Read all the questions and choose the one you think you can do best. ....1....

d Brainstorm ideas and make rough notes. ....

e Identify the reader, decide what would be a suitable style and what effect you want to produce on the reader. ....

f Analyse the question, underlining the things you must deal with and identifying your objectives in writing. ....

g Write your answer (220–260 words) following your plan. ....

h Take about 45 minutes to do the whole task. ....8....

2 Read the essay task below and underline the key points.

> Your class has watched a television documentary about the benefits of helping immigrants to integrate into their local communities. You have made the notes below.
>
> ### Areas covered
>
> - Language
> - Culture
> - Work
>
> **Some opinions expressed in the documentary:**
>
> 'Immigrants should pass a language exam before being allowed to live in the country.'
>
> 'Local culture is enriched by the diversity immigrants bring.'
>
> 'We learn new ways of doing things by working alongside people from other backgrounds.'
>
> Write an essay discussing **two** of the areas in your notes. You should **explain why the areas are important** and **provide reasons** in support of your answer.
>
> You may, if you wish, make use of the opinions expressed in the documentary, but you should use your own words as far as possible.

3 Work in small groups. Expand the opinions expressed during the documentary by

- adding reasons and examples
- saying whether you agree or disagree with each opinion and giving your reasons
- expressing a counter-argument (which you may or may not agree with).

4 Write a plan for your essay based on ideas which arose during your discussion in Exercise 3. When you have finished, work in pairs and compare your plans.

5 Read this sample essay without paying attention to the gaps. Which ideas expressed in the essay were mentioned while you did Exercise 3?

The world we live in is becoming increasingly globalised ¹... large numbers of people move abroad in search of a better life. ²... , people increasingly have to live harmoniously in multicultural situations.

³... people should acquire the necessary language skills before being allowed to settle permanently in a country. I am broadly in agreement with this point of view ⁴... learning the language of the country is the key to integrating and showing respect for the local culture. However, generally speaking it is difficult to reach a level of language proficiency until you have spent some time in the country itself, ⁵... immigrants should be provided with language lessons during the early years of their stay.

⁶... everyone gains from living in a diverse culture. ⁷... , in my country in recent years people have become much more open to foreign films and literature, while varied foreign cuisine has become a common part of people's lives. Undoubtedly, ⁸... people's minds open to new ways of seeing the world and new tastes, ⁹... enrich their lives.

¹⁰... it is co-operation that makes integration successful, so local people should welcome immigrants from outside for the diversity they bring while the immigrants themselves should make every effort to integrate into the community.

6 The phrases below link ideas together in the sample essay and also refer to the documentary mentioned in the task. Complete the essay by writing each of the phrases in the correct gap.

all of which   consequently   with the result that

to offer some examples   on the grounds that

so what I would suggest is that

it is through these experiences that

for this reason, I personally believe that

during the documentary it was suggested that

I entirely agree with the point made during the documentary that

7 Compare the essay with your plan and make any changes you wish to your plan.

8 Write your own answer to the task in Exercise 2.

Vocabulary and grammar review Unit 13

Vocabulary

1 For questions 1–8, read the text below. Use the word given in capitals at the end of some of the lines to form a word that fits in the gap in the same line.

It's easy to understand why marathons were once thought to be **(0)** ....*elitist*........ activities. **ELITE**
The first marathon runner, an ancient Greek **(1)** .... who ran from Marathon **MESSAGE**
to Athens to deliver a warning about an **(2)** .... enemy, dropped dead just **APPROACH**
after finishing his run. But mass participation marathons like the New York Marathon proved
that this was **(3)** .... The NYC event **CORRECT**
started out in 1970 when there were only 55 finishers – now there are nearly 30,000 runners
(4) .... Similar numbers are seen in **ANNUAL**
other cities around the world, like London and Tokyo.

Of course, it's hard work. A great deal of practice and **(5)** .... goes into completing a **DEDICATE**
course. The people who run **(6)** .... **SUCCEED**
are those who are very fit and who have trained consistently. They may be regular athletes, so
perhaps they already have a **(7)** .... **HEALTH**
diet and training programme. But marathon runners also include formerly **(8)** .... **WEIGHT**
or unfit folks who decided to use a marathon as an excuse to get into shape.

2 Complete these sentences with the correct prepositions.

1 Be careful what you say. He's very sensitive .... criticism.
2 As the manager of the department, you are responsible .... recruiting new staff.
3 There are more and more viruses which are resistant .... traditional antibiotics.
4 Are you familiar .... the music of Jan Gabarek?
5 If you want to be better .... playing the guitar, you'll have to practise more.
6 I can't eat omelettes because I'm allergic .... eggs.
7 I like the house itself, but it isn't very convenient .... the supermarket or the station.
8 Please let us know if our offer is acceptable .... you.

Grammar

3 Correct the errors in the use of words or phrases to express contrast.

1 He thought he had some terrible disease, however it was just a bad case of flu.
2 My sister seems to catch every cold going, although I am rarely ill.
3 Despite he didn't feel well, he went to work as usual.
4 But I exercise every day, I'm still overweight.
5 He refused to see his doctor. Although everyone he knew advised him to.

4 Complete the second sentence so that it has a similar meaning to the first sentence, using the word given. Do not change the word given. You must use three to six words, including the word given.

1 The public health service is worse than it was ten years ago.
   GOOD
   The public health service is
   .... ten years ago.
2 We don't have as many qualified nurses as we need.
   FEWER
   We .... we need.
3 My new job is not as easy as I expected.
   DIFFICULT
   My new job ....
   I expected.
4 I'm really tired. I'll be very glad when we get home.
   SOONER
   I'm really tired. The ....
   .... better.
5 I earned less money than I thought I would last week.
   MUCH
   I .... as I thought
   I would last week.
6 Your diet is just as bad as mine.
   BETTER
   Your diet ....
   mine.

Vocabulary and grammar review Unit 14

Vocabulary

1 Complete the sentences below by writing *learn*, *find out*, *know*, *provide*, *offer* or *give* in the correct form in the gaps. You can use any verb more than once.

1 How old were you when you .... your multiplication tables?
2 I've been trying to .... what I need to do to get a working visa for New Zealand.
3 I think it's the government's duty to .... free education for all young people up to the age of 21.
4 Now where are my keys? I .... they're in my bag somewhere!
5 Rebecca has been .... the chance to improve her Spanish by studying in Argentina for a year.
6 My sister has been .... a job in the company and she's considering it at the moment.
7 I don't think the police will ever manage to .... who stole the money.
8 You'll never .... to drive properly unless you go to a proper driving school.

Grammar

2 Complete the second sentence so that it has a similar meaning to the first sentence, using the word given. Do not change the word given. You must use between three and six words, including the word given.

1 We didn't have as much time as we wanted to understand all this information.
TAKE
What we wanted .... in all this information.

2 Everybody agreed that the music at Lenka's presentation was very annoying.
OBJECTED
It was the music .... at Lenka's presentation.

3 First, you complete this form and then you post it to the embassy.
FILL
What you have .... this form and then send it to the embassy.

4 Audrey is not prepared to leave her current job.
LAST
'Getting a new job is .... do!' cried Audrey.

5 Alfredo wanted nothing more than to relax when he got home.
TAKE
All Alfredo wanted to .... easy when he got home.

6 I spend most of my time doing paperwork.
TAKES
It .... most of my time.

3 Complete the letter below with adverbs or adverbial phrases from the box. Use each adverb / adverbial phrase once only. In some cases more than one answer is possible.

actually   almost certainly   apparently   hopefully
obviously   quite surprisingly   thoughtfully   to be honest

Dear Odile,

Thank you for so (1) .... inviting me to stay with you and your family for a few months later this year. I will (2) .... take you up on your offer as I've been thinking for some time of doing a gap year before I go to university. (3) .... , I need a break from studying and I think a spell of living abroad would suit me perfectly.

(4) .... , because I'm rather tired of school life, I haven't been working particularly hard this term, but (5) .... , I've managed to pass all my exams with quite good grades. (6) .... , when I go to university next year I'll have to work quite a lot harder. I already know several people on the course I want to do and (7) .... it's very demanding. So (8) .... a few months abroad will refresh me enough to really get down to work when I get back.

I'll be in touch when I've got my plans a little clearer.

Very best wishes,

Candice

Language reference

Contents

Articles

The indefinite article *a/an*

A/an is used for something general or non-specific, or when we refer to something for the first time:
*Have you got **a** bicycle?* (= any kind of bicycle)
*He's **a** good gymnast.* (= one of many)
*There's **a** tennis club in our town.*

Other uses:

- to refer to someone's job or function:
  *She used to be **a** hotel receptionist.*

- to mean one:
  *I have **a** sister and two brothers.*

The definite article *the*

The is used with any type of noun when it is clear which thing/person we are referring to. It may be specifically identified in the sentence, it may have been mentioned before, or there may be only one of these things:
*Where's **the** furniture we ordered last week?* (I'm identifying the furniture I mean)
*We ordered a table and six chairs. **The** chairs have arrived but **the** table hasn't.* (= the one(s) I've just mentioned)
*She's at **the** station.* (= the local station, the only one)
*We're meeting at **the** café later.* (= you know the one I mean – the one we always go to)

Other uses:

- to refer generally to some geographical locations, e.g. *the beach, the coast, the mountains, the sea, the road*:
  *We're spending a fortnight in **the mountains**, but I'd prefer to be somewhere on **the coast**.*

- to refer to a type of musical instrument:
  *He's learning to play **the trumpet**.*

- to refer generally to public transport and other services:
  *You can take **the train** to Edinburgh.*
  *I like reading on **the bus**.*
  *Have they contacted **the police**?*

- with adjectives used as nouns for groups of people, e.g. *the rich, the poor, the living, the dead, the blind, the deaf, the unemployed*:
  *There's a growing gap between **the rich** and **the poor**.*

No article

No article is used:

- with plural and uncountable nouns with a general meaning:
  ***Cats** chase **mice**.*
  ***Pollution** is ruining our towns and cities.*

- in certain phrases which relate to a type of place or institution, but not a specific one:
  Did you go to university?
  What did you do in class today?

Other similar phrases:
be in / go to church, court, hospital, prison, bed
be at / go to sea, school, university, college, work
be at / go home

at, *in* and *on* to express location

Use *at*

- when a place is thought of as a point, not an area (including *at home, at school, at work, at university*):
  *I'll meet you **at** the airport when you arrive.*

- to talk about an event involving a number of people:
  *Tina met Joe **at** Charlie's wedding.*

- for addresses:
  *She lives **at** number 11, Abbey Road.*

Use *in*

- when a place is thought of as an area or space:
  *Gary lives **in** a small flat at the top of a tower block.*

- for cars and taxis:
  *Let's talk **in** the car.*

- in phrases such as *in class, in hospital, in prison, in court*:
  *He studied for a degree while he was **in** prison.*

- for the world:
  *It's the tallest building **in** the world.*

Use *on*

- to talk about a position in contact with a surface:
  *We've hung the picture **on** the wall above the fireplace.*
  *She lay **on** the beach, soaking up the sunshine.*

- to talk about a position on something thought of as a line, e.g. a coast, a road, the outskirts, the edge:
  *Keyhaven is a small village **on** the south coast.*
  *There were huge traffic jams **on** the motorway.*

- with means of transport apart from cars and taxis:
  *Hi, Karen. I'm **on** the train now so I'll be home soon.*

- with some forms of technology including *television, telephone, computer, Internet, website*:
  *I've seen him **on** television.*
  *I'm afraid she's **on** the phone at the moment.*
  *You can find all the information **on** our website.*

- with *left* and *right*:
  *The post office is **on** the left just past the supermarket.*

- with these words: *premises, farm, floor* and *island*:
  *Our office is **on** the fifth floor.*

Avoiding repetition
Using pronouns

- Instead of repeating a noun or noun phrase, use a pronoun:
  *Derek Foster worked in advertising after the war. **He** became a professional painter in the early 60s.*

- Use *they/them* to refer to plural nouns and to a person in the singular when you cannot state whether the person is male or female:
  *If you ask **an artist** how **they** started painting, **they**'ll often say that one of their parents taught **them**.*

- Use *himself, herself, themselves*, etc. when the object is the same as the subject:
  *He poured **himself** a glass of water.*
  (Compare: *He poured **him** a glass of water*, where *him* refers to a different person.)

- *It, this, that, these, those* may refer to a noun / noun phrase, or to the whole of the previous clause or sentence:
  *Artists now have a vast range of materials at their disposal. **This** means that they can be much more versatile than in the past.*

  That is often used when giving reasons:
  *The artist is my cousin and **that's** why I'm here.*

One/ones, another, the other(s), both, neither, all, none

- Use *one* to refer to a singular countable noun in a group, and *ones* to refer to plural countable nouns in a group.
  *I've made some **sandwiches** – would you like **one**?*
  *There are some excellent exhibitions on. I strongly recommend **the one** at the National Gallery.*
  *Our **neighbours** are generally nice, but **the ones** in flat 4 aren't very sociable.*

  Use *a(n)/the … one* or *(the) … ones* with an adjective:
  *I've bought a lot of new **shirts** recently, but for gardening I prefer to wear **an old one**.*
  *I enjoy **romantic films**, especially **sad ones**.*

- Use *another* to refer to a second/third (etc.) singular countable noun in a group:
  *One **picture** showed a girl combing her hair. **Another** was of the same girl dancing.*

- Use *the other* when referring to the second of two things/people already mentioned, and *the others* when referring to the rest of a number of things/people:
  *Pablo has **two houses**. One is in São Paulo and **the other** is in Singapore.*
  *Most of the **actors** went to a party. **The others** went home to bed.*

- Use *both* and *neither* to refer to two things/people:
  *He's written **two novels** and **both** have won prizes. **Neither** is autobiographical.*

- Use *all* and *none* to refer to more than two things/people:
  *He's written **twenty novels** and I've read **all of them**. Mariella invited **her friends** but **none of them** came.*

who, which, whose

→ See pages 171–172: Relative clauses.

Using auxiliary and modal verbs

- Instead of repeating a whole verb or verb phrase, we can often use an auxiliary or modal verb:
  *Not many people have **read 'The Dungeon'** and I'm one of the few that **have**.*
  *A year ago I **couldn't drive a car**, but now I **can**.*

- Use a form of *do* to replace a verb in the present or past simple:
  *I really **enjoy good comedy films**, but then I think everyone **does**.*
  *Most people **liked the film**, but I **didn't**.*

Using so

- With verbs like *think, suppose, believe, hope*, etc., use *so* to avoid repeating a clause or sentence:
  *'Do you think Real Madrid will win the championship?' 'I guess **so**.'* (= I guess they will win the championship.)

- Use *do so* to avoid repeating a verb or verb phrase:
  *I told my students to hand in the essay on Monday and all of them **did so**.* (= handed in the essay on Monday)

Omitting words

- With a verb or adjective that is followed by an infinitive with *to*, it is sometimes possible to use *to* on its own, instead of repeating a whole phrase.
  *Kim suggested **going to the ballet**, but I didn't want **to**.*
  *Give me a call later if you're able **to**.*
  *I'd like to be able to **solve your problems** but I just don't know how **to**.*

Cleft sentences for emphasis

Emphasis involves showing that something is particularly important or worth giving attention to. Cleft sentences are one way of doing this. These can be formed by:

- a clause starting with *what*, linked to the rest of the sentence by *is/was*:
  I really enjoy pasta. → ***What I really enjoy is** pasta.*
  She wanted to find a job in New Zealand. → ***What she wanted was** to find a job in New Zealand.*

  Note: The verb in the *what* clause is often *do*. In this case, *is/was* is followed by an infinitive, with or without *to*:
  They advertised on television. → ***What they did was** (to) advertise on television.*

- a clause starting with *all*:
  My house only needs a swimming pool now. → ***All my house needs now is** a swimming pool.*

- a clause starting with *It is/was*, linked to the rest of the sentence by *that* or *who*:
  Mike paid the bill. → ***It was Mike who** paid the bill.*
  You should speak to the manager. → ***It's the manager (that)** you should speak to.*
  They left Poland in 2012. → ***It was in 2012 that** they left Poland.*
  I like visiting other countries, but I don't enjoy flying. → *I like visiting other countries – **it's flying (that)** I don't enjoy.*

Conditionals

First conditional		
Form	Use	Examples
If/Unless + present simple/ continuous – will/may/must, etc. + infinitive	To talk about very possible or probable situations/ events in the present or future	If you**'re** hungry, I**'ll start** getting the lunch ready. We **should get** there by midday if the trains **are running** on time.
Second conditional		
If/Unless + past simple/continuous – would/could/might + infinitive	To talk about improbable or imaginary situations/ events in the present or future	I **might miss** the city if we **moved** away from here. (but we probably won't move) If I **was driving** the car, we**'d be arriving** by now. (but I'm not driving, so we aren't arriving yet)
Third conditional		
If/unless + past perfect simple or continuous – would have / could have / might have + past participle	To talk about imaginary situations/events in the past	I **could have got** better results if I**'d taken** the photos earlier. (but I didn't take them early enough.) If it **hadn't been snowing**, we **wouldn't have got** lost. (but it was snowing, so we got lost)

Comment adverbials

Comment adverbs and adverbial phrases:

- express how certain the speaker is about something. Some common adverbs: *certainly, definitely, possibly, probably, undoubtedly*
  *She's **definitely** happier now than she used to be.*

  Some common phrases: *without a doubt, in theory, in all likelihood/probability*
  ***In all likelihood**, the meeting will have to be postponed.*

- express the speaker's attitude or opinion about what they are saying. Some common adverbs: *frankly, personally, (un)fortunately, obviously, surprisingly, strangely*
  ***Strangely**, I haven't heard from her since she moved.* (= I think her failure to communicate is strange.)
  ***Personally**, I'd prefer not to live abroad.*

  Some common phrases: *quite honestly, generally speaking, to my surprise*
  ***Quite honestly**, I don't think you should have given him so much money.*

Comment adverbials expressing opinions often go at the beginning of a sentence. However, they can also be placed:

- in a middle position in the sentence (often after the subject or after the verb):
  *Martina, **unfortunately**, didn't arrive until midday.*
  *She was, **unfortunately**, too late for her appointment.*

- at the end of the sentence:
  *Luca is thinking of going to Australia, **apparently**.*

These comment adverbials are usually separated from the rest of the sentence by commas.

- *Unless* is sometimes used instead of *if … not*, especially in first conditional sentences:
  *We'll have to eat indoors **unless** the weather improves.*
  (= if the weather doesn't improve)

- Note that *would* and *could* can be used with a conditional meaning in sentences without *if* or *unless*. The idea that we are talking about an unreal situation is understood without being explicitly stated:
  *'How **would** you communicate with someone whose language you **couldn't** speak?' 'I**'d** use sign language.'*

  Otherwise may be used with *would* or *could* to introduce a conditional idea:
  *Arsenal played well in the last 20 minutes. **Otherwise** (= If the situation had been different) they **would have lost** the match.*

Mixed conditionals

If one part of the sentence speaks about the present/future and the other part about the past, 2nd and 3rd conditionals can be 'mixed':

- *If I **hadn't met** Julia in Bulgaria last year* (past – 3rd conditional), *we **wouldn't be** married now* (present – 2nd conditional).

- *If Anastasia **didn't need** this book for her PhD* (present – 2nd conditional), *she **would** never **have bought** it* (past – 3rd conditional).

- *If you **weren't leaving** tomorrow* (future – 2nd conditional), *we **could have had** more time together* (past – 3rd conditional).

Other uses of conditionals

You can:

- give advice using *if I were you + I would + infinitive*:
  If I were you, I'd take that laptop as hand luggage.

- make criticisms or strong requests using *If you would + infinitive – would + infinitive*:
  If you'd stop making so much noise, perhaps we'd all be able to enjoy the programme.

- make polite formal requests using *I'd appreciate it / I'd be grateful if you would/could*:
  I'd appreciate it if you could hand in the report by Thursday.

Countable and uncountable nouns
Countable nouns

- Countable nouns can be singular or plural and are used for individual things which we can count.
  In our family we have a cat and two dogs.

- In the singular form they can be preceded by *a/an* or *one*, or determiners such as *this/that*, *each*, *every*:
  A human being has two hands. Each hand has a thumb and four fingers.

- In the plural form they can be preceded by numbers or determiners such as *some, any, many, (a) few, no, these/those*:
  There are a few teenagers in the room but no children.

Uncountable nouns

- Uncountable nouns are neither singular nor plural and are used for things that are not normally divided into separate items:
  We use gas for cooking and electricity for heating.

- They are used with singular verbs and can be preceded by determiners such as *some, any, no, much, this/that*:
  'Is there any coffee left?' 'No, but there's some tea.'

Note: *a/an, one, each* and *every* cannot be used with uncountable nouns.

- To refer to particular quantities of an uncountable noun, use a phrase which includes a countable noun + *of*:
  a jug of water, two cups of tea, a loaf of bread, three slices of toast, twenty litres of oil

Note: Some nouns which are uncountable in English may be countable in other languages, *e.g. accommodation, advice, applause, bread, damage, equipment, fruit, furniture, homework, housework, information, knowledge, luggage, money, news, rubbish, shopping, toast, traffic, travel.*

Nouns that can be countable or uncountable

Many nouns can be countable or uncountable, depending on how they are used.

- *Would you like some chocolate?* (= the food substance in general)
  There are only two chocolates left in the box. (= individual items)

- *French people love wine and cheese.* (= these substances in general)
  France has many different wines and cheeses.
  (= individual products)

- *I don't eat lamb or chicken.* (= general types of meat)
  I'm going to roast a chicken tonight. (= a whole bird)
  I love lambs and chickens. (= animals)
- *Coffee is expensive here.* (= the type of drink)
  Can I have two coffees, please? (= cups of coffee)
- *People are crazy about sport.* (= the general field of activity)
  Football is a great sport. (one of many individual sporting activities)

Dependent prepositions

Many verbs, nouns and adjectives are followed by a particular preposition before a noun, noun phrase, pronoun or verb + -*ing*:
The film **reminded** me **of** my childhood.
He **apologised to** them **for** damaging their car.

There are no clear rules to help you decide which preposition to use: the best strategy is to learn the preposition with the word. Examples given in a dictionary will show how they are used.

Here are some common words + prepositions (sb = somebody; sth = something).

Verb + preposition

account for	focus on
accuse sb of	help (sb) with
accustom sb to	hope for
agree with (sb/sth) about	impress sb with
amount to	include sb/sth in
apologise (to sb) for	insure (sth) against
appeal to	interfere with
apply to	invest (sth) in
approve of	involve sb in
attach sth to	link sb/sth to/with
attribute sth to	listen to
base sth on	object to
believe in	operate on
blame sb/sth for	participate in
charge sb for	persist in
comment on	prepare (sb/sth) for
compare sb/sth to/with	prevent sb/sth from
compete with	prohibit sb/sth from
concentrate on	protest against
connect sb/sth with	provide sb with
consider sb/sth as	react to/against

consist of	recognise sb/sth as
contrast sb/sth with	recover from
cope with	refer sb/sth to
dedicate sth to	regard sb/sth as
depend on	relate sb/sth to
devote sth to	rely on
differ from	remind sb of
disapprove of	resort to
discourage sb from	result in
distinguish sb/sth from	search for
distract sb from	separate sb/sth from
divide sth into/between	spend sth on
dream of	suffer from
exclude sb/sth from	think about/of
experiment on	warn sb about/against

Adjective + preposition

afraid of	kind to
angry with/about	pleased with
anxious about	prejudiced against
available to/for	proud of
capable of	relevant to
confident of	responsible to/for
delighted with	shocked at/by
dependent on	sorry about/for
different from/to	suitable for
disappointed with	suited to
good/bad/clever at	surprised at/by
independent of	tired of
interested in	upset about
involved in	

Noun + preposition

attention to	discussion about
belief in	experience of
capacity for	information on/about
confidence in	problem of/with
criticism of	reputation for
difficulty in/with	trust in

Expressing ability, possibility and obligation

Ability: *can, could, be able to*

- Use *can/can't* for abilities in the present:
  *Cats **can** see in the dark.*
  *I **can't** drive.*

- Use *could/couldn't* for general abilities in the past:
  *When I was younger, I **could** run very fast.*
  *I **couldn't** walk until I was nearly two years old.*

- For ability to do something in a specific past situation, we use the negative *couldn't*, but we don't often use the affirmative *could*. Instead of *could*, it is usually better to use *be able to*, *manage to* or *succeed in -ing*:
  *We **couldn't** open the door with the key. Eventually we **managed to** break a window and **were able to** get in.*

- For future abilities, use *will be able to*:
  *My little sister **will** soon **be able to** read and write.*

- Use *be able to* for other forms where there is no option with *can* or *could*:
  *I'd like to **be able to** see better.*

Possibility: *can* and *could*

- Use *can/could* to describe what it is possible to do. Use *can/can't* for the present and future, and *could/couldn't* for the past. We also use *be able to*, especially for the past and future:
  *Passengers **can** get to London from here in 35 minutes.*
  *Where we used to live, we **couldn't** get there by train.*
  *We **can** / We'll **be able to** discuss this at tomorrow's meeting.*

- Use *could* (but not *can* and not *couldn't*) for uncertain future possibilities:
  *I think it **could** rain later. (not ~~can rain~~)*
  But It may/might not rain tomorrow. (not ~~couldn't rain~~)

- Use *could have* (not ~~can have~~) + past participle for uncertain past possibilities:
  *I don't know where she went. I suppose she **could have gone** to the supermarket.*

- Use *can't/couldn't* + be for logical impossibility in the present, and *couldn't have* + past participle for the past:
  *It **can't/couldn't be** Paul at the door. He's in Japan.*
  *He **can't/couldn't have had** lunch yet. It's only 11:15.*

➡ See also page 169: Expressing possibility, probability and certainty, for other modals and structures to express possibility.

Rules and obligations: *must* and *have to*

Use *must* and *mustn't / must not*:

- to state rules and laws, often in a formal context:
  *Meat packaging **must** comply with the new regulation.*
  *Motorists **must not** exceed 120 kph on the motorway.*
  *You **mustn't** ride your bike without a helmet.*

- to express a personal feeling of obligation or a personal belief that something is important:
  *I **must** phone my sister today. I **mustn't** forget.*
  *You **must** see this film – it's great!*

Use *have to*:

- to describe a duty or obligation, often coming from an external source:
  *She **has to** be at a meeting at 8:30 tomorrow morning.*

  Compare these sentences:
  *I **have to** finish this report by tomorrow. (= This is something that someone else is insisting on.)*
  *I **must** finish this report by tomorrow. (= I myself feel that this is essential.)*

  *He **has to** go to the police station. (= The police have given this order.)*
  *He **must** go to the police station. (= I believe it's essential for him to go.)*

Use *don't have to*:

- to describe a lack of obligation or necessity:
  *You **don't have to** go to the party if you don't want to.*

  Compare these sentences:
  *We **don't have to** use this machine. (= We can use it if we want to, but it isn't essential.)*
  *We **mustn't** use this machine. (= We're not allowed to use it – it's prohibited.)*

Necessity

- For necessity, use *need to* or *have to*:
  *To get to the airport in time, we'll **need to** / **have to** catch the 4:30 train.*

- There are two negative forms of *need*:
  *We have plenty of time, so we **needn't hurry** / **don't need to hurry**.*

  In the past, these two forms have different meanings:
  *We **didn't need to hurry**. (= We didn't hurry because there was no need.)*
  *We **needn't have hurried**. (= We hurried but it wasn't necessary.)*

Expressing possibility, probability and certainty

Possibility

Modal verbs: *may, might, could*

- Use *may (not)*, *might (not)* or *could* (but not *could not*) to say it's possible that something is true, happens or will happen, but we don't know:
  *The photocopier isn't working – there **may** be some paper stuck inside.* (not ~~there can be some paper~~)

Note: *can* is used to say that something is a general possibility but not with reference to any particular occasion or event:
*It **can** rain heavily in this region in autumn.*
But *It **might** rain this evening.*
*Children **can** be very irritating.*
But *You **may** find my children annoying when they make a lot of noise.*

- Use *may, might, could + well/easily* to say something is a strong possibility:
  *The weather **may well** improve by the weekend.*
  *I'd better write it down, otherwise I **could easily** forget.*

- Use *may, might, could + possibly/conceivably* or *just might* to say something is a remote possibility:
  *My boss **could conceivably** change her mind and decide to give me a pay increase.*
  *I **just might** have time to finish that report this week.*

Other words and phrases

- *It's (just/quite/very/entirely) possible that* + clause:
  *It's **just possible that** we'll finish the project by March.*

- *There's (a/some / a slight / every / a good/strong/real) possibility/chance that* + clause or *of* + *-ing* verb:
  *There's **every possibility that** the business will succeed.*
  *There's **some chance that** the weather will improve tomorrow.*
  *Is there **any chance of seeing** you this weekend?*

Probability

Modal verbs: *should, shouldn't*

- Use *should* and *shouldn't* to say that you expect something is or will be true:
  *You're extremely well qualified – you **should** have no difficulty landing the job.*

Other words and phrases

- *be (quite/very/highly) likely / unlikely* + infinitive or *It's (quite/very/highly) likely that* + clause:
  *He's **unlikely to make** the same mistake again.*
  *It's **quite likely that** they'll be on the 8:30 train.*

- *There's little / some / every / a strong likelihood of* + *-ing* verb or *that* + clause:
  *I'd say **there's a strong likelihood of** him **getting** a first class degree.*
  ***There's little likelihood that** we'll manage to meet our deadline.*

Certainty

Modal verbs: *must, can't, couldn't*

- Use *must* (affirmative) and *can't/couldn't* (negative) to express things you feel certain about because you have evidence:
  *With so many customers, they **must** be making a lot of money.*
  *He didn't know what we were talking about, so he **can't/ couldn't** have read our letter.*

Note: *mustn't* is not used to express certainty (see Rules and obligations on page 168).

Other words and phrases

- *be bound + to* infinitive:
  *This machine is very badly designed. It**'s bound to break** down before long.*

Notes on modal verbs

- To talk about actions in progress now or arranged for the future, use the continuous form, i.e. modal verb + *be* + *-ing*:
  *You all **must be wondering** why I have called this meeting.*

- To talk about actions in the past, use modal + *have* + past participle:
  *Martin is abroad at the moment, so you **can't/couldn't have seen** him yesterday.*

- To talk about actions which took place over a period of time in the past, use the past continuous form, i.e. modal + *have been* + *-ing*:
  *Ulrike wasn't in when I called – she **may have been doing** the shopping, I suppose.*

Expressing purpose, reason and result

Expresses	Phrase(s)	Followed by	Position	Example(s)
purpose	so (that)	a clause	between clauses	He always dresses smartly **so (that)** people will notice him.
	for the purpose of / with the intention of	verb + -ing	after the main clause	Teresa got up early **with the intention of studying** before going in to university.
	so as to / in order to	infinitive		Carla came home early **so as not to have** an argument with her parents.
	to	infinitive		Dieter goes to the gym every day **to keep** fit.
reason	because / since / as	a clause	between clauses or at the beginning of the sentence (more emphatic)	We'd better postpone the meeting **because/since/as** Eva has been delayed. **Because/As/Since** he was feeling ill, he spent the day in bed.
	in case		after the main clause	Take your mobile with you **in case** you need to call me.
	otherwise			Candice always writes things down, **otherwise** (= because if she doesn't) she forgets them.
	because of / due to / owing to	noun or verb + -ing	at the beginning of the sentence or after the main clause	All flights have been cancelled **because of / due to / owing to** the bad weather.
	For this/that reason	a sentence	at the beginning of a sentence and referring to the previous one	Someone called me unexpectedly. **For this reason** I was late for the meeting.
result	so / with the result that	a clause	between clauses	The bridge was damaged, **so** we couldn't get across the river. Children are no longer learning their tribal language, **with the result that** fewer and fewer people speak it.
	Consequently / Therefore / As a consequence / As a result	a sentence	at the beginning of a sentence and referring to the previous one. As a consequence and as a result can also be used at the end of the sentence.	Ranjit injured himself in training yesterday. **As a consequence**, he won't be taking part in the match today. Keiko didn't write a very good letter of application. She was rejected **as a result**.
	using conditional sentences (see page 165–166) If children start learning foreign languages when they're young, they learn them effortlessly. (If clause = possible action, they learn them effortlessly = the result)			

The language of comparison
Comparative adjectives and adverbs

Use comparative adjectives or adverbs to compare two things or actions:
*This camera is **smaller** and **more compact** than mine.*
*Glíma is **less violent** than other forms of wrestling.*
*She works **more efficiently** than most of her colleagues.*

* *no + comparative adjective:*
  *Running is **no better** for you than walking fast.*

* *as + adjective/adverb + as to show similarity or equality:*
  *My younger brother is **as tall as** me.*
  *She doesn't play the piano **as well as** she used to.*

* *the + comparative adjective/adverb + the to show a process in which one thing/action depends on another:*
  *The higher he climbed, **the narrower** the path became.*
  *The faster we walk, **the sooner** we'll get there.*
  *The more I read, **the less** I understand.*

  Note: With adjectives we often leave out the verb *be*:
  The stronger the material (is), the longer it lasts.
  *The sooner we leave, **the better** (it will be).*

* repetition of a comparative adjective/adverb to express an increasing rate of change:
  *He walked **faster and faster** until he was out of breath.*
  *Food is getting **more and more expensive**.*

Superlative adjectives and adverbs

Use superlative adjectives or adverbs to put one thing or action above all others in the same category:
*Glíma is the **oldest** form of wrestling in Iceland.*
*That was the **least interesting** film I've ever seen.*
*She works **most efficiently** in the morning.*

* *the + superlative adjective + of + plural noun:*
  *It was **the simplest of** ideas.*
  *He was **the most inspiring of** teachers.*

* *the + superlative adjective + noun + imaginable/ possible/available:*
  *We had **the worst** weather **imaginable**.*

more, most, less, fewer + noun

Use *more/most + noun* to express a greater / the greatest number or amount:

* *more + plural noun or uncountable noun:*
  *There were **more people** here than there were last year.*
  *I wish I could spend **more time** with my friends.*
  ***Most sharks** are quite harmless.*
  ***Most cheese** is made from cow's milk.*

* *most of + noun/pronoun when referring to part of a specific thing or group:*
  *The pizza was awful. I threw **most of it** away.*
  ***Most of our relatives** live in Canada.*
  ***Most of the oil** in the tanker leaked out into the sea.*

Use *less/fewer + noun* to express a smaller number/amount.

* *less + uncountable noun:*
  *I'm getting **less money** now than in my last job.*

* *fewer + plural noun:*
  *There were **fewer people** than usual at today's match.*

Qualifying comparatives

To intensify or qualify comparative adjectives/adverbs use:

* *a lot / a great deal / far*
* *slightly / a bit / a little*
* *even*

*My sister is **a lot more intelligent** than me, but my younger brother is **even cleverer** than her.*
*We've had **far less** snow this year than last year.*
*Could you drive **a bit more carefully**, please?*

Linking ideas
Relative clauses

She's the woman	who that	bought our car.
	whose	son bought our car.
	from whom	we bought our car.
They've got a car	which that	runs on electricity.
This is the town	where	I grew up.
Sunday is a day	when	many people relax.
There's no reason	why	you should be worried.

* To introduce a relative clause, use *who, that, whose* and *whom* to refer to people.

  Note: *whom* is formal and is used mainly with prepositions:
  *The person **to whom** this letter is addressed lives in Athens.*

* Use *that* and *which* to refer to things.

* Use *where*, meaning 'at which', 'in which' or 'to which', to refer to places:
  *The village **where** (= in which) they live is in the middle of nowhere.*
  *This is a restaurant **where** (= to which) we often go.*

- Use *when* to refer to times:
  *I'm not sure of the date **when** they're leaving.*

- Use *why* to refer to reasons:
  *The reason **why** I'm late is that my flight was cancelled.*

- A relative clause can be at the end of a sentence or it can be embedded in another clause:
  *Madrid is the city **where I grew up**.*
  *The city **where I grew up** is Madrid.*
  *Madrid, **where I grew up**, is the capital of Spain.*

- *Who, that* and *which* can be the subject or the object of the verb in the relative clause:
  Subject: *The people **who know** me best are my friends.*
  Object: *The people **who I know** best are my friends.* (The subject is *I*.)

  Where, when and *why* are always the object of the verb:
  *We're going back to the hotel **where we stayed** last summer.* (The subject is *we*.)

Defining relative clauses

- A defining relative clause defines the noun which immediately precedes it, and is therefore essential to the meaning of the sentence:
  *The couple **who brought me up** were not my real parents.* (The relative clause tells us which couple.)

- *Who, that* and *which* can be left out when they are the object of a defining relative clause:
  *The people **(who)** I know best are my close friends.*
  *The DVD **(that)** you gave me for my birthday is fantastic.*

  When and *why* can also be left out:
  *2009 was the year **(when)** she left university.*
  *That's the reason **(why)** I'm so disappointed.*

Non-defining relative clauses

- Non-defining relative clauses give additional information, but are not essential to the meaning of the sentence:
  *The hotel, **which has a hundred bedrooms**, is on the outskirts of the city.*

- Another type of non-defining clause is a comment clause, using *which* to introduce a comment on a previous clause:
  *It had been raining nonstop for 24 hours, **which is why I didn't go out**.*
  *We were stuck in the traffic jam for ages, **which I found really frustrating**.*

- The pronoun *that* cannot be used to introduce a non-defining relative clause.

- In writing, a non-defining relative clause is separated from the main clause by commas:
  *My car, **which is seven years old**, has already done 200,000 kilometres.*

Participle clauses

Linking actions

With a present participle:
***Concentrating** on my work, I didn't realise how late it was.*

With a perfect participle:
***Having finished** his speech, he left the room.*

With a past participle:
***Seen** from a distance, the Pyramids look quite small.*

- Use a present participle clause to describe something happening at the same time as the main action or immediately after it:
  ***Opening the door**, I saw a parcel on the doorstep.*

- Present participle clauses can also be used with some conjunctions and prepositions:
  ***After watching that film**, I was too scared to go to bed.*

  In this case, the participle clause can follow the main clause:
  *She became interested in art **while travelling in Italy**.*
  *You can take the train **instead of catching the bus**.*

- Use a perfect participle clause to describe something that happened before the main action. It may provide a reason for that action:
  ***Having left our map at home**, we got lost.* (= Because we had left our map at home …)

- Use a past participle clause when the meaning is passive:
  ***Eaten in small quantities**, chocolate is good for you.*
  ***Built in 1889**, the Eiffel Tower is now a symbol of Paris.*

- Note that in all these cases the subject of the participle clause is the same as the subject of the main clause.

Used instead of relative clauses

Participle clauses can also be used instead of relative clauses. They are sometimes called reduced relative clauses.

- Use the present participle when the meaning is active:
  *There are three pictures **hanging on the wall**.* (= that/which are hanging …)
  *I noticed a man **wearing a suit** and **carrying a large box**.* (= who was wearing …, who was carrying …)

- Use the past participle when the meaning is passive:
  *Anyone **caught shoplifting** will be prosecuted.* (= who is caught …)
  *I've brought you a jar of plum jam, **made by my mother**.* (= which was made …)

Apposition

A common, economical way of linking two or more facts about the same person, thing or place is to put them next to each other in a sentence.

As with relative clauses, the second noun / noun phrase can be defining or non-defining.

- If it tells us who or what, no commas are used:
  Her friend Klaus is a computer engineer.

- If it provides additional descriptive information, commas are used:
  I'm going to see Bev Jackson, my maths tutor, this afternoon.

no, none, not

no

- No means *not any* or *not even one* and can be used with countable or uncountable nouns:
  I have no idea what you're talking about.
  There were no cars on the road at that time of night.
  There's no salt on the table.

- It can also be used with comparative adjectives or adverbs and with the word *different*:
  The traffic is no worse today than it was yesterday.
  I had to work late every evening last week, and so far this week has been no different.

none

- None is a pronoun which means *not one* or *not any*. It is usually followed by *of* + a plural or uncountable noun or a pronoun:
  None of my friends know/knows it's my birthday today.
  None of the milk in the fridge is fresh.

- It can also be used on its own:
  'How much coffee do we have?' 'None (at all). We finished it yesterday.'
  We need to buy some more eggs – there are none left.

- In formal written English *none* is considered to be a singular word and is followed by a singular verb:
  None of my colleagues speaks Japanese.

  However, in everyday speech a plural verb is more commonly used:
  None of this morning's flights have been delayed.

not

- Not is mainly used to make verbs negative and is often contracted to n't:
  You have not / haven't answered my question.
  That isn't / That's not the correct answer.
  She told me not to phone her after ten o'clock at night.
  He was silent, not knowing what to say.

- It can also make other words or phrases negative:
  I ordered tea, not coffee.
  Not many people voted in yesterday's election.
  Not everyone can win the lottery.
  Not all Canadians speak French.
  Not surprisingly, he failed his driving test.
  'Can you come out?' 'No, I'm afraid not.'

The passive

The goods	are were are being were being are going to be have been had been will be can be have to be might have been must have been	imported	from Italy.

- The passive is formed with the verb *be* + past participle.

- Intransitive verbs (verbs with no object, e.g. *appear, come, go*) cannot be used in the passive form.

- There is no passive form for the present or past perfect continuous tense or the future continuous tenses. (We do not say *The goods have/had been being imported* or *will be being imported*.)

We use the passive to focus attention on the person or thing that is affected by the action of the verb:

- when the identity of the person/thing doing the action (= the agent) is unknown or unimportant:
  My office was broken into last night.
  Tonight's football match has been cancelled.

- when it is obvious who/what the agent is:
  He was arrested and charged with theft. (Only the police can arrest and charge people.)

If we want to mention the agent in a passive sentence, we use the preposition *by*:
The goods are imported by a chain of supermarkets.

The passive is often used to describe technical or scientific processes:

*Water **was added** and the mixture **was heated** to 85°C.*

With verbs like *know, believe, think, consider, expect, report* we can use the passive + infinitive. We can also use an impersonal construction with *It* + passive + *that* + clause:

*Bill Gates **is known to be** one of the world's richest people.*
*Twenty people **are reported to have been** injured in the fire.*
__It is believed that__ the accident was caused by a gas leak.
__It has been estimated that__ average house prices will fall by 5% this year.

Structures like these are often used:

- to express an opinion that is widely accepted as true

- when you can't or don't want to identify a source of information.

We also use the passive to create a 'flow' in text:

- to put 'known information' at the beginning of a sentence:
  *The police have started to take a tougher line with petty criminals. Many of them are now **being given** prison sentences.*

- to avoid the awkwardness of a very long subject:
  The player who has won 'footballer of the year' most times addressed the club management.
  *➜ The club management **was addressed** by the player who has won 'footballer of the year' most times.*

Prepositions in time expressions

Use *at*

- with points of time:
  __at__ four o'clock, __at__ dawn, __at__ midday.

- with short periods which we think of as points:
  I'm always short of money __at__ the end of the month.

- with mealtimes:
  We can discuss it __at__ lunch tomorrow.
  (We can also say *over/during lunch.*)

- with *the weekend, Christmas* and *Easter*:
  What are you doing __at__ the weekend?
  (In American English *on the weekend* is also possible.)

- with *night* when talking about night-time in general, not a particular night:
  The traffic noise makes it difficult to sleep __at__ night.
  (Compare: *in the night* – see below.)

Use *in*

- for years, months and seasons:
  __in__ 2006, __in__ March, __in__ the autumn

- with *the* for parts of the day:
  Sam always goes shopping __in__ the morning.
  (Compare: *on Saturday morning* – see below.)
  The ground was wet because it had rained __in__ the night.
  (= during the night. Compare: *at night* – see above.)

- to say the period of time before something happens or how long something takes:
  I'll call you back __in__ 20 minutes.
  __In__ six months' time I'll have finished university.
  Clara managed to do all her homework __in__ half an hour.

Use *on*

- for particular dates or days, or parts of particular days:
  My holiday starts __on__ July 22nd.
  We're having a party __on__ Saturday if you'd like to come.
  Let's go bowling __on__ Friday night.

- with *occasion*:
  Tatiana has visited us __on__ several occasions in the past.

Reported speech
Verb tense changes

When we report what someone said, the tense of the verb is often 'further back' in time:

'I'm feeling ill.' ➜ *He said he **was feeling** ill.*
'You can borrow my phone.' ➜ *She said I **could borrow** her phone.*
'The rain has stopped.' ➜ *He said the rain **had stopped**.*
'We drove all night.' ➜ *They said they **had driven** all night.*
'We'll try to help.' ➜ *They said they **would try** to help.*

The past perfect tenses and the modal verbs *would, could* and *should* cannot move 'further back', so they remain unchanged:

*'I'd never **spoken** to her before.'* ➜ *He said he'd never **spoken** to her before.*
*'I **wouldn't go** skiing again.'* ➜ *She said she **wouldn't go** skiing again.*

The tense of the reported speech does not need to change:

- if we want to make it clear that what the speaker said is still true now or remains relevant:
  *'I **love** black coffee.'* ➜ *He said he **loves** black coffee.*
  *'Picasso **was born** in Spain.'* ➜ *She told us that Picasso **was born** in Spain.*

- if the reporting verb is in the present:
  *'I'm **looking** forward to my holiday.'* ➜ *She **says** she's **looking** forward to her holiday.*

Pronoun, possessive adjective and adverb changes

- Pronouns and possessive adjectives often need to change in reported speech, especially when the reporter is different from the original speaker:
  '*I love you*,' *Dan said.* ➔ *Dan said **he** loved **me**.*
  '*You didn't give **me** your address*,' *said Jane.* ➔ *Jane said **we** hadn't given **her our** address.*

- Time and place adverbs change if the time or place is no longer the same as in the direct speech:
  '*I'll see you **tomorrow**.*' ➔ *Jackie said she would see me **the next/following day**.*
  '*We've lived **here** for six years.*' ➔ *They said they had lived **there** for six years.*

  The adverb does not change if the time/place remains the same:
  '*I came **here** yesterday.*' ➔ *(reported the same day) He says he came **here** yesterday.*

- These are some of the time reference changes:

Direct speech	Reported speech
(ten minutes) ago	(ten minutes) before/earlier
last week/month/year	the previous week/month/year
the week/month/year before
next week/month/ year	the following week/month/year
the week/month/year after
now	at that time / immediately / then
this week	last/that week
today	that day / yesterday
on Monday/Tuesday, etc.
tomorrow	the next/following day
the day after
yesterday	the previous day
the day before

Reporting questions

- When we report a question, we change it into the form of a statement. This means that we change the word order and do not use the auxiliary *do*, *does* or *did* in the present and past simple:
  '*What are you watching?*' ➔ *He asked us **what we were watching**.*
  '*Where do you live?*' ➔ *She asked me **where I lived/live**.*

- When we report Yes/No questions, we add *if* or *whether*:
  '*Do you speak Italian?*' ➔ *He asked me **if/whether** I spoke/speak Italian.*

Reporting verbs

There are many verbs which we can use to introduce reported speech. Most of them can be followed by more than one grammatical pattern.

verb + *to* infinitive

- agree: *They agreed **to broadcast** the programme.*
- offer: *He offered **to buy** me lunch.*
- promise: *The mayor has promised **to give** us an interview.*

verb + object + *to* infinitive

- advise: *The newspaper advises **people to be** careful about using social media.*
- ask: *She asked **the reporter to repeat** his question.*
- invite: *They've invited **us to attend** the show.*
- order/tell: *The teacher ordered/told **the children to wait** outside.*
- persuade: *I persuaded **the magazine to print** my story.*
- remind: *Can you remind **me to update** my blog?*
- warn: *She warned **him not to be** late for the interview.*

verb + preposition + noun / verb + *-ing*

- complain about: *The actress has complained **about the paparazzi** outside her house.*
- apologise for: *The organisation has apologised **for publishing** misleading information on its website.*
- accuse (somebody) of: *The president accused the press **of distorting** the truth.*

verb + noun / verb + *-ing*

- deny: *The minister has denied **the accusation**.*
- admit: *He admitted **inventing** some details in his report.*
- recommend: *She recommended **doing** more research.*
- suggest: *The directors have suggested **paying** for online content with advertising.*

verb + clause

These verbs can also be followed by (*that*) + clause: *admit, agree, complain, deny, promise, recommend, suggest*:
She suggested that they should interview local people.

These verbs must be followed by an object before (*that*) + clause:
persuade, promise, remind, tell, warn:
*We warned **our audience** that they might find some of the photos distressing.*

➔ **See also page 179:** Verbs + *to* infinitive or *-ing*

Time clauses

Time clauses start with words like *when, while, as, before, after, until, as soon as*.

Referring to the future

When a time clause describes an action in the future, use a present tense (present simple, present continuous or present perfect), not a future tense:

I'll call you	when I **leave** work. (not *will leave*)
	when I'**m leaving** work. (not *will be leaving*)
	when I'**ve left** work. (not *will have left*)

Note these differences:

- *When she **goes** to Rome she **stays** with Carla.* (= She does this every time she goes to Rome.)
  *When she **goes** to Rome she'**ll stay** with Carla* (= She'll go there in the future and then she'll stay with Carla.)

- *I'll help you when you **cook** lunch.* (= I'll help you to cook lunch.)
  *I'll help you when I'**ve cooked** lunch.* (= First I'll cook lunch. Then I'll help you.)
  *I'll explain the problem while **you're cooking** lunch* (= I'll explain. At the same time, you'll be cooking lunch.)

Referring to the past

- *I called him when my train **got** to the station.* (= My train arrived and immediately afterwards I called.)
  *I called him when my train **was getting** to the station* (= I called while the train was in the process of arriving.)
  *I called him when the train **had left** the station.* (= The train left earlier. I called later.)

when and *while*

When is used:

- to show one action happening at the same time as another. It can mean 'During the time that' or 'At the time that':
  ***When** we lived / were living in Wales, I rode my bike everywhere.* (While can also be used here.)
  *Our dog always barks **when** visitors come.*

- to show one action happening immediately after another, and often as a result of it:
  ***When** I get some money I'll buy a new jacket.*
  *The snow melted **when** the sun came out.*

- to show an action interrupting or happening in the course of another longer action:
  *He was playing squash **when** he injured his wrist.*

While is always used:

- to show one action happening at the same time as another. It means 'During the time that' and it is often (but not always) used with continuous tenses:
  *She kept a blog **while** she **was travelling** in Asia.* (When can also be used here.)
  *I'll do the crossword **while** I'm waiting for you.*
  *The postman delivered the parcel **while** I **was washing** the car.* (My action lasted longer than the postman's.)
  ***While** Dad **heated** the soup, I made some toast.* (The two actions occupied approximately the same length of time.)

Other time expressions

during

The preposition *during* is followed by a noun or noun phrase. Use *during*:

- to describe an action lasting for the whole of a time period or event:
  *Bears hibernate **during the winter**.*
  *The town was lit up **during the festival**.*

- to describe an action happening at some point within a time period or event:
  *I'll be spending a week in Prague **during the summer**.*
  *Three players were given a red card **during the match**.*

meanwhile

Meanwhile is an adverb which comes at the beginning of a sentence. Use *meanwhile*:

- to introduce an action happening while another event, mentioned in the previous sentence, takes/took place:
  Paz spent two hours this afternoon surfing the Internet. ***Meanwhile**, the rest of the family went for a long walk.*

- to introduce an action happening between two times:
  I'll be home in half an hour. ***Meanwhile**, (= between now and then) could you prepare the vegetables?*

Transitive verbs

English verbs are classified as transitive or intransitive. Dictionaries identify them with the letters *T* and *I*.

- A transitive verb must be followed by an object:
  *She **found the information** on the Internet.* (the information is the object of the transitive verb *found*.)

- An intransitive verb has no object:
  *At five past seven our train **arrived**.*

- Because transitive verbs have an object, they can be used in the passive form:
  Active: *Someone **stole our car** from outside the house.*
  Passive: ***Our car was stolen** from outside the house.*

  Intransitive verbs cannot be used in the passive form.

- Some transitive verbs can have two objects, a direct object and an indirect object:
  *They will send **you an email** to confirm your booking.* (an email is the direct object of *will send*; you is the indirect object.)

  Either of these objects may become the subject of a passive sentence.
  ***You** will be sent an email to confirm your booking.*
  ***An email** will be sent to you to confirm your booking.*

- Many verbs can be used transitively and intransitively, sometimes with different meanings:
  *Could you help me **move this table**?* (transitive)
  *We're **moving** tomorrow.* (intransitive)

  *I think I **left my books** at college.* (transitive)
  *They **left** at three o'clock.* (intransitive)

  *She **runs her business** from home.* (transitive)
  *A river **runs** through our village.* (intransitive)

Verb forms to talk about the past
Past simple

The past simple tense is used to describe:

- an action that happened or a state that existed at a specific time in the past:
  *Yesterday I **felt** so tired that I **didn't go** to work.*

- an action that lasted for a period of time in the past, but is now finished:
  *I **studied** in Paris for four years from 2005 to 2009.*

- a habitual action over a specific period in the past:
  *While he was away, he **rang** his girlfriend every day.*

- actions which happened one after the other:
  *She **opened** the fridge, **took out** the milk, **gave** some to the cat and **put** some in her coffee.*

Past continuous

The past continuous tense is used to describe:

- an activity which started before and continued until an event in the past:
  *She **was driving** home when the police stopped her.* (The activity of driving was interrupted by the police's action.)

- an activity which started before and continued after an event in the past:
  *I **was cooking** lunch when I heard the news.* (And I continued to cook lunch afterwards.)

- a situation which was temporary at a time in the past:
  *I remember that summer well. I **was staying** with my aunt at the time, while my parents were away.*

  Compare the use of the past simple when the situation in the past was more permanent:
  *I **lived** in Rome when I was a child.* (not ~~I was living~~)

- something that frequently happened, with *always* or *forever*, often to express amusement or irritation:
  *My dad **was always dressing up** in funny hats.*
  *We got fed up with Jill, who **was forever complaining**.*

State verbs

We do not usually use the continuous with state verbs (this applies to all tenses). These are commonly:

- verbs which express **opinions, feelings or knowledge**, e.g. *agree, believe, disagree, hate, know, like, love, need, prefer, realise, regret, understand*
- verbs which describe **appearance**, e.g. *appear, look, seem, resemble*
- verbs which describe **senses** e.g. *smell, taste*
- these other verbs: *belong, consist, contain, cost, own*

The present perfect tenses

The present perfect tense is used:

- to describe an action that happened at an unspecified time in the past up to now:
  They've recorded a lot of albums.
  ***Have** you ever **visited** Berlin?*

- to describe a past action when the emphasis is on the result in the present:
  *Someone's **stolen** my phone! (It's not here now.)*
  *I've **told** Tim about tomorrow's rehearsal. (He knows about it).*
  *It's no wonder you're tired – you've **been working** so hard!*

- typically with time adverbs that connect the past to the present, e.g. *just, already, lately, so far, up to now, yet, today* (when it is still the same day), *this morning* (when it is still the same morning):

*Have you **seen** any good films **lately**?*
*England **has** only **won** the World Cup once **so far**.*
(**Note**: this use of the present perfect is typical in British English. In American English, the past simple may be used: *Did you see any good films lately? England only won the World Cup once so far.*)

*I've **been cleaning** the house **this morning**.*
Compare: *I cleaned the house this morning.* (It's now the afternoon.)

- with *for* or *since* to describe an activity or state that started in the past and is still continuing in the present:
  *She's **lived** in Spain for nearly ten years.*
  *They've **known** each other since they were children.*
  *He's **been driving** for three hours,*

The present perfect simple and continuous are sometimes interchangeable, although we only use the simple form with state verbs. However, note the differences in the table below.

Present perfect simple	Present perfect continuous
emphasises the result: *I've **phoned** my friends and they're coming to the party.*	emphasises the activity: *I've **been phoning** my friends. That's why I haven't done my homework.*
often describes an action that is now completed: *We've **bought** some food for the weekend. (It's in the kitchen now).* *Working conditions **have improved** a lot. (They're much better now).*	shows that an activity has continued for a period of time and may mean that it is still continuing: *We've **been buying** most of our food at the market lately.* *Working conditions **have been improving** since the new manager took over. (They're in the process of getting better.)*
says how much has been completed or how often something has been done: *I've **cooked** three pizzas.* *Sandra **has phoned** me four times today.*	says how long an activity has been happening: *I've **been cooking** all afternoon.* *I've **been speaking** on the phone for hours.*
may indicate a more permanent situation: *He's **worked** in this shop all his life.* *I've always **lived** here.*	may indicate a temporary situation: *I've **been working** on my art project for two weeks now.* *People **have been living** in terrible conditions in the refugee camp.*

The past perfect tenses

The past perfect simple tense is used:

- to indicate that we are talking about an action which took place, or a state which existed, **before** another activity or situation in the past, which is described in the past simple:
  *When Maria got home, they **had eaten** dinner.*
  Compare: *When Maria got home, they **ate** dinner.* (They ate dinner when she arrived.)

- *typically with time expressions like when, as soon as, after, before, it was the first time, etc.*
  *He went home as soon as he**'d finished** his work.*

The past perfect continuous tense is used:

- to focus on the length of time:
  *My eyes were really tired because I**'d been reading** for two or three hours in bad light.*

- to say how long something happened up to a point in the past:
  *It was two months before any of the teachers noticed that Mike **hadn't been coming** to school.*

would and *used to*

Would + infinitive and *used to* + infinitive are used to talk about things which happened repeatedly in the past but don't happen now:
*When I was small, my mother **would read** to me in bed and she**'d sing** me a song to help me to sleep. While she was reading to me, my father **used to wash up** the dinner things.*

- Use *used to*, not *would*, to talk about past states which no longer exist:
  *There **used to be** a grocer's opposite the bus station.* (not ~~There would be~~).

- *Used to* only exists in the past. It has no other tenses. The negative is *didn't use to*:
  *He **didn't use to be** so short-tempered.*

  The question form is *Did* (subject) *use to*:
  ***Did** you **use to enjoy** school when you were a kid?*

- Use the past simple, not *used to* or *would*, to specify how many times or how often something happened:
  *Charlie used to be a very successful tennis player. He **won** the junior championship three times.*

Verbs + *to* infinitive or *-ing*
Verbs followed by the infinitive

The infinitive without *to* is used after:

- modal verbs:
  *We **must hurry** or we'll be late.*

The *to* infinitive is used after:

- some verbs which are modal in meaning:
  *I **have to go** to work tomorrow.*
  *You **ought to get** more sleep.*
  *You **need to think** again. You **don't need to worry**.*

  Note: The verb *need* has an alternative negative form, *needn't*, which is followed by the infinitive without *to*:
  *You **needn't worry**.*

- certain verbs, e.g. *afford, agree, arrange, appear, attempt, choose, decide, expect, hope, intend, learn, manage, offer, pretend, promise, refuse, seem*:
  *We can't **afford to go** on holiday this year.*

- certain verbs + object, e.g. *advise, allow, ask, convince, enable, encourage, forbid, force, get, instruct, invite, order, persuade, remind, require, teach, tell, train, want, warn, wish*:
  *You can't **force people to believe** something.*
  *My father **taught me to swim**.*

  Note: After the verb *help*, the *to* can be omitted before the infinitive:
  *She **helped me (to) revise** for my exam.*

Verbs followed by the *-ing* form

The *-ing* form of the verb is used after:

- some verbs which express likes and dislikes, e.g. *dislike, enjoy, loathe, (don't) mind, (can't) stand*:
  *She **can't stand getting** stuck in a traffic jam.*

  But note the following exceptions:

  - *hate/like/love/prefer* are usually followed by the *-ing* form but are sometimes followed by the *to* infinitive (see below).

  - *would* + *hate/like/love/prefer* is always followed by the *to* infinitive:
    *I'd **hate to get up** early every morning.*

- certain verbs, e.g. *admit, appreciate, avoid, can't help, consider, delay, deny, finish, imagine, involve, keep, miss, postpone, prevent, recommend, report, resist, risk, suggest*:
  *The prime minister has just **finished speaking**.*

Verbs followed by *to infinitive* or *-ing*

A small number of verbs can be followed either by the infinitive or by the *-ing* form.

With no difference in meaning

begin, can't bear, cease, commence, continue, hate, intend, like, love, propose, start:
I've just **started to learn / learning** to ski.
He had **intended to leave / leaving** before midnight.

Note: With the verbs *like, love, hate* there can be this slight difference in meaning:
I like **to clean** my car every week. (The focus is on the result of the activity.)
I like **cleaning** my car every week. (The focus is on the activity itself, i.e. I enjoy cleaning it.)

With different meanings

- verbs expressing perception
  I **saw** the plane **land.** (= I saw the whole action.)
  I **saw** the plane **landing.** (= I saw part of the action.)

- *forget*
  I **forgot to phone** my brother. (= I didn't phone him.)
  I'll never **forget phoning** my sister that night. (= I phoned her and I recall it well.)

- *remember*
  Tom **remembered to close** the windows before he left. (= He did something he had to do; he didn't forget.)
  Tom **remembered closing** the windows before he left. (= He recalled doing it.)

- *go on*
  She won her first race when she was seven and **went on to break** the world record. (= Breaking the world record was something she did later.)
  He **went on walking** even though he was exhausted. (= He didn't stop walking.)

- *mean*
  I'm sorry, I didn't **mean to be** rude. (= intend)
  If we want to catch the early train, it'll **mean getting** up at 5:00. (= involve)

- *regret*
  I **regret to inform** you that you have not passed the test. (= I'm sorry about something unwelcome I'm about to say.)
  He now **regrets taking** the day off work. (= He wishes he hadn't taken the day off work.)

- *stop*
  We'd better **stop to look** at the map. (= stop what we are doing in order to do something else)
  There's nothing you can do about it, so **stop worrying**. (= finish worrying)

- *try*
  I've been **trying to repair** my computer all morning. (= attempt something difficult)
  Have you **tried kicking** it? (= do something which might solve a problem)

Ways of contrasting ideas
Conjunctions: *but, whereas, while, although, (even) though*

- **But** can contrast words, phrases and clauses, normally within the same sentence:
  The work was tiring **but** worthwhile.
  The work was tiring **but** it produced worthwhile results.

  However, in informal writing it may be used to start a sentence:
  We were half dead by the end of the day! **But** at least the job turned out well.

- **Whereas** and **while** are used to contrast different, but not contradictory, ideas:
  He can eat anything he likes without putting on weight, **whereas** most people have to be more careful.
  While I know she can be difficult at times, I'm very fond of her.
  The *while* clause usually comes before the main clause.

- **Though / although / even though** introduce an idea that contrasts with the one in the main clause:
  He failed his driving test **although / even though** he had practised every day for the previous two weeks.

  Even though is more emphatic than *though/although*.

- **Even if** is similar to **even though**, but adds a conditional meaning:
  I'm going to New Zealand for my holiday next year **even if** I have to save all year.

Prepositions: *despite, in spite of*

- **Despite** and **in spite of** are prepositions and therefore they are followed by a noun or an *-ing* form:
  The journey was very quick **despite / in spite** of the heavy traffic.
  Despite / In spite of feeling ill, / the fact that I felt ill, / I enjoyed the party.

Adverbs: *however, nevertheless*

- **However** is used to contrast a new sentence with the previous one(s). It normally goes at the beginning of the sentence, but may be placed within it or at the end:
  This is one possible solution to the problem. **However,** there are others. / There are others, **however.** / There are, **however,** others.

Note: Unlike *but*, *however* cannot be used to link two contrasting clauses in the same sentence.

- *Nevertheless* has the same function but is more formal. It normally goes at the beginning of the sentence:
  This is an extremely difficult decision. **Nevertheless**, *it is one that we have to make.*

Word formation
Adding prefixes

Prefixes to give negative meanings

Some words can be given a negative meaning by adding a prefix (e.g. *dis-* + *like* = *dislike*) to the beginning of a word. Here are some common prefixes which can be used to give a negative meaning:

- *dis-*: disrespect
- *in-*: inconvenience
- *un-*: unconventional

Before many (but not all) words beginning with:

- *l* we add the prefix *il-*: illiterate
- *m* and *p* we add the prefix *im-*: imperfect
- *r* we add the prefix *ir-*: irrational

Prefixes to say when something happens
- *pre-* means 'before a time or event':
  premature (= happening or done too soon, especially before the natural or desired time)
- *post-* means 'after' or 'later than':
  postgraduate (= a student who has already obtained one degree and is studying at a university for a more advanced qualification i.e. after graduating)

Prefixes to indicate attitude
- *pro-* means 'supporting or approving of something' and with this meaning it is normally used with a hyphen:
  pro-European
- *anti-* means 'opposed to' or 'against' and is normally used with a hyphen:
  anti-social, anti-terrorist

Other prefixes and their meanings
- *mis-* usually means 'wrongly' or 'badly':
  misbehave (= behave wrongly or badly)
- *re-* usually means 'again' and is often added to verbs:
  redevelop (= to change an area of a town by replacing old buildings, roads, etc. with new ones, i.e. to develop again)
- *inter-* means 'between' or 'among':
  interactive (= involving communication between people)

- *over-* can mean '(from) above':
  overview, oversee

  It can also mean 'too much' or 'more than usual':
  overworked, overspend
- *under-* can mean 'below':
  underground, undermine

  It can also mean 'not enough':
  underpaid, undervalue

Adding suffixes

Verbs, nouns, adjectives and adverbs can be formed from other related or base words by adding a suffix to the end of the word (e.g. *appear* + *-ance* = *appearance*). There are no clear rules – each word and the words which can be formed from it must be learned individually.

Some of the most common suffixes and their usual meanings are listed below.

verb → noun

suffix	verb	noun	notes
-ment	recruit	recruitment	used to form nouns which refer to an action or process or its result
-ation, -ition, -tion, -sion	accuse define distract provide	accusation definition distraction provision	added to verbs to form nouns showing action or condition
-er, -or	rule supervise	ruler supervisor	added to some verbs to form nouns which refer to people or things that do that activity
-ance, -ence	acquaint interfere	acquaintance interference	used to form nouns which refer to an action, a series of actions, or a state
-ant	contest	contestant	used to refer to a person or thing performing or causing the action
-al	arrive	arrival	used to add the meaning 'the action of' to a noun
-ee	train	trainee	refers to the person to whom the action of the verb is being done

adjective → noun

suffix	adjective	noun	notes
-ance, -ence	*significant* *convenient*	*significance* *convenience*	added to adjectives ending in *-ant* or *-ent*
-ness	*ready*	*readiness*	added to adjectives to form nouns which refer to a quality or a condition
-ity	*diverse* *liable*	*diversity* *liability*	notice that *-able* becomes *-ability*

noun → adjective

suffix	noun	adjective	notes
-y	*filth*	*filthy*	added to nouns to form adjectives meaning 'like the stated thing'
-ful	*fruit*	*fruitful*	having the stated quality to a high degree, or causing it
-ous	*number*	*numerous*	
-less	*speech*	*speechless*	used to add the meaning 'without'
-al	*nutrition*	*nutritional*	used to add the meaning 'connected with'
-ic	*idealist*	*idealistic*	used to form adjectives which say what a person, thing or action is like
-ish	*snob*	*snobbish*	

noun → noun

suffix	noun	noun	notes
-ism	*material*	*materialism*	used to form nouns which describe social, political or religious beliefs, studies or ways of behaving
-ist	*violin* *therapy*	*violinist* *therapist*	used to form nouns which describe people with a particular expertise, set of beliefs or way of behaving
-ship	*sponsor*	*sponsorship*	having the rank, position, skill or relationship of the stated type

adjective/noun → adjective / noun

suffix	adjective/ noun	verb	notes
-ify	*clear*	*clarify*	used to form verbs meaning 'to cause to become or to increase'
-ise, -ize	*general*	*generalise / generalize*	added to form verbs meaning 'to cause to become'

verb → adjective

suffix	verb	adjective	notes
-ed	*bias*	*biased*	
-ing	*grip*	*gripping*	
-able, -ible	*sustain* *neglect*	*sustainable* *negligible*	added to verbs to form adjectives which mean 'able to receive the action' or 'worth receiving the action'
-ent	*persist*	*persistent*	
-ive	*exclude*	*exclusive*	added to verbs to form adjectives meaning 'showing the ability to perform the activity'

adjective → adverb

Adverbs are almost always formed by adding *-ly* to the adjective. However, if the adjective ends in *-ic*, change it to an adverb by adding *-ally*. (Exception: *public* → *publicly*)

suffix	adjective	adverb
-ly / -ally	*immense* *heroic*	*immensely* *heroically*

Spelling rules for adding affixes

Affixes are either prefixes or suffixes.
Below are some spelling rules when adding affixes.

When adding -ed, -ing, -er, -est, -ance, -ence, -en or -y, double the final consonant in:

- one-syllable words which end in consonant–vowel–consonant:
  run – running, flat – flatten, mud – muddy
  (But w, x and y are never doubled: *flowed, taxing*.)

- verbs of two or more syllables which end in consonant–vowel–consonant when the final syllable is stressed:
  oc<u>cur</u> – occurrence, for<u>get</u> – forgetting

- verbs which end in *l* after one vowel in British English (in American English the *l* may not double):
  travel – traveller, cancel – cancellation

Don't double the final consonant when:

- there are two final consonants:
  correspond – correspondence

- there are two vowels before the final consonant:
  disappear – disappearance

- the stress is not on the final syllable:
  <u>deep</u>en – deepening

Drop the final -e:

- if there is a consonant before it and the suffix begins with a vowel (-er, -ed, -ing, -ance, -ation, etc.):
  nonsense – nonsensical, amaze – amazing, sane – sanity

  Note this exception: adding -able to words ending in -ce and -ge: *noti**ce**able, knowled**ge**able*

Don't drop the final -e:

- when the suffix begins with a consonant:
  safe – safety, arrange – arrangement, disgrace – disgraceful

  Note this exception: *argue – argument*

Change -y to i:

- in words which end in -y after a consonant when a suffix (with the exception of -ing) is added:
  happy – happiness, try – tried / trial, study – studious, family – familiar, rely – reliance

  Note these exceptions:
  *dry – drier / drily but **dryness**; shy – **shyness** / **shyly***

Change -ie to y:

- when adding -ing to words which end in -ie:
  lie – lying, die – dying

Add -es rather than -s for plural nouns or present simple verbs when the word ends in:

- -s: *bus – buses, miss – misses*
- -ch: *watch – watches*
- -sh: *wish – wishes*
- -x: *relax – relaxes*

Note: For some common nouns ending in -f or -fe the plural ending is -ves:
leaf – leaves, loaf – loaves, knife - knives

Adding prefixes

When a prefix is added (before the word), the spelling does not change, e.g. with dis-, un- and ir-:

appoint – disappoint, satisfied – dissatisfied, truthful – untruthful, necessary – unnecessary, relevant – irrelevant

Writing reference

What to expect in the exam

The Writing paper is Paper 2. It lasts 1 hour 30 minutes. You do two tasks.

- In Part 1, there is one task which you must do: an essay.
- In Part 2, you choose one of three tasks.

Part 1

You are asked to write an essay on a given subject or proposition, together with input text in the form of notes made during some form of discussion on the subject. These notes consist of three general topic areas and some quoted opinions from the discussion. In your essay you must cover **two** of the the topic areas. You can make use of the opinions if you wish, but you don't have to do so.

Length: 220–260 words

Time: approximately 45 minutes

This part tests your ability to
- develop an argument on a particular topic
- express your opinions clearly and support your ideas with reasons and examples
- write in a style that is appropriately formal for an academic essay
- organise your answer in a logical way
- write accurate English.

How to do Part 1

1 Read carefully through the instructions and the accompanying input text that you are given. (2 minutes)
2 Find and underline the points which explain the subject and context of the essay and the key points that you must write about. (2 minutes)
3 Decide which two of the three given topic areas you will focus on and whether you want to refer to any of the opinions. (2 minutes)
4 Make brief notes on what you will put in your answer and organise your notes into a plan. When writing your plan, decide how many paragraphs you need and what you will say in each one. If you are planning to use any of the opinions given in the task, think about how you can express them in your own words. (5–7 minutes)
5 Write your answer, following your plan. (25–30 minutes)
6 When you have finished, check your answer for mistakes. (5 minutes)

Part 2

In Part 2 you must choose one writing task from a choice of three. The tasks you can choose from will be three of these: an email, a letter, a proposal, a report, a review.

For each of these tasks, the instructions are much shorter than in Part 1 (a maximum of 80 words). They tell you who your text is to be written for, what its purpose is and what areas it should cover. You answer the task with your own ideas.

Length: 220–260 words

Time: approximately 45 minutes

This part tests your ability to
- organise and structure your writing
- use an appropriate range of vocabulary and grammatical structures
- use an appropriate style
- compare, make suggestions and recommendations, express opinions, justify your point of view, persuade, etc., depending on the task.

How to do Part 2

1 Read the questions and choose the task you think is easiest for you. (1–2 minutes)
2 Re-read the task you have chosen and underline
   - the points you must deal with
   - who will read what you write
   - anything else you think is important. (2 minutes)
3 Decide what style is appropriate.
4 Think of ideas you can use to deal with the question and write a plan. When writing it, decide how many paragraphs you need and what to say in each one. (5 minutes)
5 Think of useful vocabulary you can include in your answer and note it down in your plan. (2–3 minutes)
6 Write your answer, following your plan. (25–30 minutes)
7 When you've finished, check your answer for mistakes. (5 minutes)

Preparing for the Writing paper

When you do a writing task as homework or exam preparation, follow these procedures.

Set aside the time you need

In the exam you will have about 45 minutes to do each task. At the beginning of your course, spend longer doing the task and working on the writing skills needed to produce a good answer. Nearer the exam, practise answering the question within the time allowed.

Before writing

1 Brainstorm your ideas, make notes and write a plan. Your plan should have a clear structure, divided into paragraphs or sections.
2 Study the model answers in the units and in this Writing reference. Pay attention to the structure and layout of the answers, underline language you can use and read the suggestions and advice accompanying the answers.
3 Compare your plan with the model(s). If your plan is different, do you have good reasons for answering the question in a different way?
4 Use the resources at your disposal.
   - Try to use some of the words/phrases you have underlined in the unit, or copied into your notebook or from your photocopiable word lists. Take the opportunity to use new language in your answers: if you use it correctly, then you've learnt something and made progress; if you make a mistake, your teacher will give you feedback so that you can use it correctly next time.
   - Use a good learner's dictionary to check spelling, meanings and usage.
   - Try to include grammatical structures you have studied recently. This will reinforce your learning.
5 In your plan, include vocabulary and grammatical structures you want to use.
6 Read and incorporate your teacher's advice and suggestions on other pieces of writing you've done.

When writing

1 Follow your plan so that when you write, you concentrate on producing language to express ideas you've already generated.
2 Avoid repeating the same words too often – use synonyms where possible (a good learner's dictionary will help you find some of these).
3 If you need to correct something, cross out the mistake and continue writing – you won't lose marks as long as your corrections are clear. In the exam you won't have time to copy out your answer again.

After writing

1 Check what you've written: ask yourself, 'Have I expressed myself clearly?'
2 Check for mistakes, particularly mistakes you've made in previous writing tasks, and correct them (see below).

When your teacher hands back your written work

1 Go through it carefully, checking your mistakes and your teacher's suggestions.
2 Keep a section of your notebook or a computer file for noting your mistakes and the corrections. As an example, look at this extract from a student's work and the table in her computer file where she notes her mistakes.

> *cancellation*
> The cancelling of our opening speech because our actor
> *the first bad impression made on our guests*
> couldn't come was the first bad impression our guests had.
>
> I think it would be a good idea during our next activity
> *invite*
> day to host Colin Briggs, the famous footballer. This
> *children*
> would please the kids and many of their parents as well.

Mistake	Details	Correction
cancelling	Should use the noun when it exists, not verb + -ing	cancellation
the first bad impression our guests had	The collocation is 'make a bad impression on sb'	the first bad impression made on our guests
host	'Host' (verb) means 'to introduce guests or performers on a radio or television programme'	invite
kids	'Kids' is informal.	children

3 Update your list after every writing task. When a mistake disappears from your writing, remove it from the list. When you do the Writing paper in the exam itself, check for the mistakes you know are or were on your list: in the exam you're more likely to repeat mistakes you've made before than make new ones.

Essays

An essay is a piece of academic writing, produced for a teacher or lecturer, in which you have to discuss issues connected with a topic. You may previously have discussed this topic in class. You should express your opinions on the topic and the reasons for them.

You studied how to write essays in Units 1, 3, 9 and 14

Exercise 1

Look at this writing task. Underline what you consider to be the main points and then answer the questions below.

> You have watched a television discussion about methods governments could adopt to encourage people to take more exercise. You have made the notes below.
>
> > **How can governments encourage people to take more exercise?**
> >
> > - better education
> > - free facilities
> > - exercise time at work
>
> > **Some opinions expressed in the discussion:**
> > 'People already know the benefits of exercise but don't do enough about it.'
> > 'Many forms of exercise are free.'
> > 'Employers would benefit from a healthier workforce.'
>
> Write an essay discussing **two** of the methods in your notes. You should **explain which method you think is more important** for governments to consider and **provide reasons** in support of your opinion.
>
> You may, if you wish, make use of the opinions expressed in the discussion, but you should use your own words as far as possible.

1 Do you agree, on the whole, that governments have a role to play in encouraging people to take more exercise? If you do, what is your main reason? If not, why not?
2 How could education be used to achieve this aim?
   - Who should be targeted by an education programme? Children? Adults?
   - Where should this education take place? In school? On TV? Online?
3 What kinds of facilities could be made free?
4 How do you think employers and employees would react to the idea of 'exercise time at work'?
5 Do you agree or disagree with any of the three opinions expressed?

Exercise 2

Which two of these three plans are appropriate for the essay task in Exercise 1? What are the problems with the other plan?

Plan 1

Para 1   Introduction: the importance of taking exercise – otherwise, heart problems, obesity
Para 2   People of all ages need facilities that are freely available
Para 3   Idea of introducing exercise classes in schools – problems, why it won't work
Para 4   Conclusion: providing free facilities is the best thing governments can do

Plan 2

Para 1   Introduction: the general consensus on exercise and the idea of a government role to play
Para 2   How schools can do more to help solve the problem – more PE and sport
Para 3   The part parents might play in supporting these initiatives
Para 4   Benefits of more free facilities, e.g. swimming pools, bike paths
Para 5   Conclusion: why education is more important

Plan 3

Para 1   Introduction: the exercise I did as a child and how it has benefited me
Para 2   Teaching young people about exercise: inadequacies in the current education system
Para 3   Advantages of having free exercise facilities
Para 4   Exercise time at work – impractical: loss of productivity
Para 5   Conclusion: need for better education and free facilities

Exercise 3

Read the sample answer below.

1 Which method in the notes does the writer not address?
2 Which of the two methods described does the writer generally agree with?
3 Why doesn't the writer agree with the other method?
4 What reasons does the writer give for disagreeing with one of the methods?
5 Does the writer include any of the opinions included in the task description? If so, which?

It is generally accepted that people today take insufficient exercise. This, combined with a poor diet, can lead to ill health and a poor quality of life. In view of this, it has been suggested that governments should act to encourage more exercise. I shall consider two of the proposed methods.

> Write a short first paragraph introducing the topic and your angle on it.

Probably the most important action governments could take would be to introduce an education programme into all schools. In addition to publicising the benefits of exercise, this would make exercise a compulsory part of the school curriculum and get young people used to following an exercise regime. In my view, however, for this to be truly successful, there should be a corresponding programme aimed at adults. If parents took part in an exercise programme put on by the school, they would be supporting what their children were being taught.

> Discuss one of the three methods listed in the notes in the exam task. Give reasons for your opinion on this.

It has been suggested that if exercise facilities were free, there would be an increased public take-up. In theory, this seems an excellent way of encouraging adults to exercise, but in practice I am doubtful. It is based on the assumption that exercise depends on money, whereas in fact walking and cycling, two very effective ways of keeping fit, are free and can be fitted conveniently into most people's daily routine. Therefore, in my opinion, providing expensive extra facilities is unnecessary and would be a misuse of public money.

> Discuss another of the methods, again giving your opinion supported by reasons.

In view of the above arguments, I believe governments should introduce education programmes aimed at people of all ages because this is the most cost-effective means of achieving the desired goal.

> Write a concluding paragraph summarising your opinions.

When you write an essay you need to make sure that the argument you are making is clear to the reader. This means that paragraphs should follow on clearly from each other and that sentences within paragraphs should be linked in a logical, easy-to-follow sequence. Below are some of the ways you can help the reader to follow your thinking. Examples are from the sample essay.

Sentences which guide the reader

Include sentences or phrases that act as signposts to guide the reader through your essay. These often come at the beginning of a paragraph.

I shall consider two of the proposed methods.
Probably the most important action would be …
It has been suggested that …
In view of the above arguments, I believe …

Linking words and phrases

In addition to publicising the benefits of regular exercise, this would …
This seems excellent, but in practice I am doubtful.
It is based on the assumption that exercise costs money, whereas in fact walking and cycling are free.
Therefore, in my opinion, providing expensive facilities is unnecessary.
Governments should introduce education programmes because …

Pronouns and other reference words to avoid repetition

This, combined with a poor diet …
In my view, for this to be truly successful, …
If parents took part, they would be supporting what their children were being taught.
It is based on the assumption that …
In view of the above arguments, …

Lexical links

Lexical links include synonyms, near synonyms and words from the same root.

governments should act – the most important action governments could take
benefits of regular exercise – used to following an exercise regime
get young people used to following – what their children were being taught
a programme aimed at adults – If parents took part

Exercise 4

Rewrite the second sentence using reference words or synonyms to avoid repeating the words in **bold**.

1 When you engage in **physical exercise**, you **burn calories**. The more intense the **physical exercise**, the more **calories** you **burn**.
2 Do you need to **relax after a stressful day at work**? You can **relax after a stressful day at work** by taking regular exercise.
3 **Exercise** can be **fun**. **Exercise** gives you a chance to unwind, by engaging in activities that you find **fun**.
4 Find an **activity** you enjoy, and just do it. If the **activity** bores you, try something new.
5 Vigorous aerobic activity means **you're breathing hard and fast**. If **you're breathing hard and fast**, you won't be able to speak more than a few words.

Exercise 5

Find sets of three words or phrases from the box which have similar meanings.

Example: *aim – goal – objective*

accomplish   achieve   active   ~~aim~~   attain   encourage
endurance   energetic   ~~goal~~   inadequate   inspire
insufficient   motivate   ~~objective~~   scarce   stamina
staying power   strenuous

Exercise 6

Consider how you could organise these ideas for a paragraph about exercise time at work for the essay task in Exercise 1. Think about the ordering and linking of ideas and ways of avoiding repetition.

- I am not in favour of the idea of the governments requiring employers to provide exercse time at work.
- Employees would probably benefit from having exercise time at work.
- Employers cannot be forced to provide time for exercise.
- Some people say that the government should require employers to provide exercise time at work.
- The idea sounds attractive.
- Workers must take responsibility for their own health and fitness.
- The idea is impossible to implement.

Other useful language

Introducing your opinions

(Personally,) I believe/think/feel that …
From my point of view …
In my view / opinion …
I would argue that …
As far as I am concerned, …
Interestingly, …
Arguably, …

Introducing other people's opinions

It is often a good idea to show the reader how your own ideas contrast with the opinions of other people (e.g. **Some people say** the Internet has ruined our lives, **but in my opinion**, the Internet has transformed the world for the better.).

Some people suggest/believe/claim that …
It is often/sometimes said/argued/suggested that …
It can be argued that …
According to many/some people …
It has been suggested that …

Pointing out that something is obvious

When you need to express an obvious point as part of an argument, it is often useful to show that you are aware that you're not saying anything unusual.

obviously   clearly   undoubtedly   of course
Without a doubt, …
Needless to say, …
It goes without saying that …

Reviews

A review will require some description followed by a recommendation.

In a review, usually for an international magazine or newspaper, you are expected to express your opinion about something which readers may be thinking of seeing, doing or buying, e.g. a film, a concert or an exhibition. You can assume that the readers are people with similar interests to yours. You usually have to make a recommendation about the thing you are reviewing. Sometimes you will be asked to write about two things of the same type and to express your preference for one or them.

You studied how to write a review in Units 6 and 11.

Exercise 1

Read the writing task below.
1 What things should you deal with in your review?
2 Who will read it and what style would be suitable?

You see the announcement below in an international magazine.

Where to buy clothes

Our readers are interested in clothes shops to visit when on holiday or travelling. We invite you to write a review for visitors to your town comparing two clothes shops. Please describe what sort of clothes they sell, comment on the quality of the service, the value for money and how fashionable they are, and give recommendations.

Write your **review**.

Exercise 2

Read the sample answer below.
1 Does the writer cover all the points mentioned in the writing task?
2 How does the writer start the review?
3 What adjectives does the writer use to describe
   • the clothes?
   • the staff?
4 Does the writer use a formal or an informal style?
5 What do you notice about the layout?
6 Explain the writer's recommendations in your own words.

Shopping in Linz

Buying clothes might not be the first thing you think of when visiting Linz, but there are some attractive boutiques in the old town and you can come away looking fashionable and stylish. Here are my favourites.

Melanie's

Melanie's sells clothes for women and while it is a small shop, it has a wide range of styles. If you want to look really fashionable, it's certainly worth a visit. The shop has a selection of formal and casual clothes from some of the world's top designers, so they're not cheap. However, you can occasionally pick up a bargain. The staff are attentive and they'll help you to combine clothes and accessories so that you'll leave the shop looking like a million dollars, even though it may cost you a fortune!

The Parallel

If you don't feel like spending so much, The Parallel is a good alternative. This shop belongs to some local designers and sells their unique range of clothes for women at competitive prices. The clothes tend to be in distinctive bright colours, but the quality is generally good, so the shop represents value for money. You'll have to look after yourself as, apart from the security guard, the only staff you'll find are on the cash desk. While they're polite and friendly, they don't have time to give much help.

My recommendations

To sum up, for something really special, go to Melanie's, but be careful or your credit card will suffer. For bright clothes at a reasonable price, The Parallel is a better bet.

Make your review sound as authentic as possible: address the reader, give an introduction and mention the town.

Think about the details the reader will want to know and include them.

You can use a little humour to maintain your reader's interest.

You can divide the review into sections as here, but it is not always necessary.

Summarising

To summarise, … All in all, … To sum up, … In summary, …

Proposals and reports

In both proposals and reports, you are expected to write in clearly organised sections and include factual information leading to a suggestion, recommendation or conclusion.

Proposals

When you write a proposal you are trying to persuade readers to follow a course of action. Your reader may be someone in a superior position to you, in which case you will need quite a formal style; or you may be writing for colleagues or fellow members of a club, in which case the style will be a little less formal – you can address your readers more personally, using contracted verb forms. In both cases the format should be the same. You have to make a persuasive case for action(s) that should be taken, based on factual information.

You studied how to write a proposal in Units 5, 8 and 12.

Exercise 1

Read the writing task below.
1 Underline the things you must deal with in your answer.
2 Who is going to read the proposal? What would be a suitable style?

You are a member of the Students' Council at the college where you study. The principal of the college wants to make it easier for first year students from other countries to fit into college life and has invited you to send in a proposal with practical suggestions. You have been asked specifically to consider improving the range of social activities on offer and appointing student advisers to help new students.

Write your **proposal**.

Exercise 2

Read the sample answer.
1 Has the writer dealt with all parts of the task?
2 Find examples of where the writer has avoided repeating vocabulary from the exam task by rephrasing or using synonyms (e.g. *make it easier* → *facilitating*). Why is this a good approach?
3 Underline phrases used to introduce suggestions and recommendations, e.g. *I would suggest …*

Proposal for integrating new students from other countries

Introduction

The purpose of this proposal is to suggest ways of facilitating overseas students' integration into this college.

Overseas students' problems

There are two difficulties which newly arrived students have. Firstly, they are unfamiliar with the academic system in our country. Secondly, they often find it difficult to integrate on a social level with other students and the general population here.

Social activities

Judging by recent figures, it is clear that social activities organised by the college are not well attended. It has been noted that very few new students from other countries attend, especially in their first year. This may be partly due to poor publicity, but, more seriously, it may be because there are is not a wide enough variety of activities attractive to foreign students. I would recommend asking new students themselves for their ideas on the kinds of social activities they would enjoy and I suggest we should invite these students to take part in organising new activities.

Student advisers

It would also be a good idea, in my opinion to instigate a new advisory system. This, more than anything, would overcome students' problems with both the academic system and social aspects of their life at the college. A more experienced adviser or mentor would be responsible for helping new students from other countries to understand our system by giving them guidance and advice, while also introducing them to other students and helping them to make friends.

Conclusion

I suggest that we ask for volunteers to help with all the areas mentioned above.

Where possible, answer using your own vocabulary, not the words used in the exam task. Planning before you write will help with this.

Use the format of a proposal, i.e. a title, sections, headings, an introduction and a conclusion.

Don't spend a long time counting words, but keep within the word limit. If you write too little, you are probably missing important points. If you write too much, you risk being irrelevant.

Reports

When you write a report your reader may be, for example, your manager at work or a teacher, in which case you will need a more formal style; or you may be writing for your colleagues or members of your club, in which case the style will be a little less formal – you can address them more personally, perhaps using contractions). In both cases the format should be the same. You will have to give some factual information and you are often asked to make suggestions or recommendations. You must organise your report carefully and one way of doing this is to divide it into sections with headings.

You studied how to write reports in Units 2, 4 and 10.

Exercise 1

1 Read the task below. Underline the parts that tell you what points you must cover in your report and who will read it.
2 How formal should this report be?
3 When you write about what you like and dislike, do you think you should refer mainly to educational matters, to personal experiences, or to both?

You have been studying in an English-speaking country for some time as part of an educational exchange. The director of the exchange programme is interested in improving the experience for future students. He has asked you to write a report outlining why you have been doing the exchange, describing what you like and dislike about it and making recommendations for how it could be improved.

Write your **report**.

Exercise 2

1 Read the sample report. What things did the writer like and dislike about the programme?
2 Find examples of formal style in the sample report.

Pegasus educational exchange programme

Introduction

The purpose of this report is to outline my reasons for doing the exchange, the positive and negative aspects of the experience and to make recommendations for improvements.

Reasons for doing the exchange

I have been in New Zealand as part of the Pegasus programme for the last nine months. I participated in the exchange in order to do an MA in Environmental Science at the University of Auckland. At the same time I had the opportunity to improve my English.

Positive and negative aspects

For me, the benefits of doing this exchange far outweigh the disadvantages. The main professional advantage is the opportunity to exchange ideas with teachers and students from another part of the world (I come from Portugal) and with an entirely different outlook on environmental problems. This has allowed me to see such problems from a variety of angles. As a result, I believe that I will return to my country with innovative solutions to local problems. In addition, I have acquired improved language skills and increased cultural awareness.

The negative aspect from my point of view is that the programme does not receive enough financial support and, as a result, it has been very expensive for me. This is a problem which is likely to discourage prospective exchange students from participating in the programme.

Recommendations

I strongly recommend that the programme organisers should make interest-free loans available to people wishing to participate in an exchange. This would allow considerable numbers of talented students to benefit from something which they would otherwise be unable to do.

Give your report a title. Organise it in sections with section headings.

Outline the purpose of the report.

Avoid just repeating the words used in the task.

Use vocabulary and collocations appropriate to formal writing.

Explain the reasons for recommendations you make and the consequences of problems you mention.

Making suggestions and recommendations

formal	less formal
I would suggest + verb + -ing *I would suggest including this information on our website.*	*Why not + infinitive without to* *Why not phone one of your friends?*
I suggest that … + clause *I suggest that we ask for volunteers.*	*Why don't we/you + infinitive without to* *Why don't we just send them an email?*
should + infinitive without to *Its activities should be advertised more widely.*	*How about + verb + -ing* *How about meeting up after work tomorrow?*
I would recommend + verb + -ing *I would recommend canvassing students' ideas.*	*Let's + infinitive without to* *Let's have a party.*
I recommend that … + clause *I recommend that we start a social club.*	*It might be a thought + to infinitive* *It might be a thought to put on some sun cream.*
It would be a good idea + to infinitive *It would be a good idea to instigate a mentoring system.*	

Emails and letters

You may be asked to write an email or letter responding to a situation described in the task. You must use a style which is suitable for the person you are writing to, for example the editor of a newspaper or magazine, the director of a company or college. In your email or letter, you may have to include factual information and your own viewpoint in relation to this.

The types of letter you may have to write include

- a letter to the editor of a newspaper or magazine
- a letter of application, or giving a reference for someone applying for a job
- a letter to the directors of an organisation
- an informal letter to a friend.

You studied how to write letters in Units 7 and 13.

Exercise 1

1 Read the writing task below, underlining the points you must deal with in your answer.
2 Write a paragraph-by-paragraph plan for the letter. When you have finished writing your plan, check that you have included all the points that you have underlined.

> The company you work for is planning to move its Australian head office to a new city. Your manager has asked you to write to local estate agents to inquire about suitable premises in the city. Your letter should explain:
>
> - what your company does
> - what area of the city the company would like to be located in
> - what kind of premises the company is looking for.
>
> Write your **letter**.

Exercise 2

1 Read the sample answer below. Has the writer included all the points you underlined?
2 How would you describe the style of the letter?
3 Has the writer included anything which is not in the instructions? Why (not)?

Dear Sir/Madam

The managing director of my company, Secure Logistics, has asked me to contact you with a view to finding new business premises. We are currently located in a medium-sized town, but, due to recent growth in our business, we now require larger premises in a more convenient part of the country.

Secure Logistics is an established freight transport company specialising in the movement of valuable goods. We have an expanding fleet of lorries and, for this reason, we need to be located in a secure area on the outskirts of a large city with convenient transport links both to other parts of the country and to the rest of the world. We require a large parking area for our vehicles as well as extensive secure storage facilities for our goods.

In addition to this outside area, the company also needs a large office building for up to eight hundred staff. This will be our new headquarters, so we require large open-plan offices, which will be used as a call centre for customers, and a number of smaller offices for managers.

We would consider moving into an existing facility of the kind I have described, but if suitable premises cannot be found, we would be prepared to purchase an area of currently unused land on which to construct our own buildings.

I hope I have described what the company is looking for in sufficient detail, but if you require further information, please contact me at the above address. I look forward to your reply.

Yours faithfully,

[signature]

Use the first paragraph to state clearly the reason you are writing.

You will need to add substance to the information provided in the writing task by using your own ideas.

Think of a natural way to finish the letter.

Starting and finishing letters

If you know the person's name,
- start with
  - Dear Susana (if you would use their first name when you speak to them)
  - Dear Mrs Emmett (if you don't feel comfortable using their first name).
- finish with:
  - Best wishes, Regards, Kind regards (if you're writing to someone you know fairly well)
  - Love or With love (if you're writing to a close friend or a member of your family)
  - Yours sincerely or Yours (if you're writing to someone you don't know well).

If you don't know the person's name,
- start with Dear Sir, Dear Madam or Dear Sir/Madam
- finish with Yours faithfully.

Adding extra points

formal	informal
Firstly, Secondly, Finally, In addition, Moreover, Furthermore, What is more,	Besides, Also, Another thing (was that …) Apart from this/ that,

Speaking reference

What to expect in the exam

The Speaking paper is Paper 5.
- It lasts 15 minutes and has four parts.
- You do the Speaking paper in pairs.
- There are two examiners in the room; one gives you instructions and asks you questions, the other listens but does not join in the conversation.

Part 1 (short conversation)

Part 1 lasts two minutes and is a conversation between the examiner and each candidate individually. You will be asked questions about yourself, your family, sports and other leisure activities, your likes and dislikes, your education and where you live. Questions may also be about your past experiences and your future plans.

You studied and practised Part 1 in Units 1 and 11.

How to do Part 1

1 Listen to the questions carefully and give clear, direct answers. Where possible, include a few extra details, or a reason for an answer you give.
2 Try to relax. Look confidently at the examiner and smile a little when you answer the questions.
3 Take the opportunity to show how fluently you can speak.
4 Don't prepare answers before you do the exam, but do make sure that you know the vocabulary you will need to talk about the topics that are likely to come up.

Exercise

Here are some typical questions that you may be asked in Part 1 of the Speaking exam. Work through some of the questions with a partner, taking turns to be the examiner and the candidate. Try to use relevant vocabulary from the Useful language column.

Questions	Useful language
Introductory questions Where are you from? What do you do here/there? How long have you been studying English? What do you most enjoy about learning English?	I was born in … I grew up in/near … I was brought up in (place) by (people) a small / quite a large / an extended family I've been working/studying at … since (point in time) for (length of time) Actually, (+ unexpected/surprising information) I've only been learning English for two years. What I really love about (-ing) is …
Leisure time What are your main interests and leisure time activities? How important are sport and exercise in your life? What types of TV programmes do you think are worth watching? What kinds of music do you enjoy listening to?	I'm fanatical about … I … whenever I can / get the chance. quite / not terribly important (to me) I'm really keen on … / I love … I never miss … I can't stand …
Learning What is your happiest memory of school? What were the most useful things you learned at school? What do you enjoy learning? If you had the opportunity to learn something new, what would you choose?	I can remember (event) very well/clearly. Probably … / I suppose things like … I really like (… / -ing). That's an easy / a difficult question to answer. Let me think …

Future plans What do you hope to be doing this time next year? How might you use your English in the future? Would you consider living abroad permanently? Are you someone who likes to plan for the future, or do you prefer to let things happen?	*I hope to be (-ing) at (place).* *I expect I'll be (-ing)* *I'd certainly consider (-ing)* *I'd have to think carefully about …* *It's not something I'd rush into.* *I'm someone who …* *I'm (not) the kind of person who …*
Travel and holidays What kinds of holiday appeal to you most? Why? Which countries would you most like to visit? Why? Which part(s) of your country would you recommend to tourists? Why? Would you like to work in the travel industry? Why (not)?	*I (tend to) prefer … (mainly) because …* *My main reason is that …* *I've always wanted to … I don't know / can't explain why.* *I'd recommend/suggest … Firstly, because … and secondly, because …* *I've never thought about it.* *I'm not sure. I'd have to think about that.*
Daily life Which part of the day do you enjoy most? Why? What do you like to do at weekends? What do you do to relax? Do you prefer to follow a routine or do you like to do something different every day?	*I'm not very good / I'm best at/in (time of day).* *I'm a night / early morning person.* *I try to catch up on (activity); I spend time (-ing).* *Mainly / Most of the time I …* *My problem is I …* *I'd always rather (verb) than (verb).*

Part 2 (long turn)

Part 2 lasts four minutes altogether.
- The examiner will give you and your partner each a set of three photos to talk about in turn. You choose two of the photos and then speak individually for a minute about them. You have to compare the two photos and answer two questions related to them. The examiner gives you the instructions and asks the questions, which are also printed on the page with the photos.
- After your partner has spoken for a minute, the examiner will ask you to give a brief response to a question about your partner's pictures.

You studied and practised Part 2 in Units 2, 5, 9 and 13.

How to do Part 2

1 The photos will always have a common theme, so talk about the general ideas they illustrate. Don't describe them in detail.
2 You choose two of the three photos and then compare them with each other. If you are not sure what they show, speculate.
3 It is important to answer the questions the examiner asks you. These are printed on the same page as the photos.
4 Whenever possible, give reasons or explanations for the answers you give.
5 Speak for the whole minute. Don't stop until the examiner says 'Thank you'.
6 While your partner is speaking, listen but don't interrupt. The examiner will ask you a question about your partner's photos at the end. You should answer this question in two or three sentences.

Useful language

Comparing (See also Language reference page 171)
Here / In this photo, I can see / someone is / there are …, whereas in this photo …
On the other hand, this photo shows …

Giving reasons/explanations
(See also Language reference page 170)
The (main) reason for this is that …
I think / I'd say this is because …
This can be explained quite easily …

Speculating (See also Language reference page 169)
This person looks as if she's/he's …
He seems to be …
Perhaps/Maybe they're …
They're probably …
He could be / might be …

Exercise

Work through the sample question with a partner. Take turns to speak for one minute. You should each compare a different pair of photos.

In this part of the test, I'm going to give each of you three pictures. I'd like you to talk about two of them on your own for about a minute, and also to answer a question briefly about your partner's pictures.

(To Candidate A) It's your turn first. Here are your pictures. They show people shopping. I'd like you to compare two of the pictures and say what different methods of shopping they show, and why people might choose one method rather than another.

(After A has spoken for a minute) Thank you.

(To Candidate B) Which picture do you think shows the least stressful method of shopping? Why?

- What different methods of shopping do the photos show?
- Why might people choose one method rather than another?

Part 3 (collaborative task)

Part 3 lasts four minutes altogther and involves a discussion between you and your partner. The key skills being tested are fluency and the ability to participate in and maintain a conversation.

- The examiner gives you a set of written prompts in the form of a question and five related options. You and your partner discuss these together for about two minutes. During your discussion, you will be expected to exchange ideas, express and justify opinions, agree and/or disagree, suggest, speculate and evaluate.
- The examiner then asks you and your partner to reach a decision by negotiation, taking about one minute.

You studied and practised Part 3 in Units 3, 6, 8, and 12.

How to do Part 3

1 You are given 15 seconds to read and think about the task before you start. Use this time to read the question and the five options carefully.
2 Remember: the most important thing is to have an in-depth discussion, not to cover all the options.
3 Keep your focus on the question during your conversation – try not to stray away from the topic.
4 If you start the conversation, make sure you don't speak for too long. Give a brief opinion, then ask your partner for their thoughts on the subject.
5 When your partner is speaking, listen carefully. React and respond appropriately. This can include nodding and smiling, as well as speaking.
6 Try to make what you say sound like normal conversation.
7 When you are asked to decide between the options, try not to reach agreement too quickly. If you do, you'll still have to keep the discussion going until the examiner tells you to stop by saying 'Thank you'.

Useful language

Bringing your partner into the conversation
What do you think? Do you have any thoughts on this?
Do you agree (with me)? I'd say … What about you?

Keeping the discussion moving
Let's move on to … Shall we go on to next one?
So, how about …?

Agreeing and disagreeing
I (completely) agree. Yes, and (another thing) …
I (totally) disagree. I can't agree (with you there).
You've got a point (there), but (the way I see it) …

Reaching a decision
So, is that agreed? / do we agree on that?

Exercise 1

Work through this sample task with a partner. Make sure you each speak for approximately the same length of time. This should take you two minutes.

Now I'd like you to talk about something together for about two minutes. Here are some different ways of finding a first job and a question for you to discuss. First you have some time to look at the task.

(After 15 seconds) Now talk to each other about how effective these ways of finding a first job might be.

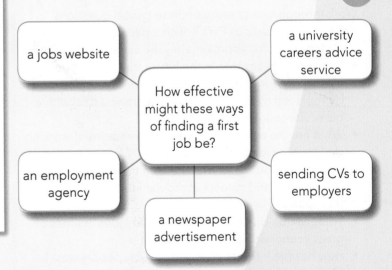

a jobs website

a university careers advice service

How effective might these ways of finding a first job be?

an employment agency

sending CVs to employers

a newspaper advertisement

Exercise 2

Now follow the examiner's next instruction.

Now you have about a minute to decide which way of finding a first job is the most effective.

Part 4 (discussion)

Part 4 lasts five minutes and is a discussion between you, your partner and the examiner. The examiner will ask you and your partner questions related to the topic you discussed in Part 3. You are expected to express and justify opinions and to agree or disagree.

You studied and practised Part 4 in Units 4, 7, 10 and 14.

How to do Part 4

1 Listen carefully to the question. The question itself may be preceded by a statement, which you are then asked to agree or disagree with or to express an opinion about. If you don't understand the statement or the question, you can ask the examiner to repeat it.
2 Answer the question with opinions and reasons. Follow the same guidelines as for Part 3 with regard to including your partner in the discussion and keeping the conversation moving.

Exercise

Work through one or more of these typical questions (related to the topic of Part 3) with a partner. Make sure you each speak for approximately the same length of time.

- Some people say that in the future traditional jobs, where you work for an organisation, will disappear and be replaced by short-term jobs, where you deal with a particular task. What's your opinion?
- What are the advantages and disadvantages of working part-time instead of full-time?
- How far do you agree with the idea that people should change jobs and careers at regular intervals throughout their working lives?
- What can be done to protect people's jobs in times of great economic change?
- How has the Internet changed the way people work?
- Many people prefer a well-paid job to an interesting job. What's your view?

Useful language

Introducing your opinion and giving a reason

Well, in my opinion … because …
I think/feel …
I'm not sure. I think …
From my point of view…
I tend to think …
I would argue that …

Presenting other people's arguments

Some people say that …
It is sometimes/often said that …
It can be argued that …
One argument often made is that …

Presenting the other point of view

Having said that, I believe …
On the other hand, I would argue that …
However, I'm not sure I agree. I tend to think that …

Giving reasons and examples

One reason why …
For this reason, …
For example, …
For instance, …
such as …